AIDING VIOLENCE

Kumarian Press

Selected Titles

AIDING VIOLENCE

The Development Enterprise in Rwanda

Peter Uvin

Kumarian Press

To Spes-Caritas Nurwaha and Hermenegilde Runambi,
whose courage, generosity,
and humor will always be with me.

May they rest in peace.

Aiding Violence: The Development Enterprise in Rwanda.

Published 1998 in the United States of America by Kumarian Press, Inc.,
14 Oakwood Avenue, West Hartford, Connecticut 06119-2127 USA.

Production supervised by Jenna Dixon
Copyedited by Linda Lotz   Typeset by CompuDesign
Text design by Jenna Dixon   Proofread by Beth Richards
Index by L. Pilar Wyman
The text of this book is set in 10/13 Adobe Sabon.
The display type is Agfa Bodega Sans.

Printed in Canada on acid-free paper by Transcontinental Printing and
Graphics. Text printed with vegetable oil-based ink.

∞ The paper used in this publication meets the minimum requirements of the
American National Standard for Information Sciences—Permanence of
Paper for Printed Library Materials, ANSI Z39.48-1984.

Library of Congress Cataloging-in-Publication Data
Uvin, Peter, 1962–
   Aiding violence : the development enterprise in Rwanda / Peter Uvin.
     p.   cm.
   Includes bibliographical references and index.
   ISBN 1-56549-083-5 (pbk. : alk. paper). — ISBN 1-56549-084-3 (cloth : alk.
paper)
    1. Genocide—Rwanda—History—20th century. 2. Rwanda—Ethnic relations.
3. Economic assistance—Rwanda—History—20th century. 4. Rwanda—Economic
conditions. 5. Tutsi (African people)—Crimes against—Rwanda—History—20th
century. I. Title.
DT450.435.U95   1998
967.57104—dc21   98-22652

07   10 9 8 7   1st Printing 1998

CONTENTS

ILLUSTRATIONS

PREFACE

This book is the third step in a reflection process that has been both intensely personal and extremely open. It is not meant to be a definitive statement; rather, it seeks to provoke discussion among Rwandans, people who have worked and lived in Rwanda, and all those committed to social change in Africa.

The first step was a discussion paper published by the World Institute of Development Economics Research (WIDER) in Helsinki, Finland (part of the United Nations University), in both English (September 1996) and French (September 1997). The second step consisted of a process of soliciting feedback on that paper from a broad variety of individuals. A grant from the Danish International Development Agency (DANIDA) allowed me to distribute the paper widely and to travel to meet people and give talks. As a result, I obtained hundreds of reactions from practitioners and academics throughout the world. Sadly, I did not feel that the political situation in Rwanda was conducive to a frank debate about these matters, so I did not organize a workshop in Rwanda, as I had originally planned. However, a great many Rwandans abroad shared their reflections with me and provided me with important insights and knowledge. I also sought and received feedback from non-Rwanda specialists; many of them told me that much of what I wrote applied to other places too.

I owe thanks to many people who have been partners in this reflection process; however, none of them is responsible for what is written here, and some of them may strongly disagree with parts of it. First of all, I thank the many people who took the time to read the earlier paper or to come to talks and share their thoughts and knowledge. I have found most of them, Rwandans and non-Rwandans alike, to be thoughtful and self-critical, willing to engage in an open reflection, willing to learn, and, above all, desperate for change. I hope that this book contributes to the kind of change needed.

A few people were especially important. Daniel Fino of the IUED (Institut Universitaire d'Etudes du Développement in Geneva) is a long-time friend and mentor who has influenced me in countless ways (including being the one to send me to Burundi and Rwanda). Antonio Donini and Norah Niland of the UN Department of Humanitarian Affairs provided crucial moral and practical support, especially in the start-up phase of this project. Through his writings and his support of this endeavor, Lindiro Kabirigi of PREFED (Programme Régional de Formation et d'Echanges pour le Développement in Bujumbura and Kigali) greatly influenced this process. DANIDA provided financial support, which made the writing of this book a much more well-informed process than would have been possible without it. A number of other people deserve special mention because they did more than they had to in order to make this book possible. They include Nancy Alexander, James Boyce, Marc Cohen, Robert Ford, Emily Fromm, Scott Grosse, Elise Keppler, Wayne Nafziger, Karthick Ramakrishnan, T. J. Ryan, Laura Sadovnikoff, and Lindsay Taub.

INTRODUCTION

This book starts with a dramatic and profoundly disturbing contradiction. From April 7, 1994, onward, a well-planned and massively executed genocide began in Rwanda, which led to the brutal slaughter of up to one million defenseless children, women, and men. This genocide was the culmination of a three and a half–year period during which a civil war instigated by the Rwandan Patriotic Front (FPR in French), as well as government-inspired militia violence, cost the lives of tens of thousands of persons, Hutu and Tutsi. Both these processes took place against the background of pervasive and institutionalized racism and the never-resolved consequences of previous episodes of violence, including a massive, festering refugee problem. As the genocide unfolded, the FPR resumed the civil war, conquering Kigali by July. Following the FPR's victory, more than two million Hutu, including most of the former Rwandan army and the militia, fled to camps in Zaire—an event that was the largest and fastest developing humanitarian emergency ever encountered (Krishna 1996; Minear and Guillot 1996). For two years, the majority of these people remained in refugee camps, dependent on the international community for survival, unwilling to return. It is only because of the civil war in Zaire (now the Democratic Republic of Congo)—itself closely related to the influx of refugees—that most of the refugees returned to Rwanda. The chances for development, however defined, in Rwanda and in the Great Lakes region in general are remote: further violence, destruction, and despair seem the only certainties.

Yet, the development community considered Rwanda to be a well-developing country. Rwanda was usually seen as a model of development in Africa, with good performance on most of the indicators of

1

development, including the usual indicators, such as growth in gross national product (GNP), manufacturing, or services; the more social indicators, such as food availability or vaccination rates; and the new bottom-up indicators, such as the number of nongovernmental organizations (NGOs) and cooperatives in the country.

Almost none of the foreign experts living and working in Rwanda expected the genocide to occur or did anything to stop it from happening. Up to the last minute, thousands of technical assistants and foreign experts were building roads, extending credit, training farmers, protecting the environment, reorganizing ministries, advising finance officials, and distributing food aid, at a cost of hundreds of millions of dollars a year—the lion's share of all government expenditures. For most of these people, up to the end, Rwanda was a well-developing country—facing serious development problems, but dealing with them much more effectively than were other countries.

This contradiction poses profound challenges for anyone who has ever worked with the development enterprise in Rwanda or in Africa in general; for me, it led to a long reflection process, of which this book is the result. What does *development* mean if a country that is seemingly succeeding so well at it can descend so rapidly into such tragedy? Why did those of us who worked there have no idea that this was coming? Is there something about our definition of development, and the indicators we use to measure it, that makes us blind to the social, political, and ethnic forces that exist in society? And, on a different, more operational, level, how did development aid, as well as the presence of an expensive battalion of technical assistants and experts, interact with the processes that led to genocide? What was the role of development, as conceived and implemented in Rwanda, in the unfolding of the processes that led to the horrible events the country went through? What, if anything, could the development community have done to stop Rwanda's slide to self-destruction?

This book seeks to understand the relationship between the 1994 genocide and the development system in that country. It takes as its starting point a question: how do situations come about in which people massively participate in brutal violence against their neighbors who have not harmed them? In other words, what kind of social processes take place that cause people to lose the values, restraints, and ethics that under normal circumstances make these actions impossible and abhorrent to contemplate? After answering these questions, the book moves on to a second, core, question: what is the role of the practice of development as implemented by its main protagonists—Third World government agencies, multilateral and bilateral development cooperation agencies, and development NGOs in the North and the South—in the processes that led to genocide?

The processes that led to the genocide, it will be argued, were multiple and complex. They cannot easily be ranked; all of them were equally crucial in leading to the genocide. They include extreme pauperization and reduction of "life chances" for a majority of the poor; an uninformed and uneducated peasant mass treated in an oppressive, authoritarian, and condescending manner; a history of impunity, human rights violations, corruption, and abuse of power; a deep-felt frustration and cynicism by many poor people; growing individual, ethnic, and regional inequality; the political strategies employed by elites in search of protection against the internal and external pressures of democratization and discontent; the existence of past and current acts of violence, including the 1990 FPR invasion; and a history of institutionalized, state-sponsored racism.

This book explains the origins and construction of these processes and moves on from there to analyze how the development enterprise interacted with them. It will become clear that the way *development* was defined, managed, and implemented was a crucial element in the creation and evolution of many of the processes that led to genocide. This does not mean that development workers, or foreign aid agencies, were solely to blame for the genocide. My aim is not to develop a conspiracy theory, pointing out the "true," evidently foreign, villains who were responsible for the genocide. Simplistic, monocausal explanations are useless here, as anywhere; moreover, the blame should not be removed from those who organized the genocide. What will become clear in this book, however, is that the process of development and the international aid given to promote it interacted with the forces of exclusion, inequality, pauperization, racism, and oppression that laid the groundwork for the 1994 genocide. In countries such as Rwanda, where development aid provides a large share of the financial and moral resources of government and civil society, development aid cannot help but play a crucial role in shaping the processes that lead to violence.

All this is sufficient reason to look closely at the relationship between the process of development and the genocide, as well as the role of foreign aid therein. However, very few people have looked at it—a remarkable fact, given that the development enterprise dominated almost all relations between Rwanda and the rest of the world. Almost all foreigners who have lived and worked in Rwanda have done so within the frame-work of—and were paid by—the development enterprise; most of the time, bilateral relations between Rwanda and Western countries were devoted exclusively to matters of development cooperation. Yet an unprecedented evaluation of Rwanda undertaken jointly by bilateral donors, UN agencies, NGOs, and social scientists (the so-called multi-donor evaluation, overseen by thirty-seven development institutions) did not address the question in any of its five reports, except for a short paragraph in the *Synthesis Report* stating that the question of "the impact of previous development aid" is a "worthwhile subject for future research and analysis" (Eriksson and others 1996, 43). The large major-ity of the evaluations of international aid's role in the Rwandan genocide, including those made by NGOs, deal with the humanitarian assistance after the crisis—not with the actions of the same organizations before the crisis began, when development was still the main game in town. Almost four years after the events, I know of only two independent evaluations of pre-genocide development aid to Rwanda. One was published in January 1996 by the Swiss Ministry of Foreign Affairs, which commis-sioned four independent specialists to study its thirty-year record of development cooperation with Rwanda (Voyame and others 1996). The other is a study commissioned by the Belgian NGO umbrella organiza-tion, which appeared in November 1997 (Brusten and Bindariye 1997).

With few exceptions (Willame 1995a; Guichaoua 1995b; Cochet 1996 for Burundi), scholars have also neglected the question. Most analyses of the 1994 crisis focus on the economic and political processes that took place in the years since 1990: the coffee and debt crisis, the FPR invasion, the threats to the elite and their use of ethnic radicaliza-tion to maintain a power base, and so forth. Although such elements are important, these studies tend to neglect the structural basis on which these processes took place. An interesting exception is a 1996 Oxfam study that states quite rightly that "poverty, the politics of exclusion, the denial of basic rights and economic exclusion are all facets of a problem that has frequently erupted into bloody conflict, culminating most recently in Rwanda's genocide and Burundi's continuing crisis" (Oxfam 1996, 5).

The reason that I propose to answer the genocide puzzle through the development angle is a personal one. Like most other foreigners, I knew Rwanda (and neighboring Burundi) only as a developing country, that is, a country receiving development aid, mainly in that unique form of social engineering known as the development project. My visits to

Rwanda and Burundi were motivated by that concern. Less than a year before the genocide, I was in the country for a "mission," as it is so revealingly called, to identify successful local development initiatives throughout the country. Like almost all the other players in the development community, I did not have any idea of the destruction to come. The pauperization was omnipresent, the racist discourse loud; fear was visible in people's eyes, and militarization was evident—but that was none of my business, for I was there for another Rwanda, the development model. Many of the people I met then, as well as some of the students I had taught before and the friends I had made over the years, are dead now; other have fled their country; all are scarred. This, then, is the profound personal reason for my interest in the issue. But there is more: the nature of my questioning goes beyond Rwanda's tragedy.

During my years of "missions" to Burundi, Rwanda, and a number of other African countries, a disenchantment with the development enterprise slowly took hold in me. The issue was not so much the sometimes manifest abuse of development aid for the political, commercial, military, or ideological interests of the donors.[1] My unease related to development aid at its best: given solely for the purpose of promoting development and managed by people who honestly believe in their noble mission. Development aid to Rwanda was, by and large, such a noble enterprise. The country's political or economic interest to any donor was close to nonexistent, with the only possible stakes being some vaguely defined historical bonds to Belgium (the former colonial power) and national-linguistic honor in France (which seeks at all costs to maintain a French-speaking empire in Africa). The failings of this "clean" development aid enterprise in Rwanda make the questions I seek to answer here all the more relevant and fundamental.

Increasingly, I faced many unanswered questions about the role of the whole enterprise: its manifest incapacity to promote genuine improvements in the quality of life for the vast majority of the poor; its top-down, external nature; and its interaction with the forces of exclusion, oppression, and powerlessness that I came to understand as the root causes of continued poverty and disempowerment. I felt that the "game" of development, played out in an almost ritualistic manner among local governments, bilateral agencies, and international organizations (with increasing NGO participation), was leading to exclusion, inequality, frustration, cynicism, and a potential for conflict. I now believe (but admittedly did not realize then) that Rwanda is an extreme example of this failure of development aid.

It is my strong belief that the questions asked here, and their answers, go beyond the extreme case of Rwanda. Throughout Africa, people are engaging in communal violence: Kenya, Liberia, Togo, Zaire, Congo, Sierra Leone, and Somalia come to mind. All these countries were, until recently, recipients of large amounts of foreign aid, and at least one of them—Kenya—was also considered a development model. I am certainly not suggesting that these countries await fates identical to Rwanda's or that foreign aid is the sole determinant of what happens in them. However, I do believe that the way development (aid) is defined and implemented interacts with processes of elite reproduction, social differentiation, political exclusion, and cultural change. I will show that this interaction carries with it a profound risk of violence. To be sure, genocide is not likely to occur in other African countries; their specific histories, the nature of their social cleavages, and the dynamics of their political processes make that unlikely. However, instances of widespread and extreme communal violence are already occurring, and I believe that many of the profound factors that brought about genocide in Rwanda are leading to violence elsewhere. For that reason, I regularly refer to other countries where processes and outcomes similar to those in Rwanda have been documented by other authors. This book, then, is written not for the small circle of Rwanda specialists only. Rather, it seeks to provide a critical reflection for all those interested in development and development aid in Africa.

Organization of the Book

This book is divided into five parts. Its structure is dictated by the arguments I wish to make. Part I consists of three chapters that provide the background to the study and the information needed to understand its core arguments. Chapter 1 presents an overview of Rwanda's history from the precolonial period to the independence era that began in 1962. Chapter 2 describes how the independent governments sought to assert their legitimacy through the use of the two discourses of "development" and "ethnicity." This chapter also analyzes in some detail the nature and functions of racism in Rwandese society. Chapter 3 presents the usual, positive vision of Rwanda in the development community and conveys a general idea of the quantitative importance of development aid in Rwanda's political economy.

Part II presents a standard explanation of the events leading up to the 1994 genocide. This synthesis begins by pointing to a series of economic and political crises taking place from the late 1980s onward. These crises constituted a profound threat to the power and privileges of Rwanda's elite. In an attempt to defend their privileges, the powers that be reverted to the radicalization of ethnicity. Radical parties, militia, youth gangs, hate media, and increased human rights violations were all stepping-stones on the path that would eventually lead to genocide. Chapter 4 ends with a critical discussion of this explanation, in which I argue that it is insufficient in some crucial respects. Although the FPR invasion, the economic crisis, the threats to the elite, the hate media, and the militia were all important elements of the process, they do not constitute a full explanation. Specifically, what is missing is an analysis of the profound structural factors underlying the events from 1990 onward.

Chapter 5 researches the behavior of the international aid community during the 1990–94 period: To what extent did it know about these processes of radicalization and human rights violations? What did it do or fail to do with that knowledge? Why? Could it have done more? Did the broader foreign policy community behave substantially differently or not? This chapter contains a detailed analysis of the uses (or nonuses) of negative and positive forms of political conditionality in societies characterized by war, human rights abuses, and racism.

In Part III, I analyze the structural basis that underlay the 1990–94 processes and made the preparation and eventual execution of the genocide easier. Chapter 6 focuses on structural violence, that is, the processes of inequality, exclusion, and humiliation that have characterized social life in Rwanda for decades. The picture that emerges shows that violence in Rwanda was not a specific set of actions that took place during the hundred days after April 7, 1994. Violence in Rwanda, I argue, is a structural process characterized by long-standing dynamics of exclusion, marginalization, inequality, frustration, and racism. This "structural violence" predates and underlies the occasions of "acute" violence we are used to focusing on. The so-called development process and the role of the international development community therein are crucial to our understanding of this structural violence and its political, economic, and psychosocial aspects. Chapter 6 also discusses the effects of structural violence on society and renders explicit the ways in which these effects laid the groundwork for violence in the 1990s.

Chapter 7 analyzes the role of the international development aid community in the processes of structural violence. It asks these questions: How did development aid affect structural violence, directly and indirectly? How can one separate the roles of local and foreign actors?

Why are aid practitioners, motivated by a sincere desire to promote the well-being of the poor, so blind to the processes of structural violence they participate in?

Part IV singles out two issues that are currently the focus of worldwide interest within the development and academic communities: the role of civil society (Chapter 8), and the role of ecological resource scarcity (Chapter 9). The case of Rwanda provides instructive and unexpected lessons for both these debates.

The final part of this book contains my conclusions. Here, I come back to the two puzzles making up this book and spell out the main theoretical and practical implications of the analysis. Chapter 10 synthesizes what we have learned about the origins of ethnic conflict in Rwanda and puts it in the context of the general literature on communal violence. The gist of the argument is that a society characterized by structural violence produces profound popular anger, frustration, cynicism, ignorance, and desire for scapegoating. This creates a fertile soil for elites to mobilize these sentiments against minority social groups. The FPR invasion and the broader economic and political threats to the elite made some of the elite choose that option to defend their power and privileges. In Rwanda in the 1990s, that option was all the easier to implement—and more violent in its outcome—because racist prejudice had been a structural feature of society for as long as a century.

Chapter 11 studies the implications of my analysis for the development aid enterprise. At different points in time, and through different processes, the development aid system interacted with the processes that underlay the genocide. Aid financed much of the processes of social exclusion, shared many of the humiliating practices, and closed its eyes to the racist currents in society. Aid was also unwilling and possibly unable to stop the processes of radicalization that took place in the 1990s. It is high time for some profound rethinking of the mission and strategies of development aid in Africa.

For this book, I drew extensively on a grey literature emanating primarily from the aid system: project evaluations, surveys, people's consultations, mission reports, annual reports, and the like. Vast quantities of this grey literature exist, and they contain a wealth of information. However, this material is located in the dusty closets of hundreds of agencies throughout the world, and it is almost impossible to unearth more than a small fraction of it. Through friendships, requests, luck, and the archival work of others, I was able to find piles of these documents—enough to cover a small wall in my office. For most readers, it would be close to impossible to find the same documents again. It is my experience, however, that whatever the source of the documents, they present largely the same information. As I explain in Chapter 3, the vision of Rwanda as a country—its challenges, its priorities, its people, its politics—is remarkably similar across agencies and people. The same holds true for the things that the aid system is interested in measuring: plot sizes, crop distributions, coffee revenues, numbers of children, and the like. There is almost no information on what people think, feel, hope for, believe in, dislike, or dream of; their social relations and conflicts; their perceptions of development, the state, or the aid system; or their resources, networks, capacities, or aspirations. Because much of this book (especially Part III) is about that, these documents offer only indirect, occasional glimpses into the realities of Rwandans as people. This is the case for all African countries and the people living in them.

Another problem is that this book describes the development aid system at large and therefore generalizes and simplifies. It is likely that for any statement I make, there have been agencies and people who acted or thought differently. Any statement about "the development enterprise" is bound to do injustice to some people and organizations. The same holds true, for that matter, for statements about "farmers," "politicians," "Hutu," or "Tutsi." I sought to respect the variation that exists in each group, but I am sure that I failed to do so for everyone involved. If you, the reader, feel that I do injustice to your point of view or oversimplify your actions, please do not discard the book immediately, but rather try to find out why your actions or perceptions differ from mine. I do not claim to possess the truth on this matter; rather, I seek to reflect, together with you, about some important questions: How can we promote or support social change in Rwanda and in Africa more generally? How can we learn from the past? How can we do better?

Finally, this book researches the causes of the 1994 genocide and the role of the international development community therein. It does not study the international community's response to the humanitarian emergency that took place after the genocide or the deadly way in which it was finally "solved" in 1997; nor does it address the political and social evolution inside Rwanda from the summer of 1994 onward or the dramatic events that have rocked Burundi since 1993. All these issues are related to the genocide, of course, and are of great importance to anyone interested in the Great Lakes region. All of them, like the genocide, represent human disasters on a staggering scale. One book cannot cover everything, however, and the task I set out to accomplish had to be focused. It should be clear to the reader that the processes of structural violence and authoritarian government I describe in Part III were not unique to Rwanda's Second Republic. They are still present now, in both Burundi and Rwanda, and produce the same effects.

Note

1. These instances exist and have been documented. See, for example, Hancock 1989; Hayter and Watson 1985; Moore-Lappé, Collins, and Kinley 1980.

PART 1

BACKGROUND

1

RWANDA BEFORE INDEPENDENCE:
A CONTESTED HISTORY

Before presenting a brief overview of the precolonial history of Rwanda, it is important to note the profound lack of agreement on the matter among Rwandans as well as among outside specialists on the region. To begin with, profound disagreement exists on the nature of the distinction among Hutu, Tutsi, and Twa. Some contend that they are distinct ethnic groups, even races. Others believe that they are socioeconomic divisions, akin to castes perhaps, or even classes—whoever acquired a sizable herd of cattle was called Tutsi and was highly considered, farmers were Hutu, and hunters and artisans were Twa (Chrétien 1985; d'Hertefelt 1971; Lemarchand 1966; Maquet 1969; Newbury 1988; Prunier 1995; Vidal 1974).

Another important issue that divides the specialists concerns the nature of the precolonial political system. Was the kingdom highly centralized and inegalitarian, as many accounts suggest, or was the power of the king theoretical rather than real outside the region immediately surrounding the capital? What were the levels of mutual control, exchange, and obligation between Tutsi and Hutu? What was the role of lineages, which included both Tutsi and Hutu, in the social and political system? When did the cattle-work exchange—a practice that many consider the centerpiece of ethnic inequality—originate, and what was its precise nature? What possibilities for upward mobility were open to Hutu (de Heusch 1994; Franche 1995; Lemarchand 1970; Maquet 1961; Newbury 1988; Prunier 1995; Vidal 1985; Willame 1995a)?

There is no consensus of scientific knowledge to answer any of these questions (Archer n.d., 5; Erny 1994, 25; Guichaoua 1995a, 19–20). This is partly due to the difficulties of recreating the history of oral societies, as well as the distortions introduced by the Eurocentric and often clearly racist accounts of the first colonizers, missionaries, and ethnographers. However, the prime cause of the difficulty in reaching any agreed-on interpretation of these issues is the fact that they have acquired a high level of contemporary political importance. Radically divergent interpretations of history provide the basis on which collective identities are built and act as powerful justifications for current behavior.

The "official" Hutu position, held by the previous genocidal government[1] and backed up by substantial scientific work, contends that the history of Rwanda is one of conquest by "foreign" Tutsi cattle rearers who gradually, through economic and military means, imposed centuries of oppression and exploitation on the Hutu. In the 1959 "social revolution," the Hutu reversed this "feudal" situation and acquired their rightful place. The inverse position, which is the "official" Tutsi position in Burundi, and is widely accepted by Tutsi in Rwanda—and by many scientists—asserts that the Banyarwanda are a single ethnic group, with the differences between Hutu and Tutsi originally reflecting no more than socioeconomic divisions. To them, it is the colonizer who is responsible for the Hutu-Tutsi divide, having created the racist categories that still exist today and having fixed rigid socioeconomic inequalities. One can argue almost any position in these debates and invoke a series of famous and not-so-famous social scientists to "prove" it.

With these caveats in mind, one can say that the most widely accepted interpretation is that the cattle-rearing Tutsi arrived in Burundi and Rwanda and neighboring regions in successive waves from the north during the fifteenth and sixteenth centuries, fleeing famine and drought. The agriculturist Hutu they met in Rwanda had immigrated to this fertile region centuries earlier from central Africa. The longest-standing inhabitants of the region are the Twa, a small and marginal group (only 1 percent of the population) engaged primarily in pottery making and hunting.

For a long time, these were the three main groups in Rwanda. Their integration had gone far: they spoke the same language, believed in the same god, shared the same culture, belonged to joint clans, and lived side by side throughout the country. There are few cases anywhere in the world of different ethnic groups sharing so many of the same characteristics. This led many to challenge the notion of the existence of ethnic groups in Rwanda. This is erroneous: ethnicity is not a matter of "objective" cultural or physical distinctions but rather is a social construct, an "imagined community" (Anderson 1991), preoccupied with the creation of boundaries between in-groups and out-groups (Barth 1969). Gurr (1993, 4) synthesizes common wisdom in ethnic studies when he writes, "the key to identifying communal groups is not the presence of a particular trait or combination of traits, but rather the shared perception that the defining traits, whatever they are, set the group apart." For decades now, distinct ethnicity has been a reality in Rwanda at the levels of public discourse, state policy, and individual sentiment. Ethnic violence has caused innumerable deaths and pain. It cannot be wished away by pointing to cultural similarities; nor can it be justified by referring to past oppression.

Originally, the interlacustrine region consisted of a number of small kingdoms that were often at war with one another. Historians have documented how one of the central kingdoms, the Nyiginya kingdom, slowly expanded, eventually controlling a territory that basically coincided with Rwanda's current one (in contrast to most other African countries, whose borders are often colonial fabrications). The expansion took two forms. One was territorial and involved the conquest of neighboring kingdoms. The other was in the degree of control exercised over the territory. The central kingdom increased its control through nomination of its own people as chiefs and through the strengthening of a religious ideology that attributed divine powers to the king.

There was one other important sociogeographic division in precolonial Rwanda. Until the end of the nineteenth century, the northwest was largely controlled by several small Hutu kingdoms in which a few Tutsi also lived, but they were politically powerless. For a long time, these kingdoms resisted aggression from the Tutsi kingdom in central Rwanda; they were incorporated into what is now Rwanda at the beginning of the colonial period with the help of the German military. It has been observed that the 1959–63 violence against Tutsi was especially widespread in the north (Lemarchand 1970; Prunier 1995). Former President Habyarimana was from that region, as was the establishment that was responsible for the 1994 genocide (Habyarimana's wife and her family, the major organizers of the genocide, were from a traditionally prominent northern lineage). It was also in this region that large-scale massacres of Tutsi took place between 1990 and 1993. From the end of the 1980s onward, internal political opposition in Rwanda came foremost from southern Hutu, who had been excluded from the spoils of power for two decades, and there were instances of popular unrest in the south since the late 1980s. Many southern Hutu opposition leaders were killed in the 1994 genocide. Therefore, this north-south division is clearly important to understand contemporary Rwanda, but by itself, it is not sufficient to explain the genocide.

Approximately a hundred years ago, a fourth ethnic group entered Rwanda, descending from central Europe. This group is commonly called the *Bazungu*, the term used for whites, but in reality it refers not to skin color but to an exclusive lifestyle. The Bazungu never constituted more than 1 percent of the population but came to own the largest share of the country's purchasing power, vehicles, status symbols, and possessions. The newly arrived Bazungu (first Germans and then, from 1916 onward, Belgians) conquered Rwanda by means of force and diplomacy. The latter essentially involved the delegation of an important, albeit subservient, political role to the king and the Tutsi rulers surrounding him in return for their cooperation. This was the famous indirect rule, consisting of the "incorporation of native authorities into a state-enforced customary order" to the benefit of the colonial power (Mamdani 1996, 18). At the same time, with Bazungu help, the central Tutsi aristocracy's control over the territory of Rwanda greatly increased. The small Hutu kingdoms in the northwest were annexed and their land tenure systems brought under monarchic control, while the other peripheral regions of the country were brought more forcefully under centralized command (Newbury 1988).[2] A few years later, the number of administrative divisions was greatly reduced, further distancing the rulers from the ruled (Feltz 1995, 284). As a result, both centralization and homogenization were greatly increased by the colonizer.

Simultaneously, the nature of the state changed to become a conduit for the rule of the colonizer, imposing onerous legislation, taxes, and obligatory cash crops to pay these taxes. "For the good of the people," compulsory work programs were started, obliging farmers to cultivate a certain number of acres of crops, dig ditches, and so forth. This infamous and often brutal forced labor was strongly resented (Franche 1995; Prunier 1995, 35; Schoepf 1995; Weinstein and Schrire 1976, 4–5; Willame 1995a, 113). During the same period, new sources of power and privilege emerged that were related to the new administration, mastery of the language of the Bazungu (French), adherence to their religion (Catholicism), and insertion into the money-based market.

Under Bazungu control, these new sources of power were reserved almost exclusively for Tutsi. During most of the colonial period, the Bazungu were convinced that the Tutsi were more intelligent, reliable, and hardworking—in short, more like themselves—than the Hutu. The Bazungu instituted a system of rigid ethnic classification, involving such "modern scientific" methods as measuring nose and skull sizes and counting the number of cattle. In 1931, they introduced obligatory identification papers stating one's ethnicity. For many scientists, and for many Rwandans, the origins of ethnic conflict and racism in Rwanda lie in this discourse-cum-practice of the colonizer; others dispute this hotly.

The Bazungu reserved education, as well as jobs in the administration and the army, almost exclusively for the Tutsi. According to oft-repeated data, in the 1950s, 31 out of 33 members of the "conseil supérieur du pays" were Tutsi, as were all 45 "chefs de chefferies" and 544 out of 559 "sub-chiefs" (Funga 1991, 24).[3] Thus, with the military backing of the Bazungu, the old and new Tutsi power holders saw their power greatly increase; as Prunier (1995, 25) writes: "Tutsi chiefs . . . , secure in the white man's support, acted as rapacious quasi-warlords" (see also Newbury 1988, 118–120). Not all Tutsi benefited from this policy, however. Prunier (1995, 24) writes that, within the Tutsi group, "it is mainly two clans that monopolize the advantages: thus 31 out of 45 'chefs des chefferies' were in the hands of the Abanyiginya clan and 5 with the Abega clan." He also quotes data that show that the average income of 287 Tutsi families in the mid-1950s, excluding holders of political office, was only 4 percent higher than the income of 914 Hutu families (Prunier 1995, 50).

Hence, under indirect rule, social relationships in Rwanda became more uniform, rigid, unequal, and exploitative than ever, with a clear hierarchy from Bazungu to Tutsi to Hutu to Twa, with each higher level having privileges denied to the lower level and with an ideology of racial superiority underlying this system of inequality (Prunier 1995, 30). Although, formally, the old monarchic political structure of Rwanda was still intact, its nature had changed; most notably, the power of some of the Tutsi had become much more absolute and exploitative (Braeckman 1994, 30 ff.; Feltz 1995, 292; Guichaoua 1989; Lemarchand 1970; Newbury 1988).[4] During this period, an ideology based on the distinctness and superiority of the Tutsi as a racial group was strengthened and implemented through decades of public policy.

Under these conditions, it is no wonder that the struggle for independence also became an ethnic struggle—a fight as much against the (remote) Belgians as against the (much closer) local Tutsi despots. In this respect, Rwanda followed the continentwide processes analyzed by Mahmood Mamdani: "the form of rule shaped the form of revolt against it. Indirect rule at once reinforced ethnically bound institutions of control [far beyond their customary reach] and led to their explosion from within. Ethnicity thus came to be simultaneously the form of control over natives and the form of revolt against it" (Mamdani 1996, 24; Mbonimpa 1994). Rwanda is a perfect example of this dynamic. For ordinary people, colonization meant a great rise in the power of local Tutsi chiefs, as well as the creation of onerous obligations due to them: taxes, obligatory labor, compulsory crops, and so forth. Popular resentment toward these Tutsi chiefs was thus as strong as, if not stronger than, the resentment toward the much more remote Bazungu.[5] For that reason, independence would be marked by ethnic violence, leading to the overthrow of the Tutsi kingdom.

Notes

1. The fact that this position was held by the previous genocidal government has brought many authors, sympathetic to the plight of the hundreds of thousands of murdered Tutsi, to unquestioningly accept a simple opposite vision— namely, that there were no ethnic groups in Rwanda and that ethnicity was a fabrication of the Belgian colonizers. For a good example, see Destexhe 1994.
2. Although in some areas, it took until after the Second World War for the Tutsi power holders to establish themselves.
3. See also Prunier (1995, 27), who claims that some of these positions were previously held by Hutu; Braeckman (1994, 36) makes the same claims, with slightly different data. This position is best argued by Chrétien 1985.
4. Prunier (1995, 234) talks about a "hardening of the social relationships." It should be clear, however, that this system served foremost the interest of the colonizer; see also Willame 1995a, 116.
5. Interview with Catharine Newbury in Pace and Schoetzau 1995.

2

AFTER INDEPENDENCE:
STRATEGIES FOR ELITE
CONSOLIDATION

At the end of the 1950s and the beginning of the 1960s, two important events occurred abruptly: the abandonment by the Bazungu of
formal political power (decolonization), and the overthrow of the Tutsi
monarchy by a few Hutu educated at the Catholic schools (the so-called
social revolution).[1] Both these processes would radically alter the face of
Rwanda. They signaled the beginning of the cycle of violence that rocks
Rwanda, and neighboring Burundi, to this date.

Decolonization was not an easy matter. The Bazungu had no intention of relinquishing control over their African territories, which they
did not consider ripe for independence. However, they were under heavy
pressure by both the United Nations and part of the Tutsi establishment.
On July 1, 1962, with little preparation, the Bazungu transferred sovereignty and power to local authorities.

The so-called social revolution consisted of the overthrow of the
monarchy and its replacement by a presidential republic. It took place
with the acquiescence, if not the connivance, of the departing Bazungu.
In the last years before independence, in the name of a suddenly discovered attachment to democracy, as well as out of fear of the much more
radical (leftist, anticolonial) Tutsi elite, Bazungu administrative and religious authorities switched their favor to the Hutu—in practice, a small
group of Catholic-educated Hutu intellectuals (Prunier 1995, 49).

The process took place in three stages (Lemarchand 1970). In late
1959, localized anti-Tutsi violence and small pogroms took place in
some provinces; hundreds were killed, and quite a few Tutsi fled the
country. In 1960 and 1961, legislative elections led to a massive victory of Parmehutu, a radically anti-Tutsi party, and the subsequent

replacement of the monarchy by a presidential regime. More Tutsi fled the country. From 1961 to 1964, some of these Tutsi refugees attempted to return militarily, launching small guerrilla assaults from Burundi and Uganda. These assaults were stopped easily but led to organized mass killings of innocent Tutsi civilians within the country, eerily resembling events thirty years later. In March and April 1962, more than 2,000 Tutsi were killed, and in December 1963, at least 10,000 more were massacred. About 15,000–20,000 people were killed between 1963 and 1964. During this time, between 140,000 and 250,000 Tutsi fled the country—40 to 70 percent of the surviving Tutsi population (Kuper 1977; Lemarchand 1970; Prunier 1995; Watson 1991). It is from their descendants that most of the Rwandan Patriotic Front (FPR) soldiers who were to invade Rwanda in October 1990 would be recruited.

Independence thus created a profoundly new and ambiguous situation in Rwanda. Although the independent state's geographic boundaries coincided more or less with its precolonial ones, its functioning, structure, legitimacy, and goals were very different. One monoethnic power system had been replaced with another, as the Tutsi totally lost their political and social power, and more than half of them either died or fled the country. Rwanda's political system was now inverted, with a small Hutu elite on top of the political power structure, the former Tutsi aristocracy dismantled, and the Bazungu withdrawn. Yet the two previously powerful groups were still physically present in the country, holding many of their previous assets. The number of Bazungu barely decreased—and after a few years, when the development enterprise took off, actually increased—and their influence on the economy and the administration remained strong, if less formal. Bazungu continued to possess the largest concentration of financial resources, well-paid jobs, foreign education opportunities, cars and fuel, brick houses, telephones, and other instruments of development and power. Tens of thousands of Tutsi also remained in the country, many of them well educated and relatively wealthy. At the same time, the lives of the large mass of Hutu peasants were unchanged: they were as poor and powerless after 1962 as they had been before.

Hence, the new power holders faced major political challenges. How could they avert challenges to their hold on power? How could they deal with the competing loci of economic and political power of the Bazungu and the Tutsi? How could they justify their hold on power to their fellow Hutu? What was their claim to power?

These questions were all the more important because, in Rwanda, as elsewhere in Africa, the state was the main if not the sole avenue for rapid wealth accumulation for the new elites (Reyntjens 1995c, 284). After independence, the Rwandan elite—the 1 percent or so of people who lived wealthy, urban, educated, Westernized, traveling lives (Bayart 1986)—was defined almost exclusively by its access to the positions of power within the state system. Africanists have used the term *state class* to describe this group of people, denoting that, unlike in Marxist thought, there was no bourgeoisie defined by its control over the means of production, but only a ruling clique defined by its control over the state. In Rwanda, as in most of Africa, the state controlled almost all avenues for enrichment and upward mobility. By far the largest share of formal-sector jobs was in the public service (the Catholic Church and the aid system being the two other main employers); even jobs in the private sector required permission and control from the Ministry of Labor (World Bank 1994b, 21). Secondary and tertiary educational opportunities in Rwanda and abroad—crucial paths for mobility—were state controlled but often executed by religious orders or financed by foreign aid agencies. The control of state revenues and development aid provided enormous opportunities for both personal enrichment and patronage (Cart 1995, 476).

Therefore, like elsewhere in Africa, a dual challenge of "state building" existed: first, the strengthening of the state as an institution with authority and capabilities, and second, the establishment and reinforcement of control over the state by the nascent elite. In the African context, the Rwandan ruling class has for a long time been exceptionally successful in meeting these challenges.

The presence of the Rwandese state has expanded into the most remote corners of the territory and of social life. Already during the colonial period, the reach of the state had been greatly strengthened, especially over the more remote areas, such as the north, where central power had been recent and incomplete at best. Simultaneously, the centralized nature of the bureaucracy had increased, as various local and regional positions had been abolished and the number of geographical units decreased. After independence, the state embarked on major programs designed to further increase its control over its territory.

The Ministry of the Interior was organized through ten provinces with centrally appointed prefects, followed by 143 communes with burgomasters appointed by the minister. Each commune was divided into about ten sectors, which were in turn subdivided into about ten cells.

Representatives of the state and of the single party were present up to the lowest level of social organization: each *colline*,[2] each extended family was constantly surrounded by centrally appointed administrators, chiefs, security agents, policemen, and local party cadres of all kinds. Cells and sectors had elected representatives, but many observed that both the social representativeness and the degree of popular involvement in the designation and control of these representatives were very low. The single party—during most of independence, only one party was allowed in Rwanda, and every Rwandan was a member of it—had a structure that mirrored that of the state, with representatives and committees on each level.

The state effectively was in charge of all fields of human endeavor and all sectors of the economy: from subsidizing prices; allocating jobs; funding research; building hospitals, schools, and vocational training centers; and registering births and deaths to prescribing social behaviors, sexual mores, or political thought—all activities previously left to the market, the family, or the church, or not done at all. Until 1990, there were no other political parties, no independent unions, no human rights organizations; in the early 1980s, all large cooperatives were also brought under state control. The Catholic Church, to which more than half of all Rwandans belong, making it a potential major source of counterpower, was closely associated with the state; its leaders were thoroughly co-opted in both state and party structures at all levels. A dense network of hundreds of kilometers of well-maintained roads, together with a fast-growing vehicular fleet, allowed the central state to relay messages rapidly to the farthest corner of the country.

It has been argued by many scholars that in much of Africa, the project of state building has been far from fully achieved and that the state is weak or soft, incapable of penetrating the social organization and economy of large parts of the rural population. Whatever the general validity of this argument—and it has been contested as both Eurocentric and factually incorrect (Olivier de Sardan 1995; Sangpam 1993)—it does not apply to Rwanda. Rwanda was in every meaning of the term a strong state, both in its capacity for effective and uncontested control of its entire territory and in the muscled nature of the exercise of this power. Much of this rise in the strength of the state was rendered possible by foreign aid: development aid constituted more than three-quarters of the state's capital budget, as well as a nonnegligible share of its current budget (see Chapters 8 and 11).

The second mandate of state building consists of the strengthening of control over the state by the powers that be. Political regimes anywhere can achieve control through the use of force or through strategies of legitimization. The Rwandan regimes were highly successful at both.

The two regimes that Rwanda has known since independence were not averse to the use of repression. The Kayibanda regime (1962–73) chased or killed most former Tutsi power holders and Tutsi politicians, even the most moderate ones, as well as many opposition Hutu politicians who did not join Parmehutu (Nkunzumwami 1996). The Second Republic under General Habyarimana (1973–94) was a military dictatorship with a weak human rights record. In Charles Humana's 1984 ranking, for example, it is classified as "poor," the lowest category (72). It killed many power holders of the First Republic (including Kayibanda), and its internal security kept a tight lid on any opposition or dissension for almost two decades. The legal system was independent in name only, and impunity was the norm (Humana 1992; ICHRDD 1995; Kabirigi 1994). Torture and arbitrary imprisonment were regularly used.[3] Elections were a farce in which Habyarimana was always reelected with more than 98 percent of the vote. Any critical press was at the risk of one's life or freedom, and intellectual and academic speech was closely regulated.

However, the main strength of Rwanda's regimes lay not in their oppression but in their capacity to legitimize themselves to internal and external forces. To achieve this, two separate discourses of legitimization were employed: one was the ethnic, "social revolution" discourse, largely tailored for domestic consumption and designed to legitimize the elite's hold on power and undercut any demand for power sharing;[4] the other was a "development" legitimization, aimed at both the international Bazungu audience and the domestic one, facilitating the maintenance of the powers that be in their position (Newbury 1992). Let us begin with the latter.

Development as Legitimization

The development ideology basically consists of an argument that the state's sole objective is the pursuit of economic development for the underdeveloped (Hutu) masses; as a result, all the "living forces" in the country, and all those abroad who are interested in promoting development, should work with the state to make that possible. This ideology serves to legitimize the government's intrusive presence in all aspects of social life and diverts attention from the real differences that exist between different classes and social groups. In other words, it diverts attention from all things political, usually replacing them with a top-down and elitist realm of technicality (Eyoh 1996, 68).

The Habyarimana regime was masterful at playing the development card. Thus 1974, the year immediately after the coup d'etat by Habyarimana, was declared the "year of agriculture and manual labor," the name of the single party was changed to Mouvement Revolutionnaire National pour le Développement (MRND—National Revolutionary Development Movement), and the parliament was renamed the National Development Council. A local journal proudly announced that, during the Council of Ministers of November 13, 1987, the president of the republic "ennobled" the term "peasant" by extending it to all Rwandans (Niyibizi 1986, 56; Ntamahungiro 1988). If all Rwandans were peasants, there were no more classes, no distinctions—except, of course, between Hutu and Tutsi, the only allowed, and never forgotten, distinction.

An excellent example of the functions of this discourse can be found in the role of the commune, the lowest level of the state. One of the first acts of the new Habyarimana regime in 1974 was the pronouncement by its president of a *discours-programme* that attributed to Rwanda's 143 communes the role of "motor of development." From now on, the communes would be the basic unit of development—forums for local-level, participatory development planning and project implementation. It was in many ways the dream of the secular development enterprise, which set out to support this beautiful project.

However, from the beginning, the structure and functioning of the commune ran counter to this development discourse. Throughout the independence period, Rwanda's communes came increasingly under centralized control: their personnel was appointed centrally (involving the offices of the president, the Ministry of the Interior, and the governor), and their freedom of maneuver was severely limited by both the central state and the party, which has an identical structure to the state and is where the real policy decisions are made (World Bank 1987, 7; Bugingo and others 1992). A World Bank report on the matter states that "communal action is the responsibility of the MRND which 'formulates the philosophy,' and the Ministry of the Interior and Communal Development, which 'has responsibility for implementation'" (World Bank 1987, 7). There is no room at all for independent behavior by commune personnel, and even less by the population. Commune personnel are not even remotely accountable to the population but solely to a vertical structure from which they receive detailed marching orders.

Interviews with communal authorities clearly show that they define their tasks entirely in terms of the interests of the Ministry of the Interior, which hires and judges them (Bugingo and others 1992; World Bank 1987). Thus, foremost among their hierarchy of tasks are the maintenance of public order and the resolution of disputes; the implementation of decrees, circulars, decisions, and instructions from the Ministry of the Interior; the collection of taxes of all kinds; the relaying of political messages from the central party level to the community ("political mobilization"); and the organization of obligatory community labor. Commune personnel are under close scrutiny from higher levels in the ministry and spend a great deal of their time in meetings and seminars in provincial and national capitals (Bugingo and others 1992; World Bank 1987, 13 ff.). For most of them, promoting development does not figure in their agenda—unless there is personal gain involved, as the previously cited World Bank report also documents. Those cases in which development matters moved higher on the agenda —and the commune became a motor for development—involved local administators of great commitment going beyond the call of duty, supported by large flows of aid money and advice. These successes typically ended when these persons were transferred or when the foreign aid flow ended.

Yet, despite the gap between rhetoric and reality, large sums of development aid were invested in this paper dream. Foreign projects painstakingly attempted to strengthen the commune, in the name of capacity building and decentralization (even the NGO sector largely did so, as documented in Brusten and Bindariye 1997, 25). High-paid consultants trained burgomasters and their personnel in methods of programming, monitoring, evaluation, and beneficiary participation; technical assistants wrote down detailed communal development plans; foreign experts wrote lengthy reports on local development—but the gap between rhetoric and reality never closed. As the technical assistants attached to communal support projects observed bitterly after years of work, "communal development projects served to allow the burgomasters to better control their population" (Voyame and others 1996, 99). The Rwandan case was even upheld as an example for other countries, such as neighboring Burundi, which later mimicked the rhetoric and the practice almost perfectly.

What is remarkable in this crude development discourse is not its local success but its widespread acceptance by foreigners (Pabanel 1995, 113). It truly allows politics to be taken out of the process of nation building and strengthening the capacities of the elites, all the while using foreign subsidies. The rest of this book provides a detailed discussion of the reasons for this acceptance. Suffice it to say here that this function of the development discourse is not unique to Rwanda; it has been observed and documented elsewhere. Ferguson (1990, xiv–xv) describes for Lesotho how the development ideology and its accompanying institutions allow for "the expansion and entrenchment of bureaucratic state power, side by side with the projection of economic and social life which denies 'politics' and, to the extent that it is successful, suspends its effects." And Chatterjee (1993, 219) argues, for the case of India, that "development [is designed to] transcend class and class conflict, as well as politics." We now turn to the second strand of legitimacy: ethnic prejudice.

The Ideology of the Social Revolution

The ideology of the social revolution can be described as the notion that Rwanda belongs to the Hutu, who are its true inhabitants but were subjugated brutally for centuries by the foreign exploiters, the Tutsi. In this view, the (majority) Hutu had wrestled power away from their (minority) former masters in 1959 and installed what amounts to, by definition, a true democracy, representative of the vast majority of the people. In other words, since the ancient regime was "feudal" and unrepresentative, the new one must be progressive and democratic (de Heusch 1994; Kagabo and Vidal 1994, 542; Chrétien 1993a, 190). This notion that the government was the legitimate representative of the majority Hutu, and the sole defense against the Tutsi's evil attempts to enslave the people again, formed the powerful core of the legitimization of the ruling clique's hold on power (Reyntjens 1994; Pabanel 1995; Prunier 1995; de Heusch 1994, 11; Kabirigi 1994, 13–14).

This ideology was, and still is, powerful in its appeal, both inside Rwanda (I discuss later the historical and social origins of this ideology) and outside. It was backed by large parts of the Catholic Church, as well as by many foreigners, who accepted its claims to progressiveness and representativeness. In its "soft" version—that Rwanda underwent a social revolution and its regime truly represents the masses—there were almost no dissenters internationally. If one reads, for example, project documents, policy statements, and analyses by foreign aid agencies or their employees, one is surprised to find, over and over again, an uncritical acceptance of the merits of the social revolution and the representative nature of the state. President Mitterand, to mention but one example, still found it necessary to insist in September 1994, after the genocide, that Habyarimana "represented an ethnic group that constitutes 80 percent of the population" (Willame 1995b, 449)—as if that, by itself, somehow made him a better kind of person. Admittedly, few foreigners were willing to openly accept the "hard" version, which argues that the Tutsi are by nature evil and unreliable. Some foreigners did take that extra step, though. The former director-general of the Swiss Development Cooperation agency, for example, described the Tutsi as an "arrogant and pitiless" group that considers itself superior to the Hutu (Heimo 1994, 196).[5] Similarly Pierre Erny, a professor of religious anthropology and ethnology at the University of Rwanda in the 1970s, states without any proof that the FPR adheres in secret to an ideology of superiority and natural leadership (Erny 1994, 39); most of his book consists of an ambiguous attempt to explain that the genocide was really the Tutsi's fault.

It is fascinating to see the extent to which these intelligent foreigners have accepted the ethnic clichés of the Habyarimana regime. It demonstrates the ease with which history can be abused, especially when the available historical knowledge is characterized by contradiction and ambiguity. If "neutral," well-trained, supposedly intelligent foreigners can accept and publish such stereotypical and racist generalizations, even after the genocide,[6] how much easier must it be for many Rwandans, who have never known anything else, to accept this picture. The next pages probe the historical and social roots of this racist ideology and the form it took under the Habyarimana regime.

The Roots of Prejudice

In this section, I probe the historical and social roots of the simple prejudicial ideology described earlier. I also seek to understand what explains the widespread acceptance of this racism, which continued for decades. After all, no Rwandan alive has firsthand experience of the "pure" Tutsi rule that existed before the arrival of the colonizer. By 1994, more than 80 percent of the population had been born after independence and the social revolution, and had never personally known Tutsi rule, not even in its indirect form under the Belgian colonizer (calculated from United Nations Department of International Economic and Social Affairs 1991). Throughout most of the period of independence, except for the first few years, the Tutsi as a group had been all but invisible in Rwanda: they had no political parties of their own, no organizations that militated for them, and no pressure groups (at least within the country), unions, or meeting places; from 1964 onward, they posed no military problem either. They seemed resigned to the discrimination they experienced in access to education and state jobs. They intermarried with Hutu, went to the same church, lived in similar houses, and earned roughly the same wages. The international foreign policy community, as well as the development aid system, totally neglected the Tutsi question and brought no pressure to bear on the government to allow the return of the refugees or to end discrimination within the country (Brusten and Bindariye 1997). And yet the notion that the Tutsi presence was a problem for Rwanda's future, that the Tutsi were an alien group with an inherent potential for evil, never disappeared. Why did this racist prejudice survive so well? What functions did it fulfill to remain so dominant in Rwandese society?

SOME REMARKS ABOUT ETHNICITY, PREJUDICE, AND RACISM

It is now widely accepted by social scientists that ethnicity—or race, for that matter—is not an "essential" category based on the objective, physical existence of genetic, linguistic, or cultural differences (although people may perceive it that way) but a socially constructed "category of ascription and identification by the actors themselves" (Barth 1969, 10), made with the tools of stereotypes, rituals, partial interpretations of history, and so forth (Schilder 1994, chap. 1). As Ted Gurr (1993, 4) states, "the key to identifying communal groups is not the presence of a particular trait or combination of traits, but rather the shared perception that the defining traits, whatever they are, set the group apart." Following this, others have written about the "imagined community" and the "invented tradition" of the nation (Anderson 1991; Ranger 1993).

It has been observed that ethnicity is foremost about setting boundaries and thus creating communities of membership and exclusion. This process of setting the boundaries is both contingent, that is, influenced by real-world events and thus changeable, and inert, meaning that it is capable of surviving even in the face of intense interaction with others and changed circumstances (Sollors 1996). Ethnicity in Rwanda perfectly illustrates this dual nature.

Although it usually invokes the past and tradition, ethnicity is highly dynamic and made up of the needs of the current. It is created out of the facts of life past, filtered through the values, aspirations, frustrations, pain, hopes, desires, lies, and remembrances of the present. As such, it cannot be understood—nor, for that matter, dispelled—by the mere presentation of historical truths, if such truths were to exist. Liisa Malkki's (1995) moving analysis of ethnicity among Burundian refugees in Tanzania shows forcefully how the contingencies of place and need—as observed through the differences between two groups of Hutu refugees, one living in a refugee camp in Tanzania and one living in a nearby city—lead to very different self-identifications and senses of ethnicity. The refugees living in camps adhered to standard racialized accounts of themselves as Hutu, eternally opposed to the evil Tutsi, whereas those living in the city identified themselves as Burundians or even as Tanzanians, with little of the racist imagery associated with the Hutu-Tutsi divide.

Although ethnicity is contingent and not eternally fixed, it is capable of persisting for a long time. Regular intermarriage between Hutu and Tutsi and the fact that they speak the same language, eat the same food, and believe in the same god (whether before or after colonization) have all been used by many observers to prove that Rwandans are not of different ethnicities or that, even if they once were, ethnic origin does not matter anymore. Yet, as Barth says, "a drastic reduction of cultural differences between ethnic groups does not correlate in any simple way with a reduction in the organizational relevance of ethnic identities, or a breakdown in boundary-maintaining processes" (Barth 1969, 33). Indeed, intermarriage—maybe the closest possible interaction between people of different ethnicities—has not erased the borders between the ethnic groups in Rwanda. Children from biethnic marriages take over the ethnicity of their fathers—they do not become ethnicity-less. Chrétien and his colleagues (1995) showed that images associated with intermarriage—especially the myth of Tutsi conspiracies using the beauty of their women to entrap Hutu elites, and the general notion of a loss of purity when Hutu men marry Tutsi women—constituted a core element of the genocidal rhetoric and imagery. Thus, rather than being an element of integration, intermarriage was a cornerstone of the racist discourse, keeping the borders alive instead of weakening them.

Recent work by psychologists clarifies the individual-level processes that underlie widespread prejudice. Marc Ross, in a fascinating book on what he calls the "culture of conflict," makes a comparative analysis of ninety cultures and the factors that cause conflict within them. He concludes that "psychocultural" factors, that is "assumptions, perceptions, and images about the world that are widely shared with others and not idiosyncratic" are crucial (Ross 1993, 10).

> [Such] interpretative processes, even though they are most often described in psychological terms, are also profoundly cultural. The notion of a culture of conflict draws attention to how people in communities develop and share interpretations rooted in psychocultural dispositions. The approach forces one to consider the common formative experiences and explicit values and practices shared by people growing up together and to appreciate the importance of the common identities, self-concepts and out-groups which serve as acceptable targets for externalization and projection. (Ross 1993, 111–12)

Recognition of ethnic difference, however, is different from prejudice. For it to evolve into prejudice requires two processes: first, the reduction of people's identity to their ethnicity, with disregard for their other features; and second, the attribution of moral judgments to these identities. As such, prejudice feeds on reduction and generalization, by which every person becomes "a Hutu" or "a Tutsi" and thus smart or stupid, lazy or hardworking, dishonest or trustworthy, good or bad.[7] As social scientists, although we do not necessarily take over these moral judgments, we often write and think in terms of the same "totalizing classificatory grid" (Anderson 1991, 184) that pits "the Hutu" against "the Tutsi" and is a continuation of the mind-set of the racists themselves.

In Rwanda, basic psychocultural images of the Tutsi and the Hutu have been—and still are—the basic building blocks of society. These profoundly ingrained, widely shared images treat Hutu and Tutsi as radically and unchangeably different in their history and in their personal, intellectual, and moral attributes. These images can be observed in—and from childhood are transmitted by—a multitude of proverbs, stories, and myths regarding the differential nature of Hutu, Tutsi, and Twa (FIAU 1996, 9).

This prejudicial ideology can properly be called racist, for it is widely perceived as referring to races.[8] Old myths of Tutsi being not only "foreigners" but also of a genetically different, so-called Hamitic race, and "scientific evidence" related to height, blood factors, lactose digestion, and food habits, were being used until 1994—even discussed by Rwanda's émigré intelligentsia on the Internet.[9] The notion that the difference between Hutu and Tutsi is a racial one probably dates from the colonial period, when the Hamitic hypothesis was introduced. However, as I explain later, the images of social and moral differentiation in all likelihood predate colonization.

THE SOCIAL NATURE OF PREJUDICE

The above images predate the so-called social revolution of 1959–62; rather, they enabled it to take place. It is fascinating to look at the terms in which, from 1955 onward, the nascent political debate in Rwanda was cast, and at the images that were developed in the first political texts from that time, which are still referred to today. The 1957 Hutu Manifesto, written by a small group of Hutu intellectuals, including Rwanda's later president Kayibanda, is without doubt the most important of them. It was to be the founding document of "Hutu consciousness" and of the independent state. Its central passage states that "the problem is basically that of the monopoly of one race, the Tutsi . . . which condemns the desperate Hutu to be forever subaltern workers." In return, the circle of notables around the king wrote that there could never be fraternity between Hutu and Tutsi, for the Tutsi had conquered the Hutu and the latter would always be subservient.[10] Hence, from completely opposite perspectives, these people followed identical images.

These profound, divisive images were largely shared by all Rwandans (Prunier 1995, 9, 37 ff.). This helps explain the widespread popular participation in the Tutsi massacres in the years just before and after independence, during which tens of thousands of Tutsi were killed, their houses looted and burned, and more than 100,000 forced to flee. These events pose considerable problems for those authors who argue that the Hutu-Tutsi conflict was created out of nothing by elites who were intent on accessing or retaining power. As Kuper says in *The Pity of It All* (1977, 106, 249; see also Schilder 1994, 73),

> I have no difficulty in accepting an emphasis on the significant role of the elites in inflaming and manipulating ethnic hatreds, as Tutsi leaders sought to maintain their dominant position and as Hutu politicians challenged

that domination and the increasing "Tutsisation" of high office. But I would add that they were harnessing real social forces, embedded in the structure of the society, and in the perceptions of many of its members.

For Kuper, these forces were structural, that is, corresponding to real differences in power and prestige between the two groups (Kuper 1977, 104, 252). I argue that this generally shared psychocultural image was the more profound force.

There exists considerable divergence as to the origin of this prejudice: is it a construction of the colonizer, or did it precede colonization? It seems most probable that images of fundamental distinction between Hutu and Tutsi (accompanied by real-life socioeconomic differences) already existed when the colonizer "discovered" Rwanda. Although the first ethnographers, missionaries, and colonial administrators profoundly misinterpreted much of what they saw, they did not invent these images ex nihilo (Lemarchand 1970, 45; Feltz 1995, 286–88). This is not to say that these images necessarily bear a close resemblance to reality; they may have been the ideology of an expanding Tutsi kingdom seeking to add historical legitimization to its recent conquests and centralization of power (Chrétien and others 1995, 85). Hence, an ideology of the god-given superiority of Tutsi was evolving in the second half of the nineteenth century, in line with the actual conquest and centralization of power by Tutsi kings then under way. Like elsewhere, this ideology was in flux, "the outcome of a contest between various forces" (Mamdani 1996, 22). It seems likely that when the first Germans came, the king was more than happy to make them believe in the long-standing and accepted nature of his rule; indeed, the Germans, by conquering new territories in the north, greatly helped the king extend his power (Prunier 1995).

The colonizer rigidified this ideology both through the use of racist images describing Hutu and Tutsi as two distinct races, with greatly differing intellectual and moral capacities, and through the institution of indirect rule, which forcefully implemented these images (Elias and Helbig 1991; see Schilder 1994, 128–31, for the same practice in what is now Cameroon). Both the administrative authorities and the church shared these images of Tutsi as naturally superior and born to rule and of Hutu as the opposite in all respects (Franche 1995). The colonizers also helped these ideas become realities and influence everyday life. For decades, Tutsi men were treated as the natural rulers of society and were given almost exclusive rights to so-called customary power and privilege, whereas almost all Hutu people were excluded from these opportunities (also observed in Somalia by Simons 1995, 33, 44). It is no wonder that both sides came to believe in these images, projecting them back to time immemorial. At the same time, under Belgian orders, the Tutsi "native authorities" implemented forceful and constraining policies, including taxation, forced labor, forced cultivation, and forced migration (Braeckman 1994, 30 ff.). By the time Rwanda gained independence, a century of myths and associated practice had created the ideology that was to underlie the postindependence instability.

Under these conditions, it is no wonder that the struggle for independence also became an ethnic struggle—a fight as much against the (remote) Belgians as against the (much closer) local Tutsi acolytes (Mamdani 1996). Although not all Tutsi were wealthy and powerful under colonial rule, it is clear that almost no Hutu were; it is equally clear that the vast majority of the Hutu suffered greatly from the increased demands (including onerous taxation and forced labor) placed on them during colonial rule. In that respect, Burundi and, especially, Rwanda followed the same continentwide processes described so well by Mamdani (1996, 24):

> The form of rule shaped the form of revolt against it. Indirect rule at once reinforced ethnically bound institutions of control and led to their explosion from within. Ethnicity thus came to be simultaneously the form of control over natives and the form of revolt against it. . . . The anti-colonial struggle was first and foremost a struggle against the hierarchy of the local state, the tribally organized Native Authority, which enforced the colonial order as customary.[11]

After independence, the new regime used the social revolution ideology as the primary strategy for legitimization of its control of the state. This ideology constituted both a reversal and a continuation of these long-standing psychocultural images. It was a continuation to the extent that it persisted in its depiction of the innate and profound differences between the Hutu and the Tutsi as homogeneous, mutually exclusive, categories. It was a reversal in that the moral and social privilege associated with the Tutsi—the natural-born rulers, the chosen people—was turned on its head, with the Tutsi now in the position of alien, inferior outsiders to be contained. As Erny states when discussing the so-called social revolution of 1959, unlike in the French Revolution, the distinctions between people were "inverted and not overthrown" (Erny 1994, 59; Chrétien and others 1995, 88). Braeckman (1994, 51), from a very different ideological perspective, writes that "independent Rwanda defined its identity by denying the right to existence of the other, by defining as stranger the one who is his internal double."

Violence, finally, rigidified ethnic prejudice further. Ethnic violence along Hutu-Tutsi lines took place in both Burundi in 1965 and 1972, when hundreds of thousands of Hutu were slaughtered by the Tutsi-dominated army, and Rwanda in 1959–63 and, to a lesser extent, 1972–73. Violence was perpetrated by both Tutsi (in Rwanda, through attacks by the refugees, and in Burundi, through the monoethnic army) and Hutu. Violence solidifies ethnic prejudice in different ways. First, people struggle to make sense of violence. This also holds for the perpetrator, who needs to explain and justify his or her acts of violence. This can well be achieved through further dehumanization and increased emotional distance from the target of the violence (Warren 1993, 9; Lauer 1989, 480–81). Second, the incidents of violence in Burundi and Rwanda became a traumatic part of the identity of both Hutu and Tutsi—in both cases, and for both sides, creating self-images of vulnerability and weakness. In the words of Volkan (1994, xxv), "the group draws the mental representation of a traumatic event into its very identity. It passes the mental representation of the event—along with associated shared feelings of hurt and shame, and defenses against the perceived shared conflicts they initiate—from generation to generation" (see also Malkki 1995, 94 ff.). Hence, although these occurrences of violence along ethnic lines initially may have been a strategy of aspiring elites to conquer or maintain power, they became a traumatic component of the culture of prejudice in both countries and reinforced mutual images of the other as inherently aggressive and immoral. As Prunier (1995, xiii) eloquently states, "in 1959 the red seal of blood put a final label of historical unavoidability on this mythological construction, which from then on became a real historical framework." In this context, it is important to note the vicious dynamic between the two neighboring countries, with events in each country presenting to the other, in a kind of distorted mirror, the proof of its worst fears, its worst nightmare.

The Institutionalized Structure of Prejudice

In line with its ideology of the social revolution, the new Hutu elite developed a policy of systematic discrimination against Tutsi, especially in areas of direct political importance and vertical mobility. "The army, diplomatic service and parliament, with rare exceptions, were always reserved for Hutu's" (Physicians for Human Rights 1994). Under the Habyarimana regime, according to Prunier (1995, 75), "there would be not a single Tutsi burgomaster or prefect, there was only one Tutsi officer in the whole army, there were two Tutsi members of parliament out of seventy and there was only one Tutsi minister out of a cabinet of between 25 and 35 members. The army was of course the tightest and its members were prohibited by regulations from marrying Tutsi women."[12] The system of ethnic identity papers introduced by the Belgians was kept intact by the postcolonial governments (USAID 1992) and continued to exist until the 1994 genocide, greatly facilitating its execution. The return of the Tutsi refugees—whose numbers grew to more than half a million by the 1990s, as a result of natural population growth—was categorically denied, with the argument that there was no more space in Rwanda (Adelman and Suhrke 1996, 12). A quota system was installed whereby access to higher education and state jobs for people with Tutsi IDs was limited to a number supposedly equal to their proportion of the population.

This quota system was usually only partly implemented. Most authors seem to agree that in the public sector—but not at the highest levels, and not at all in the army—Tutsi remained represented beyond the 9 percent they were theoretically allocated. Moreover, in other sectors of society—commerce and enterprise, NGOs, and development projects —they were present beyond that proportion (Schürings 1995, 496; Guichaoua 1995a, 34). Hence, they were subject to discrimination in schooling and access to jobs, but that discrimination was hardly foolproof or absolute. Oft-repeated data "prove" that the predominance of Tutsi in secondary schools decreased, but that they remained overrepresented throughout (Funga 1991; Munyakazi 1993).[13] In all likelihood, during the last two decades, most Hutu from the south were as discriminated against in access to schools and universities, for example, as were most Tutsi.

These quota systems and ethnic IDs, then, served to keep the distinctions alive (Chrétien talks about maintaining the "stranger-ness" of Tutsi) and to allow for social control by the state rather than for actual direct discrimination. These policies were part of the institutional structure of Hutu power, administrative "proofs," or reminders, of the fact that the Tutsi were different from everyone else, and the state was watching out for the interests of the majority Hutu.

As such, these institutionalized structures of discrimination were both an outgrowth and a facilitator of prejudice. What Fein (1993, 37–38) wrote about the Holocaust describes a reality that is remarkably similar to the situation of the Tutsi in Rwanda before 1990:

One condition that may predict genocide is in the making is the practice of denying groups access to political and/or economic positions. In Germany before Nazi rule, the Jews were only marginally integrated politically. Economically Jews were over-represented in the professions, but traditionally they had been excluded from the guilds and civil service. The anti-Semitism that denied Jews access to political office, education, and the professions eroded slowly during the 19th century, only to reemerge at the end of the century. Prior discrimination and prejudice made the Jews a convenient target for Nazi ideologues.

In normal times, the "institutionalized structure of discrimination" served less to carry out direct discrimination than to provide general legitimization, but in crisis times, it provided a tool that could effectively be activated against Tutsi. This is what happened in 1972–73, when the Kayibanda regime was facing popular discontent. Suddenly, mass campaigns were orchestrated to strictly implement quota policies: thousands of Tutsi youth were kicked out of schools, adults lost their jobs, and people were killed. It happened again in the 1994 genocide, when the ethnic IDs allowed the perpetrators of the genocide to compile lists of Tutsi locality by locality or to check people's "Tutsiness" at checkpoints and slaughter them.

In Rwanda, as in other African countries, the ruling clique in power (at the heart of which was the *akazu*, "the little house"—that is, the relatives and allies of President Habyarimana, who controlled the top positions in the government, the army, and the parastatal sector) sat on top of a state machinery. The composition and power base of this ruling clique were highly regionalistic and ethnic, or, to be more precise, northern and Hutu.

This state class sought to strengthen its power and privileges through the use of force and control, on the one hand, and through legitimization, on the other. For the latter, it drew on two ideologies: one of development, and the other of ethnic distinction. Médard (1991, 94), writing about Africa in general, states that "ideological legitimacy is expressed through myths, foremost the myth of development and the one of national unity, as well as slogans, and stereotypical, constantly repeated, discourses [*langue du bois*]." Rwanda reflects these continentwide tendencies, with the exception that, instead of national unity, a particular form of national disunity was crucial to Rwanda's ideological legitimization strategy.

Racist prejudice in Rwanda fed on more than a century of myths and images of inferiority and superiority that predated colonization but were greatly strengthened and modified during the colonial period. At the time of independence, the power positions were inverted, but not the images. Hence, the social acceptability of racist prejudice was based on its deeply ingrained nature in Rwanda's social and political history; it became strengthened with every occurrence of violence in neighboring Burundi and at home.

The political acceptability of racist prejudice was probably as much a matter of a profound sharing of these images by most of the elite as of a realization of their convenience for the powers that be. Indeed, this prejudiced, ethnic strand of legitimacy served the prime function of diverting attention from the majority's poverty and inequality under the veil of joint belonging to the "imagined political community" of the Hutu (Physicians for Human Rights 1994; see also Pabanel 1995, 114). This has been pointed out by Anderson (1991, 7) in his definition of nationalism as an imagined political community: "regardless of the actual inequality and exploitation that may prevail in each, the nation is always conceived as a deep, horizontal comradeship." Later in his work, he rightly observes that racisms "justify not so much foreign wars as domestic repression and domination" (Anderson 1991, 150; see also Stavenhagen 1990, 16; Bayart 1991; Eyoh 1996).

This ideology has always contained genocidal elements, as one can witness in a 1964 Kayibanda speech, suggesting to the Tutsi refugees that if they seek to obtain political power again, they may well find that "the whole Tutsi race will be wiped out" (Erny 1994, 62–63). During most of the 1970s and 1980s, this ideology lay dormant—it had not disappeared, but its salience to public life decreased. In the 1990s, this ideology became radicalized rapidly and reached a genocidal level by 1994. This process of radicalization of prejudice—its socioeconomic basis and its political mechanisms, as well as the role of development aid therein—is the core of the remainder of this book.

It is important to note that, to my knowledge, no aid agency has ever pushed the government to change these policies. Alison des Forges, one of the foremost American specialists on the Great Lakes region and a human rights activist (working for Africa Watch), bitterly laments the fact that all foreign aid agencies accepted the continuation of the ethnic IDs and did not pressure the government to abandon them—not even in 1992, when it became clear that they were being employed to target Tutsi for harassment and extermination (des Forges 1994).[14] Already in 1972–73, thousands of Tutsi working for foreign aid projects, embassies, and households lost their jobs or were killed, yet development aid continued as usual—in fact, it greatly increased immediately thereafter. In 1973, TRAFIPRO, for example, the country's largest cooperative managed by the Swiss Development Cooperation agency, lost all ninety-one of its Tutsi employees. Yet the next year, the same agency recommended increasing its assistance and "rwandanizing" the project, without so much as mentioning the risk of further marginalization of the Tutsi. More fundamentally, the issues of widespread racism and the refusal to allow for the return of hundreds of thousands of refugees seem not to have been on the intellectual agenda of the development community; these were not problems and were not discussed, either inside the community or with Rwandans (CIDSE and CARITAS Internationalis 1995, 10).

Notes

1. It is useful to clarify just how few people had received any education at all during the colonial period. According to data by Nzisabira (1992, table 4.4), in 1992 there were forty-nine persons in Rwanda enrolled in tertiary education (amounting to seventeen per million, or less than 0.002 percent). By 1985, that figure had increased to no more than 0.09 percent. The proportions for high school were 0.2 percent and 0.6 percent, respectively.
2. Literally, "hill"—the prime geographic and social point of reference in Rwanda.
3. Braeckman (1994, 85, 94, 99) describes a strong portrait of a violent police state, quite at odds with the more generally prevailing opinion.
4. Tetzlaff (1991, 18) observes that throughout Africa, the politicization of ethnicity has been part of the nation-building process.
5. There is no doubt that feelings of superiority, born out of privilege as much as fear, can be encountered among people of Tutsi origin—just as they are absent among many other Tutsi. However, these are individual-level sentiments, unlike the racist imagery that underlay the genocide.
6. Note that by no means all foreigners accepted this discourse, especially its hard, anti-Tutsi version. Note also that, especially after the genocide, many foreigners came to accept uncritically the opposite image of ancient ethnic unity and harmony.
7. Kressel (1993, 238–39), discussing genocide, writes that "victims are deprived of the two qualities essential to being perceived as fully human and included in the moral compact that governs human relationships: identity—standing as independent, distinctive individuals, capable of making choices and entitled to live their own lives—and community—fellow membership in an interconnected network of individuals who care for each other and respect each other's individuality and rights."
8. See Pierre van den Berghe's (1967, 9–10) famous definition of race as "a human group that defines itself and/or is defined by others as different from other groups by virtue of innate and immutable physical characteristics."
9. See Chrétien and others (1995) for an in-depth analysis of these primitive racist images; Elias and Helbig (1991) provide interesting quotes illustrating

how the colonizers, up to now, described Hutu and Tutsi as different races. See also Grosse 1994b for a discussion. Erny (1995) documents how many basic concepts—such as short/tall or north/south—have major, although usually unspoken, ethnic connotations in Rwanda. Malkki (1995, 79 ff.) documents the widespread acceptance of racist images among Burundian Hutu in a refugee camp in Tanzania.

10. For the full text of these documents, see Mkundabigenzi 1961.

11. See also the Catharine Newbury interview in Pace and Schoetzau 1995: "Stratification became more pronounced during the colonial period and the kinds of demands that the state made on common citizens, most of whom were Hutu, increased as part of the whole colonial apparatus. The accumulated resentment of rural people at the way they were being treated by chiefs was channeled and built up in a movement during the 1950s as it became clear that Belgium would be leaving and independence would be coming."

12. Note that the latter observation, although widely circulated, is unproved. Others, such as Kabirigi (1994), have suggested that the same interdiction also applied to those who wanted political appointments.

13. These data should be interpreted with the utmost caution, given their extremely political nature.

14. The replacement of the old IDs by new, nonethnic ones was at least discussed at some point in the 1990s between the government and the U.S. Agency for International Development (USAID) mission.

3

THE IMAGE OF RWANDA IN THE DEVELOPMENT COMMUNITY

This chapter presents some basic data on the importance of aid in Rwanda's economy and society. Rwanda received a large amount of aid: in this small country, there was no *colline* and no public service where one did not find the four-wheel-drive vehicles of foreign experts within view. In many ways, neither the machinery of the state nor the emerging structure of civil society could function without the massive amounts of development aid that went into the country. This international generosity was partly related to the very positive, generally accepted image of Rwanda as a model developing country, in which government and citizens were actively, wisely, and successfully committed to development. I present this image through an analysis of the rhetoric of the world's major intellectual and financial contributor to development policy, the World Bank, as well as through an overview of the standard data by which "development" is measured (data also published primarily by the World Bank). A short final section briefly describes the way the development aid system has coped with the major contradiction between the positive image of Rwanda as a stable, well-developing model country and its subsequent rapid descent to genocidal violence and social disintegration.

The Importance of Development Aid in Rwanda

Until the genocide, Rwanda was one of the most aided countries in the world. Development aid to Rwanda was vastly larger than private investment and commercial exports combined (see Figure 3.1)—although the

Figure 3.1 Financial Flows into Rwanda, 1977–93

Source: Compiled from United Nations, *African Statistical Yearbook* (New York: United Nations, various years).

data include money for technical assistance, much of which never reaches the country (Voyame and others 1996, 51). According to the Organization for Economic Cooperation and Development (OECD 1991, 189), official development aid accounted for 11.4 percent of Rwanda's gross national product (GNP) in 1989–90—above the average for Africa and the least developed countries. And in the 1990s, the size of development aid, if anything, increased further: from an average of $45 per person in the 1980s to $80 and more—primarily due to a great increase in structural adjustment–related program aid and later emergency aid. For comparison's sake, at 1992 exchange rates (US$1 equals RF 120), this means that the average six-person household received a theoretical RF 57,600 in development aid, or more than its entire income for the same year.

In total, there were approximately 200 donors in the country: about 20 bilateral ones, 30 multilateral ones, and 150 nongovernmental organizations (NGOs). Together, they managed more than 500 projects in 1986, ranging from the very small to the very large (Hanssen 1989, 25;

Voyame and others 1996, 60 ff.). The aid system was omnipresent in Rwanda, both physically and geographically. At the end of the 1980s, Rwanda was the largest recipient of aid from both Belgium and Switzerland. It had the highest density of technical assistants (foreign experts living in the country) per square kilometer in Africa. Hanssen (1989, 161) counted 881 of them in 1988, most of them with their families. United Nations Development Programme (UNDP) data show that, excluding expatriates working for NGOs, there were 757 foreign technical assistants in 1989 (Bizimungu and others 1991, 8). The Ministry of Foreign Affairs and International Cooperation calculates that in 1990, there were 210 volunteers and 453 technical assistants working for government services (Ministère des Affaires Étrangères et de la Coopération Internationale 1990). If one adds to that the foreigners working for NGOs, the missionaries (many in the business of development at least part-time), and the hundreds of specialists on short-term missions, one gets an idea of the strong physical presence of the foreign aid system. There was almost no corner of this small country (about the size of Maryland) where a four-wheel-drive vehicle with some technical assistant in it would not pass on a daily basis.

This development aid supplied the fuel on which the machinery of the state ran. According to the World Bank, "foreign assistance financed over 70 percent of public investment" in the 1982–87 period (World Bank 1989b, 11), and the figure rose afterward. On a macroeconomic level, it was this enormous increase in development aid that allowed the Rwandese state to import far more than it exported (see Figure 3.2).

The Image: Development against the Odds

The image of Rwanda created by the development community was an idyllic one. In brief, it was the image of a country of subsistence farmers faced with daunting economic and demographic challenges but endowed with a government that followed the right policies, the fruits of which the hardworking population enjoyed.[1] It was the image of a country in which things were good for all those in the business of development. The construction and repetition of this image can be uncovered by examining the language of the World Bank—the agency that certifies good behavior, the pinnacle of the development profession.

In 1976, the "for official use only" *Memorandum on the Economy of Rwanda* stated that "despite these handicaps [that is, low income, an

Figure 3.2 Rwanda's Imports and Exports

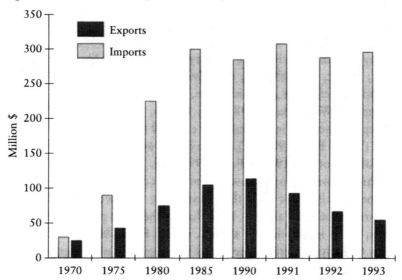

Source: Based on United Nations, *African Statistical Yearbook*
(New York: United Nations, various years).

embryonic modern sector, a land shortage, rapid population growth, and its inland position] the present Government . . . has made perceptible progress in developing a strategy to lift the economy from its present low level" (World Bank 1976, 1). Fifteen years later, Rwanda was presented in the same terms: "despite these constraints, Rwanda has made a creditable effort toward economic and social development" (World Bank 1991f, 468). In a revealing circular remark, the same paragraph goes on to say that "Rwanda has been able to attract substantial volumes of external aid from a great diversity of sources, confirming donor perceptions that the government is development-oriented and pursuing generally appropriate objectives." These dual elements—the forbidding nature of the development task in Rwanda, and the relative success of the government in tackling it—are repeated over and over in all descriptions of Rwanda, like an endless prayer, a ritual in the development religion: although "the task was forbidding, . . . Rwanda's approach to economic and social development could be considered as successful" (World Bank 1989b, 3; Voyame and others 1996, 57).

The forbidding obstacles that Rwanda had to overcome are common to almost all underdeveloped countries: "the principal problems come from the vicious circle of poverty, high population growth and pressure on the environment. In this cycle, the poor are the chief victims and the chief culprits" (World Bank 1994b, 29).

Rwanda's assets to overcome these obstacles are always the same, too. They invariably include the country's political stability (World Bank 1984, 1; 1986c, 2; 1989b, 3), the government's concern for the rural population, its effective administration, and its prudent, sound, realistic management (World Bank 1989a, 2; 1989b, 3; 1991c, 1; 1991d, 1). Other reports mention in passing "the cultural and social cohesion of its people" (World Bank 1986c, 2), or the ethnic and socioeconomic homogeneity of the country (World Bank 1991c, 3).

All this shows not only how images are constructed and repeated over time but also how little the consultants who write these reports really care about these aspects. Even during the most peaceful period in Rwanda, it was impossible for anyone, except for willfully blind people, to stress the cultural, ethnic, or social homogeneity of its people—and note that some of these reports were written in the 1990s, when that myth had long been shattered. Ethnicity has for decades been one of the major stakes in Rwandan society; yet in a hundred-page historical and policy analysis of "the role of the communes in socioeconomic development in Rwanda," there is only one line that euphemistically mentions that independence was "accompanied by widespread disturbances in the countryside"—and this in a policy discussion of the nature of the state and its relation to the population in a context of decentralization (World Bank 1987, 5). More generally, no aid agency ever denounced the official racism or the quota system or the ethnic IDs—not even in the 1990s, when it was clear that they were being used to prepare for mass killings (Guichaoua 1995a, 19). Thus the apolitical image of Rwanda as a generic—and at the same time exemplary—developing country was kept intact until the genocide.

This image is not accidental or the result of the incompetence of the specialists writing these reports. World Bank experts, and their colleagues in the other aid agencies, are every bit as qualified and intelligent as any academic or professional, including the author of this book. Rather, according to Jonathan Ferguson, who made a similar analysis for Lesotho, these simple, if not outright false, images are crucial in the construction of Rwanda as a "development problem" that can, predictably, be solved by just the kind of aid that the World Bank or any other development aid institution happens to possess. Such development problems preferably take the shape of national, "plannable," subsistence agriculture economies in which training, credit, infrastructure, planning, public health interventions, and agricultural research and extension constitute the solutions—solutions that the experts in the aid system luckily happen to have ready (Ferguson 1990, chap. 2). As Philip Quarles von Ufford (1993, 140) writes:

> The capacity to control definitions of what is supposed to be happening locally is of the utmost importance to the agencies as, in a way, they constitute their organizational identity and their "logo" in the development market. Such representations provide the means for the agencies to gain political support and access to funding in their own constituencies. The need to construct notions of manageability is also related to this. . . . The images of the local scene must be made to fit organizational needs.

Ethnic inequality; institutionalized, state-organized racism; regional politics; lack of dignity and self-respect; the generalized presence of impunity and fear and the absence of justice; human rights violations; the oppressive presence of the state, and the like are emphatically not parts of this "solvable problem" or of the mandate of development agencies; they are thus evacuated, ignored, considered not to exist.

The "myth of apolitical development," as Paul Nelson (1995, 9) calls it, has other functions too. It allows the "[World] Bank to avoid the full implications of its actions within a society" (Levinson 1992, 62) by blocking out part of reality from the realm of the visible. It situates the World Bank in a technocratic realm above or outside of politics, which allows it to avoid making politically painful judgments or having to adapt its policy prescriptions to political realities—all of which invites trouble, both with member governments and with the international capital markets (Wade 1996).

This image is not unique to the World Bank. Most other development aid agencies also considered Rwanda a model country (Schürings 1995, 495; Renard and Reyntjens 1993, 11, 18; Guichaoua 1995a, 33; Willame 1995b, 436, 445). Brusten and Bindariye (1997, 12 ff.) document how, until 1989, the Belgian NGO community, without any noticeable dissent, adhered to exactly the same image of Rwanda as the World Bank—an uncommon occurrence. And a Swiss evaluation of three decades of bilateral aid to Rwanda observed that Rwanda was widely considered a stable, noncorrupt, efficient, and serious development partner (Voyame and others 1996, 61, 64), while the annual report of the Swiss Development Cooperation agency in 1991 mentioned its "admiration" for "the government's seriousness in its desire to develop the country." Hence, the rosy image of Rwanda was shared by NGOs as well as bilateral and multilateral aid agencies.

Note, however, that among the multilaterals, the World Bank seemed to be the one with the strongest love affair with Rwanda. The reason for the intensity of this relation was in all likelihood that Rwanda's economic policies overall were quite liberal and thus very much in line with the Bank's ideology, which was a rarity in Africa before the second half of the 1980s. Most other multilateral agencies adopted the more usual policy of avoiding any judgmental remarks about government policy and political issues in their official documents. Indeed, the large majority of project reports on Rwanda contained no information at all on its past, its constellation of power, or its social or political struggles. If any attention was paid to anything political, it was usually limited to a few paragraphs outlining the administrative structure of the country or the ministry concerned. Project documents of the International Fund for Agricultural Development (IFAD) and the Food and Agriculture Organization (FAO), for example, never mentioned the nature of the government beyond a small paragraph on the organization of the Ministry of Agriculture; the population density and agricultural nature of Rwanda, in contrast, were always discussed at length.[2]

Many academics, following the same ideology of development, accept the same image of Rwanda. Rwanda is repeatedly called a model developing country by social scientists (Willame 1995a, 12; Guichaoua 1995a, 14; Chrétien and others 1995, 91). A few examples among many will suffice. Hubert Rossel (1992, 30) writes, interestingly enough: "contrary to other Third World countries that were really 'under-developing' countries ('pays en voie de sous-développement'), Rwanda was truly developing . . . in the eyes of those who do not confuse purely economic growth with development." Robert Ford (1993, 179), who lived for years in Rwanda, writes about Rwanda's "good governance" and the way it is "well organized" and calls it a "unified country." The prime problems the country faces are considered to be erosion and over-population (observed by Gaud 1995, 13); the scientific literature on these issues is vastly larger than on any other issue, with the possible exception of the preservation of Rwanda's gorillas.

The Data

At first sight, the figures seem to confirm this picture. Table 3.1 presents data on Rwanda's macroeconomic trends, the usual indicators for development. Table 3.2 adds some "alternative" social indicators of

Table 3.1   Economic Development Indicators

Indicator	Period	Growth Rate (%)
GNP per capita	1965–88	1.5
Industrial growth	1980–88	3.6
Services growth	1980–88	3.4
Agricultural growth	1980–88	0.3
Energy production	1980–88	5.5
Gross domestic investment	1980–88	7.4
Annual exports	1960–80	7.8

Sources: World Bank, *Republic of Rwanda. First Education Sector Project. Staff Appraisal Report* (Washington, D.C.: Population and Human Resources, South Central and Indian Ocean Department, 1991); World Bank, *World Development Report 1995* (Oxford: Oxford University Press, 1995).

Table 3.2   Some Social Indicators of Development

Indicator	1970	1980	1990 or 1992
Access to safe drinking water (%)	67	55	69
Access to sanitation, urban (%)	—	60	88
Access to sanitation, rural (%)	—	50	56
Infant mortality per thousand	142	—	110
One-year-olds vaccinated against diphtheria, tetanus, and pertussis (%)	—	36	85
One-year-olds vaccinated against polio (%)	—	25	5
Women vaccinated against tetanus (%)	—	5	88

Sources: Data are derived from Bernard Barrère, Juan Shoemaker, and others, *Enquête Démographique et de Santé, Rwanda 1992* (Kigali, Rwanda: Office National de la Population and Demographic and Health Surveys Macro International Inc., 1994); UNDP, *Human Development Report 1995* (Oxford: Oxford University Press, 1995); UNICEF, *State of the World's Children 1995* (Oxford: Oxford University Press, 1995); and World Bank, *World Development Report 1995* (Oxford: Oxford University Press, 1995).

development, providing information about both the availability of social services and, to a lesser extent, their impact. In both cases, data are presented for the years up to 1990 or 1992, after which came the civil war that preceded the genocide.

These data—to the extent that they are correct, and there is serious doubt about that[3]—show overall good performance, as commonly defined, certainly within the African context. Economic growth per capita progressed nicely; the important indicators of modernization—

industrial production, services, domestic investment, exports, paved roads, telephone lines, electricity consumption—were all growing fast, especially for African norms. Between 1965 and 1987, industry's contribution to GNP rose from 7 to 23 percent, and services from 18 to 40 percent (IFAD 1990, 1). Vaccination rates, often considered important indicators of so-called human development, were also up significantly; in fact, Rwanda in 1990–93 was among the three most advanced countries in sub-Saharan Africa. Even for those development practitioners who like to think of themselves as more alternative, bottom-up people, who believe that development is a matter of civil society taking development into its own hands, Rwanda was a highly successful country. By the beginning of the 1990s, Rwanda had one of Africa's highest densities of NGOs: according to my calculations, there was approximately one farmers' organization per 35 households, one cooperative per 350 households, and one development NGO per 3,500 households (see Chapter 8 for a detailed discussion). Hence, according to the different indicators used by different development theories and models, Rwanda was clearly on the path to development.

Of course, there were worries in the development community. The prime fear was that agricultural productivity was stagnating while erosion and soil depletion were on the rise—as was Rwanda's total population. Nobody saw quick remedies to that trend: agricultural research, the promotion of antierosion techniques, agroforestry associations, and the like had all been the subject of decades of work and seemed to have reached a limit in terms of their effectiveness. The promotion of rural and urban industry and regional agricultural specialization were discussed as alternatives but seemed either slow to come about or unrealistic.

From the middle of the 1980s onward, the agricultural sector, and the countryside in general, entered a profound crisis (discussed in more detail in Chapter 4). Rwanda's food security and food self-sufficiency—prime objectives of all the postindependence development plans and policies—were increasingly endangered. Moreover, agricultural export crop production (essentially coffee and tea) provided the backbone of the government's foreign currency earnings. Any slowdown in production in this sector could have immediate impacts on the strength of the Rwandese state, as was shown by the economic consequences of falling, or rising, coffee prices from the middle of the 1970s onward (Uwizeyimana 1996).

A second problem with Rwanda's development trajectory was the rise in government deficits and, following that, in external debt. As repeated in countless World Bank reports from the 1980s onward, the government "failed to realize that the high tax revenues of the 'coffee boom' (1979–80) were only temporary, not justifying a permanent increase in expenditures" (World Bank 1989b, 4). Naturally, this led to an unavoidable need for structural adjustment, which took years to negotiate and finally came about by 1990 (Cart 1995).

From Development to Relief: Explaining the Transition

This growing, increasingly modern economy with a liberal government, an improving infrastructure, and a vibrant civil society filled with foreign aid experts self-destructed in a matter of months, falling victim to the most brutal, widespread, and systematic killing spree the world has ever witnessed (the Holocaust and the Cambodian genocide seem to have been more organized from above, with less widespread popular participation, killing a smaller proportion of the total population). There clearly existed a major contradiction between development practitioners' image of Rwanda as a stable, well-developing model country and its subsequent rapid disintegration in extreme violence. How are the two reconciled? With the benefit of hindsight, how do development practitioners now look at the development process in Rwanda? Do they see any relation to the genocide?

The dominant position, adhered to by most of the international development community, is that Rwanda *was* indeed developing quite nicely (although the agricultural situation was worrisome) and that an external factor (beyond the field of development) caused all this to collapse. That factor is usually considered to be the Rwanda Patriotic Front (FPR) invasion, but for some, it may also be the collapse in coffee prices, the influence of the international community (premature pressures for democratization or French, Zairean, and Ugandan military involvement and arms trade), or the general nastiness of the *akazu*, the small clique around President Habyarimana's family that planned the genocide.

There is no doubt that all these factors are important in understanding the 1994 genocide. However, they are also very limited. All these explanations are alike in that they acknowledge no link between Rwanda's development process (and the role of the foreign aid machinery therein) and the 1994 genocide; the latter, they conclude, was due to some unfortunate deus ex machina that disrupted an otherwise excellent development process. This book demonstrates in detail how faulty that analysis is.

Notes

1. Note how, after the FPR came to power, this image was being repeated by some. See, for example, Judith Matloff, staff writer of the *Christian Science Monitor*, in her article "Kagame New Rulers, U.S. Plan Give Africa a Future" in mid-June 1997: "Kagame and his men set an almost puritanical example, free of the excesses of other African states. The country he leads is an earnest one where schools function, streets are clean, bribery is frowned on, and hard work rewarded."
2. See, for example, IFAD 1988, 1990, 1992; FAO 1982, 1983, 1990. When these agencies describe Rwanda's rapid economic growth in the 1960s and 1970s, they never single out the high quality of the government's policies; rather, they mention good agroclimatic conditions, massive foreign aid, and positive trends in the international coffee market.
3. See Uvin 1994a for population data; World Bank 1986a, 4, for GNP data, and World Bank 1986a, 99, for agricultural production data.

PART II

CRISIS, ELITE MANIPULATION, AND VIOLENCE IN THE 1990s

4

POLITICAL AND ECONOMIC
CRISES AND THE RADICALIZATION
OF SOCIETY

From the middle of the 1980s onward, Rwanda's economy entered a severe and multifaceted economic crisis that negatively affected almost all social groups. This economic crisis was first agricultural (affecting both food crops and export crops) and then became financial. It was followed by a series of political crises: a rise in political discontent within the country, caused at least in part by the economic crisis; the civil war instigated by the Rwandan Patriotic Front (FPR) beginning in October 1990; and international pressure for democratization. Together, these crises profoundly threatened the power and privileges of the regime's dignitaries. The radical elements within the regime took recourse through the usual defense—the revival of ethnic hatred, made all the easier by the FPR invasion. Through a series of human rights abuses, racist propaganda, and the militarization of society, Rwandese society moved toward the genocide.

In the first two sections, this chapter details the nature of the economic and political crises. The third section analyzes the processes through which genocidal violence became possible, and the fourth critically analyzes the explanation presented here, pointing to some deficiencies that are addressed in the next part of the book.

Economic Crises

Although food production in Rwanda had greatly increased between 1960 and the middle of the 1980s, it began stagnating between 1985 and 1990 (see Figure 4.1). Maize production, for example, fell from 110,000 tons in 1983 to 90,000 tons by 1986 and subsequently stagnated in the 90,000 to 100,000-ton range. Similarly, sorghum production, another staple, which was at 213,000 tons in 1982, slid erratically downward to approximately 140,000 tons in 1988 and 1989. According to recent research, "over the period 1984–1991, kcal. produced by Rwandan farmers dropped from 2,055 per person per day to 1,509" (Clay and others 1995, 1)—from an already low level to an intolerable level (World Resources Institute 1996, table 10.1). From 1991 onward, the civil war (see below) further strained Rwanda's agricultural system. In 1993, when up to one million persons were displaced as a result of an FPR offensive, Rwanda's food production totally collapsed: maize production, for example, fell to 74,000 tons, and sorghum to 109,000 tons (FAO on-line data). Commercial and concessional food imports, although on the rise, did not make up for the post-1985 decline in production.

The production of cash crops fared slightly better. Despite a few years of bad weather, wheat and rice production, for example, slowly increased from 2,100 and 4,400 tons, respectively, in 1980 to 11,000 and 10,000 tons in 1990. The volume of coffee and tea production also rose steadily until 1988–89. However, from 1985 onward, a decade-long decline in the international price of coffee, Rwanda's major export, began; tea also lost up to 40 percent of its value. As Figure 4.2 shows, coffee export receipts fell from $144 million in 1985 (admittedly an exceptionally good year) to $30 million in 1993 (FAO 1994). All this greatly reduced the foreign exchange earnings of the Rwandan state—which was still more than 80 percent dependent on coffee and tea—as well as the purchasing power of most rural households (Marysse, Ndayambaje, and Waterloos 1992, 45). Also during the mid–1980s, the companies in charge of Rwanda's few other exports—cassiterite and bauxite—folded, depriving the state of their revenue (Marysse, De Herdt, and Ndayambaje 1995). The available data indicate that the aggregate gross domestic product (GDP) per capita decreased from $355 in 1983 to $260 in 1990—a 7 percent annual decline (Uwizeyimana 1996, 104; see also Marysse, De Herdt, and Ndayambaje 1995, 31). According to a 1994 World Bank report, poverty in Rwanda greatly increased, from 40 percent in 1985 to 52 percent in 1992 (World Bank 1994b, i, 10).

During these years of reduced revenue due to the coffee crisis, Rwanda's government resorted to increased borrowing to keep up its expenditure pattern. As a result, foreign debt, until the 1980s low by African standards, began increasing rapidly, rising from 16 percent of the gross national product (GNP) in 1980 to 32 percent in 1990. From late

Figure 4.1 Food and Agricultural Production Index (1989–91=100)

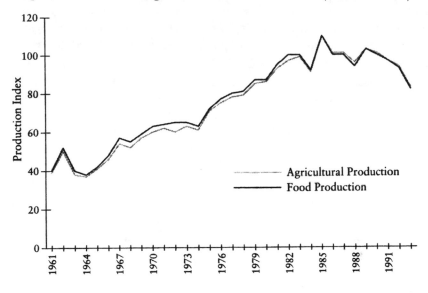

Source: FAO online data.

Figure 4.2 Coffee and Tea Exports

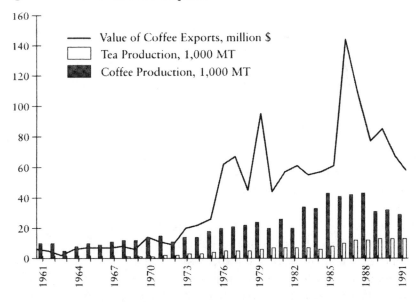

Source: Compiled from FAO online data.

1990 onward, the civil war instigated by the FPR further aggravated the economic crisis and rendered Rwanda's public finances truly disastrous.

The population displacement from a major food-producing region contributed to Rwanda's decline in food production and created demands for emergency food and housing. The international community helped fulfill these needs, but only from 1992–93 onward, and partly at the cost of ordinary development aid. The decline in agricultural production in the northwest region also greatly reduced government revenue, as the region was a major tea- and coffee-producing area (Percival and Homer-Dixon 1995). The closing off of the major transport road to Mombasa rendered exports and imports more expensive. Finally, the government began devoting an increased share of its resources to the war effort; the number of soldiers in the Rwandan army grew from 3,000 to 5,000 to 30,000 to 40,000, and expenditures on arms soared (although military aid, especially from France, softened the cost). As a result, military expenditure rose from 1.6 percent of the GNP between 1985 and 1990 to 7.6 percent in 1993 (UNDP 1995, table 14; SIPRI various years); by 1992, the military consumed 38 percent of Rwanda's government budget (World Bank 1994b, 24). According to Reyntjens (1994, 117), the total increase of Rwanda's public debt between 1990 and 1992 was equivalent to the rise in military expenditures.

Thus Rwanda entered a profound economic crisis, felt both by the state and by most farmers. Data on fertility suggest just how severe the crisis was for most people. Between 1983 and 1992, Rwanda's total fertility rate rapidly and dramatically fell from 8.4 to 6.2 children per woman; during the same time, the desired family size fell from 6.3 to 4.2 (Barrère and others 1992, 30; Grosse 1994a, 13, documents that the decline took place primarily from 1986 onwards). Usually, reductions in fertility are taken to be reflections of increased income or well-being, effective family planning programs, or both. However, neither of these trends occurred in Rwanda; contraceptive use increased only slightly during the same period and never came close to involving even 10 percent of the population. It has been documented that very rapid declines in fertility can, in fact, be due to severe crisis, reflecting people's sense that the future is so uncertain and threatening that it is better to postpone marrying and having children. A major study on the demographic effects of economic reversals in sub-Saharan Africa, for example, concluded that severe economic crisis, especially in single-export-dependent countries, tends to delay marriage and childbearing (Working Group on Demographic Effects 1993). It seems likely that the economic crisis sparked a similar response in Rwanda, explaining the dramatic decline in fertility (André and Platteau 1995, 10; Olson 1995, 219).

THE CAUSES OF THE CRISIS

The agricultural crisis was the result of a combination of factors, conjunctural and structural. The conjunctural factors included drought in 1984, excessive rain in 1987, plant disease in 1988, and the effects of the war from 1991 onward, particularly in 1993 (Willame 1995a, 3l).[1] The more important causes were structural, however, reflecting long-standing trends and constraints. They included the effects of land pressure, erosion, and poverty, combined with the exhaustion of a top-down, immobilizing development model that had been followed for decades. All this had rendered the Rwandan peasantry increasingly unable to cope with shocks.

Similarly, the state's financial crisis contained both conjunctural and structural elements. The effects of the war were the main unpredictable and temporary factors. The foremost structural constraint was Rwanda's export dependence on coffee, which had not changed since the colonial period, making the country highly vulnerable to international price swings in this commodity. Another structural factor was Rwanda's nascent industrial sector, which was largely mismanaged and very expensive, both in import content and in subsidies.[2] More generally, since the early 1980s, the state faced a persistent balance-of-payment deficit, as well as an increasing dependence on foreign aid, indicating that its problems had begun before the coffee crisis. By and large, its situation resembled that of most other African countries. It must be observed, however, that in 1982 the government had already implemented an austerity program, which rendered both the balance of payments and the public-sector budget positive by 1984–85. The collapse of the mining sector, however, together with the fall in coffee prices, brought about a new, more severe crisis, which the government could not control.

STRUCTURAL ADJUSTMENT

In 1991, after long and difficult negotiations (Cart 1995, 475), Rwanda signed a $90 million structural adjustment program (SAP) with the World Bank. In 1992 and 1993, additional sectoral adjustment loans were negotiated but only partially implemented. These programs were identical to many other such programs in Africa. They sought to promote fiscal and monetary discipline; the withdrawal of government from all economic sectors except human resources, justice, and environment; increased production for exports (to reimburse debts and allow imports of agricultural inputs); the liberalization of domestic and international trade; and, more specifically for the case of Rwanda, free internal labor migration (World Bank 1994b, 1991c).

One of the cornerstones of the SAP, designed to boost coffee exports and to reduce imports, was the devaluation of the Rwandese franc by 40 percent in November 1990 (before the actual signing of a SAP agreement, and just a few weeks after the FPR invasion) and by an additional 15 percent in June 1992. The devaluations had an important inflationary effect. Inflation rose from 1 percent in 1989 to 19.2 percent in 1991 (Chossudovsky 1994, 21). While the consumer price index (1987 = 100) had been quite stable before 1990, rising from 97 in 1985 to 104 in 1989, it rapidly increased to 130 in 1991 and 160 in 1993 (World Bank on-line Social Indicators of Development; Marysse, De Herdt, and Ndayambaje 1995, 32).

At the same time, the state had to cut expenditures. In 1990, the producer price of coffee—the price the state guaranteed (at least theoretically) for coffee farmers—was lowered from RF 125 (where it had been since 1987) to RF 100 per kilogram (Uwizeyimana 1996, 94).[3] As a result of inflation, many of those with jobs saw their incomes erode, and many people in the urban areas became noticeably poorer. Meanwhile, the devaluations could not compensate for the further decline of the price of coffee on the international markets.

In general, however, only a small part of the SAP as negotiated with the International Monetary Fund (IMF), the World Bank, and the U.S. Agency for International Development (USAID) was implemented. The expansion of public-sector jobs was halted, but the agreed-on cutbacks never materialized; the rapid increase in the size of the army ended up greatly expanding public employment. Most of the decontrol measures—engaging the government to free the markets for goods and services, exports and imports—were never implemented. As a result, the disbursements came to a halt: according to Marysse, De Herdt, and Ndayambaje (1995, 36), only 8.7 of the 30.6 SDR (special drawing rights) promised by the IMF was ever disbursed, and only $60 million of the $90 million promised by the World Bank was granted.

Meanwhile, the government had been adopting an increasing number of policies, usually with aid money, that, although not formally part of the SAP, reflected its philosophy. These included programs of improving the health sector and the water supply through raising users' fees (Bugingo and others 1992, 61). Combined with taxes, *umuganda* (obligatory community labor), school fees, and obligatory contributions in kind to the construction of schools and health centers, these policies exacerbated the already severe pressure on most farm households.

The sectoral adjustment loans did not pull Rwanda out of its economic crisis. By 1993, for example, Rwanda's debt as a percentage of GNP had skyrocketed from 32 percent in 1990 to 62 percent; it amounted to 838 percent of 1993 exports (from 103 percent in 1980) (World Bank 1996). Structural adjustment did not cause these problems; rather, it was largely irrelevant to their resolution,[4] for two reasons. One, stressed by the World Bank itself, is that Rwanda never implemented most of the SAPs. This argument, used by the Bank and the IMF against nearly all criticisms of structural adjustment, has some validity in the case of Rwanda. Apart from the devaluations and the abolition of some export and import controls, the size of the state was not reduced, and its degree of intervention in the economy hardly decreased. This is especially evident if one looks at government policy from the mid-1980s onward, when the agricultural and economic crises had already hit Rwanda (and not solely from 1991, when Rwanda finally signed its SAP agreement). In the Bank's 1994 *Adjustment in Africa* study, comparing the fate of twenty-nine adjusting countries that began adjustment between 1987 and 1991, Rwanda is one of the few African countries whose policies actually deteriorated during the 1985–93 period (from the Bank's point of view, that is). Its final rating on most policy categories is "poor."

The other reason why structural adjustment did not solve Rwanda's problems is that these problems were enmeshed in crises that were beyond the program's ability to address. The SAP was to be implemented while the country was facing an economic crisis without precedent and simultaneously going through a civil war and a democratic transition. Too many variables intervened to modify or undermine the potential impact of the SAP, or even its likely implementation. The World Bank did not take into account the political crises facing Rwanda but acted, in traditional fashion, as if politics did not exist. As we will see, in so doing, it was not alone; none of the international development aid agencies changed their policies in response to the disintegration of Rwandese society during the 1990s.

Political Crises

At the beginning of the 1990s, three political crises occurred that, added to the economic crisis, greatly threatened the stability, if not the survival, of the regime. The year 1990 stands as the turning point: in that one year, Rwanda faced the introduction of a multiparty system, the beginning of a civil war, and the adoption of structural adjustment—a case of "simultaneous transitions," as it is termed in the political science literature, that was extremely disrupting to the system as it had evolved over the last decades. The regime and its dignitaries were under attack from all sides and took recourse in the usual, time-tested manner: the revival of ethnic hatred. The Table 4.1 at the end of this chapter summarizes most of the events discussed in the following pages.

POLITICAL DISCONTENT

The first challenge to the regime was the rise of internal discontent, emanating mainly from disgruntled Hutu urbanites but also spreading to the countryside. It was widely known that the dignitaries of the regime had become increasingly corrupt during the 1980s, as evidenced by the abuse of public enterprises; the smuggling of drugs, arms, and gorillas; and kickbacks on construction (Braeckman 1994, 102 ff.; Gordon 1992; Reyntjens 1994, 32; 1995c). Widespread corruption, disappointment with the slow pace of development, and the occurrence of local famines all combined to challenge the regime from within (Guichaoua 1995a, 28; Percival and Homer-Dixon 1995). Opposition took place partly along regional lines, with political opposition coming mainly from the south and the center; the prime positions of power and privilege in the Habyarimana regime were almost fully monopolized by people from the president's district in the north, and most public investments took place in that region (see Chapter 6). In December 1991, contrary to its usual mutism, even the Catholic Church spoke out against the regime. In a pastoral letter, the bishop in Kabgayi, Rwanda's most important diocese, reproached the government for its bad management of public affairs, corruption, social injustice, and human rights violations (Reyntjens 1994, 114).

In 1990, the regime grudgingly allowed the creation of new political parties, although a few of the larger and more important ones had not even waited for the declaration. By 1992, a set of new human rights organizations and fifteen political parties had been created, and the first coalition government was established. As was usually the case in Africa at the time, the new parties were quite alike. They all shared a desire for change, not necessarily of the political system but of the power holders within the National Revolutionary Development Movement (MRND) (Prunier 1995; Reyntjens 1994). Their political programs included few specifics besides affirmation of the need for alteration. Most of the parties were headed by political heavyweights from the former single party and could hardly be said to represent the large majority of the country: the farmers. The latter, not surprisingly, were largely unconcerned with the so-called democratization (Reyntjens 1994; USAID 1992).

FPR INVASION

The second major event was the October 1, 1990, invasion from Uganda by the FPR, composed largely, but not exclusively, of the descendants of the 1959–63 wave of Tutsi refugees who had settled in Uganda.[5] In the beginning, the FPR had little more than a few thousand soldiers, but it was well armed and trained. Many of its soldiers had fought for years with Museveni in Uganda; from this, they had obtained experience and arms. They almost reached Kigali but were halted by the Rwandan army, supported by rapidly flown-in French and Zairean soldiers. Approximately 500 civilians died, and as many as 350,000 temporarily fled their homes. After this initial surprise attack, the FPR was pushed back into Uganda and the national parks at the border. Many refugees returned home, and the civil war entered a guerrilla phase, with the FPR controlling small but varying parts of the northeastern region and constituting a permanent threat to the regime.

From 1991 onward, negotiations for a cease-fire and power sharing took place in Tanzania, first in Dar es Salaam and then in Arusha. These negotiations were torturously slow and permeated with double-talk and broken promises on both sides (see Table 4.1 at the end of this chapter for a detailed chronology). A cease-fire was agreed on in June 1992 and went into effect in August of the same year. It was violated in February 1993, when the FPR launched a major attack (justified by the massacre of 300 Tutsi a few weeks before) that killed hundreds of civilians and pushed hundreds of thousands of others into camps in and around Kigali. New negotiations began, and a new cease-fire was negotiated in

August 1993. At that time, a new peace agreement was signed, which included provisions for a twenty-two-month transitional government and parliament, ending with multiparty elections and integration of the FPR forces into the Rwandan army and gendarmerie. The agreement also proposed the creation of a blue-helmet peacekeeping force, which was approved on October 5 by the UN Security Council. Its mandate included assistance in providing security for Kigali so that the broad-based government could be installed, monitoring government and FPR observance of the cease-fire and adherence to the peace accord provisions on the integration of the armed forces, providing security for returning refugees, and monitoring the security situation in the period leading up to elections.

The FPR invasion profoundly affected the Rwandan political and economic landscape. Immediately after the outbreak of the war, the interests of the regime were probably served, in that the invasion increased the government's legitimacy, and large parts of the population rallied around it (Reyntjens 1994, 93, 150, 181). There is also evidence that the FPR arbitrarily killed civilians, and images to that effect were strongly exploited by the government (Misser 1993). And as I already outlined, the invasion greatly contributed to the economic crisis that Rwanda was facing. Moroever, the people who were displaced by the fighting, and those living in the regions that the displaced moved into, were understandably hostile to the FPR and open to ethnic radicalism (Rwanda: Wrapping Democracy 1992).

INTERNATIONAL PRESSURE

Following the end of the cold war, the international community suddenly rediscovered a strong attachment to democracy and put pressure on the regime to democratize and to negotiate power sharing with the FPR and the domestic opposition as a first step to free elections. This pressure is generally credited with providing the impetus for the Arusha negotiations, which led to guarantees for the return of the Tutsi refugees, as well as power-sharing mechanisms (Reyntjens 1994; Prunier 1995).

This pressure was exercised as Rwanda was facing both a civil war and the introduction of structural adjustment. Some observers have questioned the expediency of this pressure under these difficult circumstances (for example, Renard and Reyntjens 1993). Moreover, important and powerful factions within Rwanda who disagreed with and were afraid of the outcome of the negotiations in Tanzania were neglected. Reyntjens (1994, 189 ff.) provides a well-informed clarification on the composition of these factions. At the heart was the so-called *akazu*, the small clique of high dignitaries around Habyarimana and his wife. A second group consisted of racist radicals, often intellectuals. A third group was composed of cadres of the MRND, the former single party, for which democratization meant a likely loss of power. While the international community was concentrating all its attention on the documents being prepared at Arusha, these factions prepared to use violence to reverse the externally inspired changes. In the externally driven rush for multiparty elections, defined as the solution to all problems, these forces inside the country did not confront one another (Adelman and Suhrke 1996). The conversion to democracy was the donors', not the elites'.

From Elite Fear to the Incitation of Genocide

All these processes threatened to deprive the Habyarimana regime and its cronies of their control of the state. As Adelman and Suhrke (1996, 17) wrote: "ideologically and politically, the BBTG [broad-based transitional government, negotiated at Arusha] represented a frontal attack on the power base erected by the Habyarimana regime during 20 years of rule—a denial of authoritarian rule, of 'Hutu power,' and especially Northwestern-based Hutu power which was the regional constituency and political backbone of the regime." The regime was under attack from all sides, and parts of it looked to ethnic hatred as the usual solution to its problems. Ethnicity could serve to unite the large majority of the population around the government, take the momentum away from the opposition, combat the FPR, and render elections impossible. Ethnicity was to be the tool of the elite, as it had been for the last thirty years (de Heusch 1994, 17; Guichaoua 1995a, 29). This was all the easier to achieve because the FPR invasion, besides creating death and misery, seemed to confirm old racist images of Tutsi as aggressive and dangerous (Braeckman 1995, 8).

Under the leadership of the *akazu*, a variety of dynamics was created that sought to radicalize racist prejudice (see Table 4.1 for a detailed chronology). The first was the extension of the FPR threat to all Tutsi (Chrétien 1993a; Uwizeyimana 1991). The best-documented expression of this strategy came immediately after the FPR invasion. On the night of October 4, 1990, the army staged an all-night shooting attack on Kigali and blamed it on the Tutsi. This fooled the world for quite some time (it was only unmasked months later) and strengthened a sense of psychosis against "the enemy within" (Braeckman 1995, 8). It was used to justify the imprisonment, during the next few weeks, of some 8,000–10,000 Tutsi, mostly intellectuals, priests, teachers, businessmen, and opponents to the regime (Reyntjens 1994, 95). Most of them were freed only after months of international pressure; many were tortured, some killed, or their possessions stolen (Prunier 1995; Pabanel 1995, 118; Braeckman 1994, 115). In early 1991, a similar fake attack was also used to justify the killing of hundreds of Tutsi in Kibilira (Human Rights Watch 1995, 17). Thus, a direct link was created between the rebels and all Tutsi in the country, and fear of all Tutsi, even those unconnected to the war, was promoted (Nkubito 1992, 22).

More generally, at political rallies, in speeches, and in extremist local-language newspapers and radio stations, Tutsi were constantly the subject of hateful propaganda (Chrétien and others 1995, 190–95; Chrétien 1991; Article 19 1996; Dupaquier 1996, 150). Much of the freedom of press that was suddenly (and only partly) allowed was invaded by newspapers with an incendiary and racist position. The most (in)famous cases were *Kangura*, a radical newspaper created in early 1990, and Radio-Télévision Libre des Mille Collines, created in mid-1993,[6] but more than twenty papers regularly published racist editorials and cartoons; the official Radio Rwanda often produced similar material. This propaganda included explicit and regular incitations to mass murder, verbal attacks on Tutsi, the publication of lists of names of "interior enemies" to be killed, and threats to anyone having relations with Tutsi. These genocidal and extremist voices were not only tolerated, but also morally and financially supported by people at the highest levels of the establishment, including the government (Reyntjens 1994; Braeckman 1994, 152 ff.).

During the same period, extremist political parties were created that openly preached hatred and violence, again with support from the highest echelons. These included the CDR (Commité de Défense de la Révolution, a party to the right of, but close to, Habyarimana's party) and, from mid-1992 onward, a set of armed militia—foremost the infamous *interahamwe* ("those who attack together") and *impuzamugambi* ("those with a single purpose")—linked to Habyarimana's party and the CDR, respectively (Human Rights Watch 1994b; Prunier 1995; des Forges 1994; Braeckman 1994, 143). These parties and groups were supported, trained, and armed by the *akazu* and served to radicalize and divide the opposition and to slow down the process of the Arusha negotiations.

Radicalization and division of the opposition proved to be easy to achieve. From the beginning, most opposition parties were little more than vehicles of individual politicians—almost all of them former MRND dignitaries—with little on the agenda beyond the quest for their own power and advantages. They were more than willing to embrace radical and racist tactics if this could help their cause (Reyntjens 1994, 122, 125; Braeckman 1994, 131). Most political parties created their own youth militias and used force against their opponents—often within the party. By 1993, almost all opposition parties had split between radical, so-called Hutu power wings that were close to the CDR and its discourse, and moderate wings. During the genocide, most of the leaders of the moderate factions were slaughtered; many of the radical so-called opposition party members participated, often in positions of power.

During this time, Rwandese society became increasingly militarized. Between late 1990 and early 1992, the size of the regular army increased from 3,000 to 5,000 to 30,000 to 40,000 soldiers, and large amounts of arms were imported into the country. The government distributed many of these arms in the areas closest to the war, to allow for "popular defense" of the county. By 1992, the militias were created, and they too were well armed and trained in the use of these arms. Finally, in late 1993, a massive campaign was initiated to distribute arms to "self-defense groups" in all communes in the country (Braeckman 1994, 154 ff.; Human Rights Watch 1994a).

From the very beginning of the civil war, frequent massacres of Tutsi were committed. On each occasion—October 1990, January 1991, February 1991, March 1992, August 1992, January 1993, March 1993, and February 1994 (see Table 4.1)—hundreds of Tutsi were slaughtered by mobs and militiamen directed by local administrative authorities, national politicians, the police, and the army (Reyntjens 1994, 117; Centre Nord-Sud 1994; Human Rights Watch 1994b; U.S. Department of State 1993). In between these massacres, a reign of terror was launched against Tutsi, in which occasional killings, rapes, imprisonment, or harassment could befall anyone at any time. Many fled the country; there was no Tutsi family in Rwanda that did not live in permanent fear.

These processes were orchestrated at the highest levels, their execution passed on with Rwanda's typical efficiency through the usual channels to local authorities. As the Commission Internationale d'Enquête sur les Violations des Droits de l'Homme au Rwanda depuis le 1er octobre 1990 observed, "these massacres . . . have never been the result of chance or spontaneous popular movements or even the result of competition between different parties. There seems to be a central hand, or a number of hands, that master the genesis and the unfolding of these events."

All these processes resemble similar processes in past genocides elsewhere in the world (Du Preez 1994, 83, 101–7). They successfully sought to spread ethnic fear throughout society, to organize and legitimize the forces of violence and genocide, and to desensitize people to violence. Kelman and Hamilton (1993, 235), who have done some of the best work seeking to explain the social processes that allow large numbers of people to participate in violence, distinguish three phases in the preparation of mass violence. These phases, designed to overcome moral inhibitions against violence, are authorization, which absolves the individual of the responsibility to make moral choices; routinization, when the action becomes so normalized that there is no opportunity to raise moral questions; and dehumanization, which occurs when the actors' attitudes toward the targets and toward themselves become so structured that it is neither necessary nor possible for them to view the relationship in moral terms.[7]

The routinization of violence has been described by many social psychologists. In the context of apartheid South Africa, Hoffmann and McKendrick (1990, 17) discuss people's capacity for "neutralizing, disregarding, minimizing, rationalizing, and misjudging" the extent of violence in society. And Sabini and Silver (1993, 212–13) state in their study of the psychology of genocide that "once brutality becomes standard procedure within an organization, it takes on an added legitimacy."

When, in April 1994, the plane carrying Habyarimana from a peace negotiation in Arusha was shot down, the scenario unfolded along predictable lines. The army was ready, as were the militias, as were the victims. The violence started the same night in Kigali and was largely executed by the presidential guards, the militias, and the army. In a few hours, thousands of people were killed, including the prime minister (as well as the ten Belgian UNAMIR soldiers guarding her), opposition politicians, and large numbers of Tutsi. The carnage spread to the rest of the country at varying speeds. In some areas, it started immediately; in others, where provincial governors, communal burgomasters, or ordinary citizens resisted, it took weeks. In the latter case, the so-called interim government replaced civil servants with new, extremist ones and flew in the militia from the capital. Hundreds of thousands of defense-less children, women, and men were killed.

Beyond the Standard Explanation

These events constitute the standard explanation of the origins of Rwanda's genocide. Although every factor discussed here—the economic crisis and its impact on the poor, as well as on the state; the political challenges to the regime; the FPR invasion; the international pressure for democratization; the hate propaganda; and the militia and the role of the *akazu* therein—is important, this is not the whole story. Specifically, this account begs three questions.

First, this account tells us nothing about the deeper social basis on which the processes of manipulation and radicalization rest. All the attention focuses on the causes and the strategies of the manipulation of ethnicity by the elites; at the same time, there is little discussion of the people who perpetrated the violence, the world they inhabited and the reasons they might have had for obeying the messages.

Yet it is clear that messages of hatred broadcast by elites—or by radios controlled by elites—are not simply received by passive recipients who automatically follow the wishes of their beloved leaders. People, even those living in poverty, have a capacity to choose the messages they will respect and to modify them according to their own preferences (for some excellent work based on that premise, see Long and Villarreal 1993; Olivier de Sardan 1995). After all, these are the same people who spent an inordinate amount of time and energy disobeying the messages that came from above: dissimulating their assets or selling products on the black market to escape taxation, ripping out coffee plants and inter-cropping them with food crops or badly maintaining them (all forbid-den by law), or not showing up for obligatory community labor and party meetings. Moreover, by the 1990s, the legitimacy of the elite was very low: it was generally seen as a corrupt, distant group, interested primarily in self-preservation and enrichment (Netherlands Development Cooperation 1992, 49). Thus, contrary to a widespread vision of Rwandese peasants as obedient executioners of orders from above—even if these orders involved killing their neighbors—they should be seen, like all people, as independent actors, facing constraints, to be sure, but capable of making decisions. Their willingness to carry out orders to kill must be scrutinized, its roots analyzed.

Second, and closely related to the first criticism, the analysis is too short term, suggesting that the occurrence of the 1994 genocide can be understood in reference to events and trends no older than a few years. Yet it is clear that both the racist ideology on which the genocidal edifice was built and the political processes that allowed the *akazu* to manipulate society are part of long-term social, economic, and political processes occurring in Rwanda. Without understanding those processes, we will always be limited to a mechanistic vision of the Rwandan—or, for that matter, the Serb or Croatian—as a simple, manipulable puppet.

Third, genocide is a qualitatively different phenomenon from "ordinary" forms of violence, no matter how severe. The hundreds of thousands of people killed in Rwanda in 1994 were not the regrettable if unavoidable casualties of a civil war (although extremist propaganda to this day presents it that way); they were the victims of a genocide—innocent women, children, and men slaughtered for the simple reason that they were, or looked like, Tutsi. Why were ordinary Rwandans willing to kill neighbors, students, colleagues, and total strangers? What kind of social processes had taken place that could bring people to lose the values, restraints, and ethics that under normal circumstances make these actions impossible to do and abhorrent to contemplate?

To answer these questions, more is needed than an understanding of threats to the elites and their strategies for survival. If messages of hatred and extremism spread so well, it is because they fell onto fertile ground—ground tended by ordinary people. There are two factors that need understanding: the role of a long-standing and institutionalized racist prejudice, and the condition of what we call "structural violence." It is these factors that provided the foundation on which extremist propaganda built its genocidal edifice. Without them, one cannot understand Rwanda's genocide. Chapter 2 already contained a discussion of the nature and strength of racism in Rwandese society—a crucial, yet oft neglected part of the explanation. The next part of this book (especially Chapter 6) examines the world of the ordinary Rwandans—the faceless, ragged-clothed, skinny, poverty-stricken people who did so much of the killing, the same people the development enterprise sought to help for years, the same ones who fled the country from the summer of 1994 onward, and the same ones who were kept for years in refugee camps and then forced back to Rwanda or killed in 1997.

But first, Chapter 5 analyzes the role of development aid during the tumultuous years 1990–94. To what extent did the development community influence the processes that led to genocide? Did it seek to prevent it but was incapable of doing so? Did it not react? If not, why? And how did the actions or inactions of the development community relate to the wider international political context within which they occurred?

Notes

1. IWACU (1991, 9, 25) argues that average temperatures and rainfall for the periods 1974–81 and 1982–88 were barely different, but in the second period there was famine, suggesting that structural and not climatic factors were the important ones.
2. All three reasons were put forward by Voyame and others 1996, 58, 127, 132, 140. According to some data, each job in the industrial sector cost the state RF 5 million. See also Ministère du Plan 1989, 4.
3. From 1980 to 1985, it had been at RF 120. In 1991, the price increased from RF 100 to 107, and in 1992 to RF 115—below the rate of growth of the consumer price index, though (FAO on-line data).
4. This is quite a different conclusion from the often heard radical charge that the World Bank's SALs actually caused the economic crisis or the genocide; see Chossudovsky 1994; McCullen 1995.
5. The FPR was financially backed by a broad "Tutsi diaspora" throughout the world, including the United States.
6. It must be noted that, according to recent data (Barrère and others 1994, 20), only 30 percent of rural households possessed radios, as opposed to 62 percent in the urban areas. The same proportion emerges from an analysis in rural Gitarama (Groupe de Labeaume 1985, 65). UNICEF 1995, table 4, documents that 6.4 percent of the people had radios.
7. Bar-Tal 1990 adds trait characterization, in which groups are characterized as possessing traits that are unacceptable to society.

Table 4.1   Chronology of Political Events, September 1990–April 1994

Year/ Month	Developments in the War	Democratization	Militarization
1990			
Sep.			
Oct.	∎ 1: The Rwandan Patriotic Front (FPR) invades Rwanda ∎ 4: Rwandan armed forces (RAF) fake an FPR attack		∎ 1.5% of GDP go to military expenditures during this year ∎ Size of RAF forces before the war: 3,000
Nov.		∎ Habyarimana promises a multiparty system	
Dec.			∎ Radical journal *Kangura* publishes the "10 command-ments of the Hutu," inciting genocide
1991			
Jan.	∎ FPR attacks a prison in Ruhengeri		∎ 4.1% of GDP to military expenditures during this year
Feb.	∎ RAF stages fake FPR attack		
Mar.	∎ 29: Cease-fire signed at N'Sele	∎ First opposition party created (Mouvement Démo-cratique Républicain, MDR)	
Apr.	∎ 5–6: Continued talks in Dar es Salaam		
May			
June		∎ 10: Multiparty system incor-porated into new constitution ∎ Major political parties (PSD, PL) are formed	

Human Rights Violations	Human Rights Coverage	Press Coverage
	∎ 30: The Association Rwandaise des Droits de l'Homme (ARDHO) is formed	
∎ 4: Tutsi and political opponents detained (8,000 between Oct. 1990 and Apr. 1991) ∎ 300 Tutsi slaughtered in Kabila ∎ Tutsi-Hima disappear in Mutara		∎ 20: *De Standaard* (*DS*) documents massive arrests of Tutsi
∎ 23: 500–1,000 Bagogwe (Tutsi subgroup) massacred in Kinigi ∎ Others executed after being released by FPR from a prison in Ruhengeri		∎ 26: *Le Monde* (*LM*) notes the circulation of racist anti-Tutsi propaganda
∎ 300 Tutsi massacred in retaliation in Bigogwe ∎ 3,000 detainees released as a result of international pressure	∎ U.S. Department of State publishes report detailing arbitrary detention of 5,000 Rwandan civilians	∎ 7: *LM* focuses on the unfair treatment of those detained since the Oct. RPF invasion; also notes the racist propaganda that implores Hutu to avoid Tutsi in all their affairs
∎ 5,000 detainees released		∎ 7: *LM* notes that there have been "irregularities" committed in the judicial process against Tutsi
		∎ 1: *LM* notes the unwarranted detainment of political prisoners in Rwanda since the Oct. 1990 invasion ∎ 25: *LM* notes the anti-Tutsi propaganda in *Kangura*
	∎ Amnesty International publishes report detailing detainment of 8,000 after 1990 FPR invasion and torture and rape of civilians	

(cont.)

Table 4.1 Chronology of Political Events, September 1990–April 1994 (cont.)

Year/ Month	Developments in the War	Democratization	Militarization
1991 (cont.)			
July			
Aug.	▮ 8–9: African subregional summit held to discuss the Rwandan war		
Sep.			
Oct.		▮ 13: New prime minister nominated	
Nov.			
Dec.		▮ New government (MRND and 1 PDC [Parti Démocrate Chrétien] member) is formed; widespread contestation	
1992			
Jan.		▮ 16: Talks are held among new political parties in London	▮ 6.2% of GDP applied to military expenditures during this year
Feb.			▮ Size of RAF: 30,000–40,000
Mar.	▮ 14: Habyarimana agrees to create peace with FPR	▮ CDR is formed	

Human Rights Violations	Human Rights Coverage	Press Coverage
▋ 7 Tutsi detained and 4 never return	▋ Association Rwandaise pour la Défense des Droits de la Personne et des Libertés Publiques (ADL), Association pour la Promotion de l'Union par la Justice Sociale (Kanyarwanda), Association des Volontaires de la Paix (AVP); Ligue Chrétienne de Défense des Droits de L'Homme au Rwanda (Lichredor) created	
▋ 16 Tutsi arrested and never return ▋ 11 Tutsi arrested and 8 do not return ▋ 4 arrested and handed over to military for beating		
▋ 7 Tutsi attacked in the Rwankuba sector of Murambi commune: 1 killed, 3 raped, 12 beaten		
▋ Continued attacks: 2 beaten, 1 killed, 7 arrested ▋ Tutsi hide in bushes throughout the night in fear of their lives		
	▋ UN Human Rights Commission's Committee of Five examines Rwanda during this year	
▋ 300 Tutsi massacred in Bugesara	▋ Human Rights Watch publishes report detailing conditions of detainment of 8,000 after the 1990 FPR invasion; massacres in Kibilira (1990), northwest Rwanda (1991) ▋ U.S. Department of State publishes report detailing the Jan. 1991 racially motivated massacre of Bagogwe	

(cont.)

Table 4.1   Chronology of Political Events, September 1990–April 1994 (cont.)

Year/ Month	Developments in the War	Democratization	Militarization
1992 (cont.)			
Apr.	▌6–7: Negotiations in Paris	▌16: Five-party coalition government formed	▌Militia groups *interahamwe* and *impuzamugambi* formed
May			
June	▌5: Cease-fire agreed on		
July	▌12: Arusha talks begin: Organization of African Unity (OAU) 50-person Neutral Military Observer Group (NMOG) is formed to monitor cease-fire		
Aug.	▌1: Cease-fire goes into effect ▌10–17: Arusha Protocol on rule of law, political pluralism, and respect for human rights is made	▌10–17: Agreement on rule of law, political pluralism, and respect for human rights	
Sep.			▌Guns are distributed by the government to civilians in Kiyomba and Bwisige
Oct.			
Nov.		▌15: Habyarimana declares that the agreements with the FPR "are but a piece of paper" ▌22: Mugesera, high MRND dignitary, gives major genocidal speech	
Dec.			

Human Rights Violations	Human Rights Coverage	Press Coverage
▮ 22 murdered by assassination and grenade attacks		
▮ Killings in Ruhengeri and Gisenyi		
		▮ 1: *New York Times (NYT)* mentions 8,000 detained without cause immediately following FPR invasion
▮ 15–17: 300 Tutsi murdered in Kibuye		
	▮ Comité de Liaison des Associations de Défense pour les Droits de l'Homme au Rwanda (CLADHO) is formed as an umbrella organization for all human rights in Rwanda	
		▮ 20: *DS* describes militia and terror against Tutsi
▮ 2 Tutsi murdered in Kibilira	▮ ADL publishes report detailing massacres of and human rights violations committed against Tutsi	▮ 12: *NYT Magazine* has lengthy story on civil war in Rwanda, with references to French fighting on behalf of the Rwandan army, French arms sales to Rwanda; Africa Watch reports government troop "killing sprees"

(cont.)

Table 4.1   Chronology of Political Events, September 1990–April 1994 (cont.)

Year/ Month	Developments in the War	Democratization	Militarization
1993			
Jan.	▮ 10: Arusha protocol on power sharing is negotiated		▮ 7.6% of GDP applied to military expenditures this year
Feb.	▮ 8: FPR violates cease-fire; 1 million people in northwest Rwanda are now displaced (figure declines subsequently)		▮ 193 guns are distributed by the government to civilians in Mutura
Mar.	▮ 6–8: Negotiations between FPR and government in Dar es Salaam		
Apr.			

Human Rights Violations	Human Rights Coverage	Press Coverage
■ 4: 5 young girls raped and killed ■ 21: 300 massacred (Tutsi and political opponents) in north-west Rwanda	■ 7–20: International commission of NGOs comprising Human Rights Watch, International Federations of Human Rights, Inter-African Union of Human Rights, and International Center for Human Rights and Democratic Development conducts mission in Rwanda; hundreds are interviewed, and mass graves are excavated ■ UN Human Rights Commission's Committee of Five examines Rwanda during this year	■ 29: *LM* discusses accusations made against the Rwandan army of gross human rights violations against Tutsi
■ Violence, rape, detainment, and torture against Tutsi civilians during this month: 18 Tutsi murdered in Mukingo 13 Tutsi murdered in Rwinzu 5 Tutsi murdered in Tumba 8 Tutsi murdered in Mbogo	■ International commission of NGOs publishes report detailing that over 2,000 Tutsi have been murdered since the FPR invasion for the sole reason that they are Tutsi; documents massacres in Kibilira (1990), northwest Rwanda (1991), and Bugesara (1992) by civilian groups with the support of the regime; notes that extremist rhetoric is widespread; militia groups have been formed; appeals for international response are made ■ U.S. Department of State publishes report detailing massacres of Tutsi in Bugesara (Mar. 1992), massacre of Bagogwe (Jan. 1991), disappearances of Tutsi youth and enlargement of the army	■ 5: *LM* discusses international commission report, including the number of massacres of mostly Tutsi who were murdered for the sole reason that they were Tutsi and that there will be reprisals for those who helped the commission ■ 17: *LM* (interview with M. Marcel Déharge) questions why France has not reacted to the massacres that have been committed by the regime; Déharge says that the international commission report will not be ignored
■ Violence against Tutsi; overall, 147 killed and hundreds more beaten, arrested, and raped	■ International commission of NGOs presents report in Paris and Brussels	■ 4: *LM* discusses the role of France in supporting a regime that has committed massive human rights violations ■ 17: *LM* questions French military assistance to RAF in light of the international commission's report detailing massacres of innocent Tutsi ■ 8, 15, 27: *DS* documents the NGO report, as well as the fact that Habyarimana discards it fully
	■ 8–17: B. W. Ndiaye, UN special rapporteur, conducts an investigation of human rights violations in Rwanda	

Table 4.1   Chronology of Political Events, September 1990–April 1994 (cont.)

Year/ Month	Developments in the War	Democratization	Militarization
1993 (cont.)			
May	▌9: Arusha protocol on refugees and displaced persons is made	▌Radical Parmehutu wing splits off MDR	
June	▌23: United Nations Observer Mission Uganda-Rwanda monitors arms flows to Rwanda as per UN Resolution 846		▌Radio Libre Mille Collines (RLMC) begins broadcasting
July			
Aug.	▌3: Arusha protocol on the integration of the armed forces is made ▌4: Arusha accords are signed; UN assistance mission is proposed		
Sep.	▌Contingent of 600 FPR soldiers arrives in Kigali		
Oct.	▌5: UNAMIR approved in UN Resolution 872		
Nov.		▌27–29 Talks held between political parties in Nairobi	
Dec.		▌28: Transitional government imple- mentation is delayed	

Human Rights Violations	Human Rights Coverage	Press Coverage
∎ 18: Samuel Gapyisi, MDR leader, murdered		
	∎ Human Rights Watch publishes report detailing massacres in northwest Rwanda (Jan.–Feb. 1993), killings in Feb. and Mar., extremism on the radio, and arming of civilians and reiterates the findings of the international commission of NGOs—that 2,000 innocent Tutsi have been murdered since the 1990 invasion and that massacres have been committed by civilian groups with the backing of the regime in Kibilira (1990), northwest Rwanda (1991), and Bugesara (1992)	
∎ 21: Rwambuka, confidant of Habyarimana (and accused of having inspired the Bugesara massacres), is murdered	∎ UN special rapporteur's report is released; identifies that the massacres that have taken place fulfill the treaty definition of genocide; violence is increasing; extremist propaganda is rampant; militias are organized	
∎ Attacks on judges and human rights activists; bombs explode in Kigali		
		∎ 6: *DS* mentions Belgian parliamentarian asking questions about *akazu* implication in violence and corruption
∎ Nkubito, president of human rights association, severely wounded in car bombing		
∎ At least 22 schoolchildren killed by bombs	∎ ADL publishes report detailing massacres of and human rights violations committed against Tutsi	

(cont.)

Table 4.1   Chronology of Political Events, September 1990–April 1994 (cont.)

Year/ Month	Developments in the War	Democratization	Militarization
1994			
Jan.		▮ 5: Habyarimana sworn in as president (boycotted by opposition)	
Feb.	▮ 17: UN threatens to withdraw peacekeeping troops unless transitional government is implemented	▮ 19: Political parties agree to implement transitional government Feb. 22 ▮ 22: Habyarimana fails to show up for swearing in of government; postponed until Mar. 25	
Mar.		▮ 25: Habyarimana releases a report with plans for the installation of transitional government	
Apr.	▮ 6: Habyarimana's plane is shot down		▮ 7: Genocide begins

Human Rights Violations	Human Rights Coverage	Press Coverage
	▌ Human Rights Watch details arms sales to Rwanda from France, South Africa, and Egypt and reiterates that 2,000 innocent Tutsi have been murdered since the 1990 invasion in numerous massacres with the backing of the regime ▌ Ndiaye's report is presented to the UN Human Rights Commission; report is integrated into a general human rights report	
▌ 21: Félicien Gatabazi, PSD leader, is assassinated; Martin Bucyana, CDR leader, is murdered in retaliation ▌ 37–50 civilians (predominantly Tutsi) murdered by militias	▌ U.S. Department of State published report detailing massacres of Tutsi (Jan.–Feb. 1993) and existence of death squads	▌ *LM* discusses the massacres, the role France has played in supporting and enlarging the army, and the anti-Tutsi propaganda ▌ 23: *DS* discusses Gatabazi killing
▌ 7: Genocide begins		

5

UNDER THE VOLCANO:
THE DEVELOPMENT COMMUNITY
IN THE 1990s

The reaction of the aid community to the events in Rwanda was marginal. Mostly, the business of development continued as usual. A few small gestures apart, most aid agencies continued the same projects, without questioning or redefining their goals, approaches, or allocation patterns. Any changes in the way development business was executed during the years immediately before the genocide were due to dynamics that were entirely unrelated to the civil war, the human rights violations, the racism, and the militarization of Rwandese society. Indeed, the prime evolution observable in the aid business was one toward increased amounts of program funding linked to structural adjustment. Also, from 1993 onward, there was a significant rise in emergency aid to cope with the rising numbers of people displaced by Rwanda's civil war and the arrival of hundreds of thousands of refugees from Burundi.

Of course, one cannot understand the development business in isolation from the broader political relations between Rwanda and the international community. From early 1991 onward, the international diplomatic community was quite strongly engaged in trying to bring about the peaceful resolution of the civil war and to promote democratization inside Rwanda. To that effect, it used both diplomatic pressure and positive support. Simultaneously, however, the international community remained almost entirely passive toward Rwanda's deteriorating human rights record, the increase in racism, and so forth. It was only in mid-1993, immediately after the publication of important human rights reports, that there was a brief episode of serious pressure on the Rwandan government to change its ways. Parallel to that, Western countries, particularly France, sold arms, trained the Rwandan military, and generally remained diplomatically close to the Habyarimana government.

Human rights nongovernmental organizations (NGOs), both local and foreign (and occasionally some development NGOs), were the only actors that did seek to stop the human rights violations and the preparations for genocide. In 1991, they began publishing a series of reports detailing the killings and arrests, as well as the pattern of government involvement and racist propaganda behind them. In 1993, several large international human rights NGOs considered the situation in Rwanda so worrisome that they took the unique step of sending a joint mission to Rwanda and publishing a major joint report. Yet their voices were not heard, or at least not heeded.

This brings us to a common argument in any discussion of the international community's (in)actions before the genocide. It is often said that nobody in the foreign policy establishments of the world's major countries saw the genocide coming, and that it thus makes no sense to reproach foreign governments and international organizations for having been passive or acquiescent. This argument—that the genocide was unpredictable, even for the Rwandan Tutsi themselves (otherwise, they would have left the country)—is sufficiently important to be dealt with first.

On Knowledge and Ignorance

Did the international community—mainly the governments of Belgium, France, and the United States, and the UN political headquarters—know that preparations were under way for a full-scale genocide in Rwanda? If so, when was this known? If not, could the international community have known it?

Most authors who have studied the matter answer the first question affirmatively. Most prominent are Adelman and Suhrke, who argue that, from late 1993 onward, foreign embassies and the UN Assistance Mission in Rwanda (UNAMIR) troops—and through them, the governments of Western countries and the highest levels of the UN—possessed clear information about an upcoming genocide and could have stopped it if they wanted to (Adelman and Suhrke 1996, 38; des Forges 1995, 456).[1]

Analysts have documented that anyone living in Kigali, both diplomats and aid officials, would have been aware of the increasing potential for genocide in Rwanda. The rise in tension and violence, the wide distribution of arms to civilians and militia, and the increasingly vehement anti-Tutsi propaganda broadcast by Radio Libre des Mille Collines, all indicated the growing potency of ethnic hatred. These facts, combined with explicit warnings to Western and African diplomats by important people at the heart of the Habyarimana government, further clarified the nature of the violence that would follow.

Adelman and Suhrke (1996) also argue that the UN secretariat was well informed of the intention of extremists and the extensive preparations to commit genocide. From January 1994 onward, General Romeo Dallaire, head of the UNAMIR, made repeated requests for more troops and equipment, as well as for permission to confiscate known illegal arms imports to protect civilians. All these requests were denied. On January 11, 1994, Dallaire sent a cable to the UN secretariat that detailed credible evidence from a Rwandan government informer of a plan to kill Belgian UNAMIR troops and then murder all Tutsi living in Kigali; the informer also detailed the location of secret arms caches for this purpose.

Finally, two major human rights reports published in 1993 detailed massive arms distributions to the population, increasing extremist anti-Tutsi rhetoric, the existence of militia groups, and massacres of over 2,000 Tutsi with the consent of the government. The first report was written by four human rights NGOs that, in response to the escalating human rights crisis in Rwanda, created a joint commission of inquiry (Africa Watch and others 1993). In August, a UN special rapporteur's report (United Nations 1993) confirmed the findings of the joint commission report and stated further that "the cases of intercommunal violence brought to the Special Rapporteur's attention indicate very clearly that the victims of the attacks, Tutsi in the overwhelming majority of cases, have been targeted solely because of their membership in a certain ethnic group, and for no other objective reason. Article II, paragraphs (a) and (b) [definitions of genocide in the Geneva Convention on the Crime and Punishment of Genocide], might therefore be considered to apply to these cases." These reports, along with the experience of diplomats and UNAMIR forces in Kigali, seriously challenge the assertions by the international community that it was utterly surprised by the outbreak of civil violence in April 1994.

In contrast, the degree to which this information was widely known and conclusively interpretable is subject to dispute. It is quite likely that few people in the international community could have seen the genocide coming, for a variety of reasons. The most fundamental explanation is that it is hard to imagine or expect a genocide. There is a fundamental, hard-to-grasp, qualitative difference between "ordinary" killings and a genocide. The Swiss Development Cooperation agency reflects this sentiment in the introduction to its 1994 annual report: "we cannot say we were badly informed; those running our Coordination Office in Kigali did remarkable work in providing information, making contacts, and issuing warnings. They probably knew as much about the situation as the best informed Rwandans. But how many amongst those foresaw a catastrophe of such enormity?" Adelman and Suhrke (1996, 9), in their otherwise critical analysis, as well as Kagabo and Vidal (1994), Prunier (1995, 211), Willame (1995b, 443), and des Forges (1995, 457), all argue the same point.[2] Moreover, the usually mentioned warning signs of the events that would begin April 6, 1994, occurred only in late 1993 and early 1994, that is, within a few months before the actual genocide—too late for ordinary processes of policymaking to move into action in time to stop the genocide.

A second reason why it may have been hard to predict the genocide, even if one was aware of the human rights violations, involves the potential for confusion with "ordinary" political violence. The last years were characterized by broad and widespread political violence: the assassination of opposition leaders, the creation of militia by all political parties, random acts of terrorism, and so forth. It may have made sense for many observers—most of whom were not specialists on Rwandese society—to lump all occurrences of violence in the broader category of political violence and to believe that the latter would be solved by bringing the peace-cum-democracy negotiations in Arusha to a good end. This can also explain the inaction of the UN secretariat toward General Dallaire's information about impending genocide: the former UN secretary-general has argued that such plots are often exposed in conflict regions and communicated to the secretariat, only to be uncovered later as false alarms (Boutros-Ghali 1996, 31).

The debate will always remain inconclusive. However, even if we accept that the international community could not have foreseen the genocide that began on April 6, 1994, and thus could not have been expected to act to prevent its occurrence, the debate on its role and responsibility is not closed. Before April 6, there were forty months of widespread violence and massive human rights abuses in Rwanda, directed against innocent Tutsi based solely on their ethnicity. These instances of violence were instigated by the highest levels of government and accompanied by widespread racist and genocidal discourses.

Table 4.1 shows that these instances of violence were well known throughout the world. There were no less than six major, internationally published reports on the human rights situation in Rwanda presented at press conferences, distributed to government officials and embassies, and so forth. The two discussed earlier—one by a consortium of NGOs and one by the UN—explicitly mentioned the killings against the background of the genocide convention. Human rights agencies inside Rwanda published still more reports and documents (des Forges 1996). Even the U.S. Department of State's annual human rights reports contained a wealth of information on the matter. At the same time, prestigious newspapers in the European press (but hardly any in the United States) regularly reported on the same processes in the same terms. Finally, the climate of hatred and fear was visible to all the foreigners living in the country—to diplomats and, especially, to technical assistants, who were usually much more in touch with what was happening "in the field." Many U.S. citizens living in Rwanda met weekly with the U.S. embassy staff and amply discussed these facts. People of Tutsi origin, many of whom worked for aid agencies and embassies, were without exception deeply afraid for their lives and often told their foreign employers and colleagues about their fears. Many of those who could do so fled the country.

Thus we can establish with certainty that the regular occurrence of murderous violence against innocent people, and that this violence was both racially motivated and organized from the highest level of the state, was widely known even to casual observers, and even more so to those living in the country. These facts by themselves—regardless of whether they would eventually lead to genocide—were serious enough to require action. Most development aid agencies have explicit policies that oblige them to act in the case of massive human rights violations in recipient countries. When these processes involve high-level government harassment and killing of innocent people—often employees of aid agencies or partner NGOs—under a highly racist ideology, there is even more reason to speak out forcefully and clearly and act accordingly. Finally, when a society is falling apart due to racism, violence, hatred, and lawlessness, this should cause at least a profound rethinking of the development assistance mandate and the current portfolio of projects, and a search for innovative ways of dealing with these problems. No such thing happened, however. The aid community largely continued business as usual, as if oblivious to the challenges facing Rwandese society. The broader international foreign policy community, meanwhile, sent conflicting and confused signals.

The 1990s Development Community

From 1990 to the end of 1992, the international aid community seems to have been largely passive toward the processes described earlier. The sole engagement I am aware of was a 1990 letter signed by more than a hundred technical assistants, including foreign NGO personnel, defending the regime against criticism and asking for military support against the Rwandan Patriotic Front (FPR) (Reyntjens 1994, 102; Brusten and Bindariye 1997, 14). At the time, the extent of the killings inside Rwanda was not immediately known; the fake attack on Kigali in October 1990, for example, was uncovered only months later, as was the January 1991 extermination of the Bagogwe. At the same time, the FPR invasion clearly killed people and created hundreds of thousands of refugees. Finally, the popularity of the regime, and its highly positive image within the development community, made it much harder for people to realize, and to believe, what was going on or to react decisively (Willame 1995b, 436; Renard and Reyntjens 1993, 18).

In fact, in quantitative terms, development aid to Rwanda in 1991 and 1992 greatly increased. The prime reason for that was totally separate from the war and the political crises that were rocking the country: Rwanda's structural adjustment–inspired policy changes were accompanied by great increases in so-called program aid. Indeed, structural adjustment loans (SALs) from the World Bank consist of program aid, which is money given without a specific purpose (unlike more ordinary project aid, which is donated for specific inputs in a previously agreed-on project) to facilitate or induce the often painful policy change. In addition to the Bank's SAL, many bilateral donors provided additional program aid (under headings such as balance-of-payment support, debt relief, and structural adjustment support) to the government to encourage it or to reward it for taking the path of economic policy adjustment. In the case of Rwanda, again reflecting its popularity within the aid community, this support was massive, just when general aid levels to Africa were declining. In 1991, the year that the SAL agreement with the World Bank was signed, Belgium gave BF 200 million and financed BF 400 million of a World Bank loan to Rwanda; Switzerland awarded SwF 10.9 million in 1991 to "un pays ami en difficulté" (a befriended country in difficulty, in the words of that year's annual report); the United States provided between $10 million and $25 million; the European Community (EC) between $15 million and $40 million;

France between $12 million and $14 million; and even tiny Austria lent between $6 million and $10 million (almost doubling its total aid to Rwanda).[3] In 1992, Germany added $16 million, Japan $6 million, and Belgium BF 720 million. As late as January 1994, just before the genocide, Japan managed to commit itself to approximately $7 million of debt relief–cum–structural adjustment. Most of this program aid was in addition to normal, ongoing project aid, causing total aid volumes to rise significantly, by as much as one-quarter in 1991 (Chossudovsky 1994, 21). Hence, the Rwandan government saw a great increase in program funds—coincidentally, just when it began importing large amounts of weaponry and spending vastly more money on the military.

Most of these funds were accompanied by detailed and heavy economic conditionality. As elsewhere, the International Monetary Fund (IMF) and World Bank imposed the original conditionality, and many donors simply attached those conditions to their funds. Others, such as the U.S. Agency for International Development (USAID), listed in detail their own conditions. The conditions of a 1991 grant, for example (officially termed "Production and Marketing Policy Reform") read as follows: "prior to the first ($15 million) tranche, the GOR [government of Rwanda] will replace its existing foreign exchange allocation and licensing system with an interim managed system, to ease the shock of decontrol. Other conditions precedent to the first tranche are to remove controls on price and profit margins (except for monopolies), abolish fixed prices for most goods and services, and reduce tariffs, custom duties, and import surcharges. Conditions to the second tranche include implementation of an open licensing system and a comprehensive review of export policies."[4]

The second main trend in the aid community in the 1990s was one toward greater government "ownership" and control of the aid resources. This trend, too, was entirely unrelated to the war and the disintegration of Rwandese society; in fact, these processes greatly hampered its execution. This trend was the result of dynamics internal to the aid system and, more specifically, of the desire among more progressive aid managers to increase local ownership of aid projects and programs. The Belgian bilateral aid agency, for example, was adopting a so-called partnership approach, in which control over aid negotiations and management was gradually transferred from Brussels headquarters to Kigali, with greater opportunities for government involvement. Rwanda had been chosen as one of the prime countries in which the new policy would be carried out beginning in 1990, and attempts (all unsuccessful) to do so were made until 1993. The Swiss Development Cooperation agency, similarly, sought to move away from working directly with the population and toward strengthening local government structures in Rwanda, a process that was similarly moving along with great difficulty. In August 1993, when any resemblance to a functioning government had disappeared, the United Nations Development Programme (UNDP) launched a NATCAP (Programme de Renforcement des Capacités Nationales de Conception et de Gestion de l'Assistance Technique) program, designed to give government the capacity to plan its human resources requirements (including technical assistance) in the long run. This program, too, never took off.

Thus, as Rwanda's farmers were facing crises without precedent, as inequality and corruption reached endemic proportions, as hope for the future was extinguished, and as violence, hatred, and human rights abuses became government policy, the international community was congratulating Rwanda for its improved capacity to overcome its "limited absorptive capacity," to "improve its capacity to design and implement development projects" (World Bank 1989b, 18)—in short, to play the aid game. This may sound too cynical: these policies were truly progressive within the aid community, and no development can take place without local public structures taking their responsibilities. However, one wonders if their continuation during these years was a priority or reflected any understanding of the disintegration of Rwandan society and its structures of governance.

The third trend in the development community in the 1990s, linked this time to the war, was the rise in emergency aid. Contrary to what could be expected, emergency aid to Rwanda did not rise by much during the early 1990s: the overall proportion of emergency aid for all Organization for Economic Cooperation and Development (OECD) members was no more than 2 to 3 percent in 1990 and 1991. Emergency aid began in earnest only in 1992 and 1993, when the FPR resumed the civil war and caused hundreds of thousands of people to flee again. Also in 1993, hundreds of thousands of Burundian refugees entered Rwanda, fleeing violence in their country after the first democratically elected president was killed. The largest donor was the World Food Program (WFP), which supplied $54 million of food aid in 1993,[5] followed by the United States with $28 million of food aid; France, Belgium, Germany, the Netherlands, the EC, and the International Committee of the Red Cross (ICRC) also became major donors of emergency aid, primarily food aid in the form of maize, wheat, and milk, but also blankets, medical aid, and sometimes more innovative measures. The Swiss, for example, began to supply fuelwood to the refugees so that they would not destroy local forests. Accusations were heard by people in the camps that the Rwandan government pocketed part of the emergency aid; in August 1993, the International Red Cross suspended its food aid for that reason (Geen voedselhulp 1993).

For the rest, the international community continued largely unchanged, with few exceptions. In 1991, as an expression of its worries about the political situation in Rwanda, the Swiss Development Cooperation agency decided to renew its aid commitments on a year-to-year basis only; previously, it had been one of the more progressive donors, committing itself to projects of three to five years. Overall, the United States acted most forcefully: citing human rights violations, it cut aid to Rwanda in 1992, but the amount was still far above historic trends (see Table 5.1). The following year, the United States dramatically increased the amount of humanitarian aid, channeled primarily through U.S. NGOs and through the WFP. Strangely enough, however, it chose to leave its military assistance to the regime unchanged. In March 1993, after a cease-fire, the United States announced that it would bring its aid back to the (very high) level of 1991, dependent "on the satisfactory handling of public affairs and continuance of democratization."[6]

In 1992, a handful of development NGOs also spoke out about the deteriorating trends, publishing a declaration discussing the massacres and asking for sanctions against the authorities. In the same year, a group of Belgian development NGOs publicly made the same diagnosis in a Belgian newspaper (Reyntjens 1995a, 269). And during 1993, some foreign development NGOs, including Oxfam, Aide et Action, and Catholic Relief Service, in collaboration with some Rwandan human rights organizations, made a few declarations to the government expressing (in carefully worded terms) their worries about the human rights violations and the situation of internally displaced persons.

For the other donors, we have to wait until mid-1993, and the publication of the major NGO consortium report detailing the nature of the human rights violations, for any action to occur. Immediately after the publication of that report, there was a flurry of diplomatic activity, some of it involving development aid. The governments of Belgium and Germany briefly threatened to cut aid to Rwanda unless the human rights situation improved (Reyntjens 1994, 194). Both countries, however, never executed these threats (Reyntjens 1994, 94, 195).

Table 5.1   Development Aid, 1987–93

Donor	1987–89 Average	1990	1991	1992	1993
Belgium					
Total aid (million $)	30	43	56	48	41
Program aid (%)		15	42	17	4
Emergency aid (%)	4		4	0.5	11
Switzerland					
Total aid (million $)	10	10	17	14	20
Program aid (%)		6.1	44.6		
Emergency aid (%)					
Germany					
Total aid (million $)	25	33	45	46	42
Program aid (%)		30		35	
Emergency aid (%)					
United States					
Total aid (million $)	13	13	40	22	35
Program aid (%)			50+		
Emergency aid (%)		1	0	0	81
OECD					
Total aid (million $)	235	287.9	366.4	351.5	352
Program aid (%)		8	35	29	8
Emergency aid (%)		3	2	14	12

Sources: Compiled from OECD on-line data and various AGCD, GTZ, SDC, and USAID annual reports.

Switzerland also expressed its displeasure but did not change its aid allocation, apart from granting some funds to Rwandan human rights NGOs. Canada announced that it would drastically reduce aid to Rwanda; this later occurred but was justified by general budgetary considerations, and no more pressure was brought to bear on the Rwandan government (moreover, the volume of aid to Rwanda in 1993 still largely surpassed the level before the 1990s). The World Bank refused to give Rwanda more funds (both the latter tranches of a second SAL and an already prepared third one) until an established government was set up to negotiate and implement serious commitments (the Bank thus did not cut its aid on human rights grounds but on managerial ones). The European Parliament finally "condemned and called for a halt to abuses"; the ACP-EC (African, Caribbean, Pacific–European Community) commission also condemned the abuses and asked the EC to drop price supports for Rwandan agricultural products until the human rights situation improved. None of this ever happened.

All in all, then, very little happened. A few weeks after the publication of the report, after some conciliatory words by the Rwandan government, the storm died, and no more attempts were made to use development aid to pressure the Rwandan government into respecting human rights or silencing the voices of genocide. The development business proceeded at its usual pace, hampered only by the increasing disintegration of the government—the prime partner for practically all bilateral and multilateral development projects. In November and December 1993, for example, the *Africa Research Bulletin* mentions four new aid agreements with Belgium in the health sector, worth BF 81 million; a new $9.5 million loan from the International Fund for Agricultural Development (IFAD) to finance a rural management project in the highlands of Buberuka; and two new International Development Association (IDA) credits totaling $25 million for agricultural research and for private business support.

It has been argued that there were good reasons for not applying a stronger conditionality on Rwanda. Alienating the government undoubtedly could have hampered the peace negotiations in Arusha, which were sponsored by the same Western countries that were Rwanda's most important donors. Moreover, to the extent that a reduction in aid hurts the majority of the population, cutting aid would have hurt the chances of democracy taking root in Rwanda rather than advancing it (Suhrke, personal communication). These observations cannot be dismissed out of hand; as a matter of fact, they resemble the usual discussions about the merits and limits of negative conditionality, and judgments about these dilemmas always come easily to those who look at them after the fact, without responsibility for making the decisions (see Chapter 11 for more discussion of this matter).

However, confronted with racism, massive government-instigated human rights violations, widespread fear, random violence, and the slow disintegration of Rwandese society, donors could have done more than simply (threaten to) cut aid. They could have rethought their goals and approaches, created new projects that specifically sought to intervene in these areas, or modified and adjusted the execution of existing projects— practices that are sometimes called positive conditionality (McHugh 1995, 14 ff.; Wozniak Schimpp 1992). Yet almost none of this happened. By and large, the same projects continued in the same way; no agency fundamentally rethought its mission or goals or practices. Some funds went to support the new human rights NGOs; a few conflict-resolution seminars were organized by an occasional NGO; some crumbs were allocated to strengthening the judicial sector; a handful of legal experts was hired by various agencies to write and rewrite electoral laws; and the Belgians, who had been trying to sell a TV station to Rwanda as part of their development aid (against strenuous objections from the World Bank), now justified it as a contribution to democracy (Mattheiem 1991). OECD data on commitments reveal that only two donors, Switzerland and the United States, added some new "civil society strengthening" and "democracy" projects in 1992 and 1993.[7] The most interesting of these was the Democratic Initiatives and Governance Project, designed by USAID in late 1992, which was supposed to strengthen civic associations, the free press, and the National Assembly in order to "facilitate and broaden popular participation in shaping the terms of a new social contract and the institutions through which that contract will be carried out."[8] This project remained largely a dead letter, however.

Thus the development business continued largely as usual, and whatever change took place was unrelated to the disintegration of Rwandese society, resulting rather from its own internal dynamics, such as the need for structural adjustment or the desire to strengthen partner institutions.

It is interesting to note that in 1995, after the genocide, the aid community spent significant amounts of aid money on some of these matters. Suddenly, "peace-building" projects were started by Australia ($400,000) and Belgium ($280,000). The latter country also put $1.6 million into "strengthening civil society" projects, and Canada contributed $3.3 million.[9] "Human rights monitoring and education" projects now received $750,000 from Belgium and $600,000 from the Netherlands; "legal and judicial development" projects got more than $3 million from Canada, $800,000 from Switzerland, and $8 million from the United States. Apart from Switzerland and the United States, none of these countries had had any significant activity in these areas before; as a matter of fact, they are never mentioned in a twenty-four-page OECD-compiled list of projects from 1990 to 1994.[10]

The record of the UN development agencies illustrates the same inertia. An analysis of the UNDP *Compendium of Ongoing Projects* (various years) in Rwanda shows that nearly all projects by UN agencies in the 1990s continued unchanged, year after year—the only impact of the country's disintegration being that many of these projects were incurring years of delays. As in the case of the bilateral donors, great increases in program aid were the prime observable trends in the 1990s. In 1991, the IMF accorded Rwanda a $41 million credit line to finance a three-year economic reform program,[11] and the World Bank provided $90 million for its SAL. In the same year, the Bank began an expensive school rebuilding project, and two adjustment-related government policy reform programs received a total of $38 million in 1992. In 1991–92, the African Development Bank provided a $15.2 million SAL. The few new projects that were added related to structural adjustment and to capacity building. Under the category "social conditions and equity projects," we find an unchanged list of three women's projects for a total of half a million dollars (with a total government contribution of $20,000). The list includes not one project that seems directly related to the disintegration of Rwanda's society, except for an increase in emergency aid and some assistance for the preparation of an electoral law. The annual reports of the UN resident coordinator (various years) never mention the political and social disintegration of Rwanda, focusing instead on the usual aid interests: donor coordination, government strengthening, and humanitarian relief.

All aid agencies, from headquarters in Western capitals to local offices, were aware of the rapid deterioration of Rwanda's human rights record (from already low levels) and of the rise in racism and violence; similarly, all development experts were daily confronted at the personal level with the fear, hatred, and insecurity that characterized daily life in Rwanda in the 1990s. None of them, though, felt that the development assistance mission ought to be, or could be, fundamentally rethought. The development aid system knew of the disintegration of Rwandese society; saw the many Tutsi working for aid agencies or partner NGOs being harassed, threatened, or killed (Schürings 1995, 496); discussed these matters and surely regretted them; but seemingly felt that it was outside its mandate or capacity to intervene, that all it could do was to continue business as usual. Thus aid continued to muddle through, trying to make its usual projects work with a faltering government, until the day the genocide began.

The Broader Picture

It may be argued that it is unjust to single out the development aid enterprise in this analysis—that condemnation of human rights abuses and action to end them belong to the foreign policy establishment's prerogatives more than to the development aid system. Although I do not fully agree with this statement, I believe that it is useful to briefly look at the evolution of the broader relations between Rwanda and the main Western powers, which also happen to be its main donors.

There was no single or consistent policy of the international community toward Rwanda. Mostly, though, the international community was actively engaged in seeking to promote both an end to the civil war and democratization within Rwanda. From late 1990 onward, both African and Western countries sought to provide occasions for the government and the FPR to meet, to negotiate cease-fires, and, later, to work out a peace agreement (Adelman and Suhrke 1996, 14; des Forges 1995, 455). Through the provision of neutral places for meetings and negotiations, the presence of intermediaries and observers at the negotiations, and the application of private and not-so-private diplomatic pressure, the international community sought to nudge the peace process forward in many ways.

The civil war broke out in Rwanda in late 1990, one year after the end of the cold war. As has been widely documented, it was at this time that the international community became more interested in promoting democracy and respect for human rights in the Third World. As a result, the international community put pressure on Rwanda to democratize. However, such pressure did not come solely from the international community. As already documented, major internal (Hutu) discontent beginning in the late 1980s forced the Habyarimana regime to make some concessions by early 1990. Also, the FPR claimed to have an agenda of democracy and respect for human rights. Once the peace negotiations began, all these pressures became intricately linked, as the path to peace was based on the creation of a broad-based transitional government and the inclusion of the FPR therein, followed by democratic elections.

Adelman and Suhrke (1996, 18) argue, probably rightly so, that without this international involvement, the peace process would not have advanced as fast as it did—and there may not have been any negotiated settlement process at all. In all likelihood, without the international involvement, the issue would have been decided on the battlefield, and it is unclear what the outcome would have been. As it is, a peace agreement was negotiated that included a major democratization of Rwandese society that constituted a profound threat to the powers that be. The early months of 1994 saw broad pressure being applied by France, Belgium, the United States, Canada, Tanzania, and Germany, among others, to move forward with the implementation of this agreement

and, most notably, with the creation of a coalition interim government—and there was equal, successful resistance by the regime against
doing so. All in all, then, the international community undertook some
serious and sustained efforts to end the war peacefully and promote
democratization in Rwanda.

At the same time, however, the international community adopted
other behaviors that were inconsistent with these efforts. First, as
already documented, the international community reacted only mini-
mally to the increase in government-sponsored human rights abuses in
the country. There were only two short-lived times that these well-
documented violations became the subject of major diplomatic activity.
The first was in late 1990–early 1991, when foreign diplomats lobbied
for the release of the 8,000 to 10,000 Tutsi who had been illegally
detained immediately after the October 1990 invasion. That pressure is
generally considered to have been successful, leading to the release of
most of the people detained and even a few judiciary actions against
those who were responsible for it (Renard and Reyntjens 1993, 19). The
second time was after the publication of the joint NGO human rights
report in early 1993, when the international community expressed serious concern over the human rights violations documented in that
report. Belgium and Switzerland briefly recalled their ambassadors, and
the international community made some noise of disapproval. Again,
this is generally thought to have been quite effective: the government
promised that it would look into the allegations, and for the next year
or so, fewer massacres were committed. Hence, on those few occasions
when the international community set out to pressure the government to
improve its human rights record, results were achieved. This makes the
overall neglect of these issues all the more regrettable.

Second, even though the Rwandan government was implicated in
racist and genocidal violence against Tutsi, the international community,
while pushing for peace and democratization, also continued and even
stepped up its military collaboration with the regime. As already mentioned, the United States continued its military collaboration and support to the regime until 1994 (although at $200,000, it was never very
important). Belgium sent some troops to evacuate its nationals in 1990
and then increased its military assistance to Rwanda until 1994,
although it stopped the provision of lethal weapons in 1991 (Braeckman
1994, 152). Both these countries' roles were small, however, compared
with that of France. From the FPR invasion onward, France greatly
stepped up its military support to the Habyarimana regime. Active

involvement of its troops is generally credited with helping to halt both the October 1990 invasion and the March 1992 FPR offensive. However, French military advisers were involved in many more ways in the operation of the army; the French military's involvement in advising the president, training new recruits, defending important installations, manning roadblocks, and interrogating prisoners has been widely documented (Adelman and Suhrke 1996, 14–15; Braeckman 1994, 159; Reyntjens 1994, 175; Rwanda: Third Degree 1991; Rwanda: French Agenda 1992; Verschave 1995). At the same time, the Habyarimana regime embarked on a campaign of rearmament, again with prime support from France. Arms were imported from Egypt and France with credits from French nationalized banks, and other arms were bought from South Africa (Braeckman 1994, 149). As mentioned earlier, these arms were used to equip the army and the militia and were even widely distributed to ordinary citizens throughout the country. Human Rights Watch documented that during the genocide, arms were shipped from France to Rwanda, in contravention of a UN arms embargo.

Third, the international community that supported and helped negotiate the Arusha peace agreement was unwilling to authorize an effective UN peacekeeping operation. Article 54 of the Arusha accords reads that a neutral force was expected to contribute to the security of Kigali by protecting civilians, searching arms caches, and neutralizing militias. The successful transition to peace in Rwanda depended heavily on the speedy deployment of this mission. Nevertheless, both UNAMIR's mandate and its troop size were woefully insufficient to satisfy this need.

For one thing, the mandate given to UNAMIR by the UN Security Council was significantly more restricted than the one negotiated by the same actors in Arusha. UNAMIR was sanctioned as a mission that could only contribute to security in Kigali "within a weapons secure area established by the parties" and monitor the cease-fire (see United Nations 1996).[12] In accordance with this mandate, UNAMIR was not provided with either a human rights cell or an intelligence unit. As Adelman and Suhrke (196, 7) note, the militia members "were not going to disarm themselves," but UNAMIR was not authorized to take the necessary action and, consequently, to contribute to security or protect civilians (Adelman and Suhrke 1996, 7). When the location of arms to be used in future violence against Tutsi was disclosed, the UN Department of Peacekeeping Operations still refused to give General Dallaire permission to seize these weapons (Adelman and Suhrke 1996, 39). In addition, when the genocide finally began, UNAMIR, in the name of neutrality, did not seek to intervene; a few weeks later, its size was greatly diminished.

The size of the approved mission was insufficient to attain even the narrow goals of the approved mandate. Dallaire's estimated necessary troop size of 4,500 (a figure that had already been reduced from 8,000 to avoid veto of the mission entirely) was decreased further by the Security Council to a force of 2,548. However, the contributing countries did not provide enough troops and equipment to bring this already compromised force up to strength. UNAMIR resources were so insufficient that four months after forces began arriving in Kigali (eight months after the peace agreement had expected the mission to commence operations), only 1,260 of the possible 2,548 had been deployed. Promised equipment never arrived in Kigali (Adelman and Suhrke 1996, 36).

The failure of UNAMIR—the gap between its promise and its reality—is symbolic of a pattern by the international community of pushing for major changes in the Third World but not providing the resources to back them up when they are threatened. The international community was willing to pressure Rwanda and the FPR for peace and power sharing and promised its support in the form of guarantees for the security of Rwanda's citizens, human rights monitoring, military interposition, and so forth. However, from day one, UNAMIR was not given the resources necessary to execute its mission—a fact that did not escape those who were preparing the genocide. It has been said that many Rwandans counted on UNAMIR to protect them. UNAMIR, and the international community behind it, failed miserably in its task (des Forges 1995, 463).

In sum, the policies of the international community toward the civil war and the slide of Rwanda toward genocide were contradictory. On the one hand, a serious and consistent effort was made, led by Tanzania and supported by the concerned Western countries, to promote a peaceful and negotiated end to the war. At the same time, and in line with general trends after the end of the cold war, pressure was exerted on the regime to democratize. Peace and democracy became inexorably linked in the Arusha negotiations, which ended with an agreement that included the creation of a broad-based transitional government, demilitarization, and elections. These were important and laudable goals, hailed by many Rwandans, and the international community deserves credit for helping to make this happen.

On the other hand, military and diplomatic support to the regime continued unabated or, in the case of France, increased greatly. The international community remained almost totally passive toward the human rights abuses taking place in Rwanda, organized by the government and backed by widespread racist and genocidal propaganda. Rwanda remained a respected member of the international community—in fact, it was a member of the UN Security Council at the time the genocide began. Only twice during those four years was there some serious diplomatic effort to curtail human rights abuses, and in both cases it was remarkably successful—not surprising, given that the Rwandan regime depended entirely on international aid for its survival. The most crucial contribution that the international community could have made to the peace process and to which it had committed itself, the establishment of UNAMIR, received a significantly smaller mandate and fewer resources than foreseen in the Arusha negotiations. This may have encouraged extremists to go ahead with the genocide, and it rendered the international community powerless when it broke out.

In the end, the widespread human rights violations and the preparations for the genocide never made it to the international agenda. They did not become linked to the development enterprise nor to the peace and democracy process nor, for that matter, to the UNAMIR mandate. The behavior of the international community in April and May 1994—its focus on evacuating its nationals, its withdrawal of UNAMIR in the face of genocide, its refusal even to acknowledge the genocide despite massive evidence, its foot-dragging in deciding on any intervention, and its acceptance of France's blatant actions to shelter the genocidal regime—makes one doubt the willingness of the international community to protect the lives of innocent people who are being slaughtered in far-away countries. In all likelihood, nobody cared enough about the people who were at risk and were eventually killed to commit resources to their protection.

What was the specific role of development aid in all this? Throughout the early 1990s, development aid continued its own well-intentioned, separate life, following its internal dynamics, almost totally unrelated to the political trends discussed earlier. For reasons unrelated to the war, program aid rose greatly in 1991 and 1992, dramatically increasing the total financial resources available to the government. Up to 1994, with few exceptions, projects in the pipeline were executed without change; no human rights conditionalities were added to overall aid disbursements or specific projects. To the extent that projects or programs were halted, that was done on managerial grounds. No major attempts were made to stop the racism, violence, hatred, and fear spreading through Rwandese society. The aid system continued its usual mission, separate from society and largely blind to its major stakes.

My argument about development aid, then, has two elements. One relates to negative conditionality, which is what one usually thinks of in any discussion about the relation between development aid and human rights. In the years leading up to the genocide, few attempts were made to use the international community's aid leverage to halt the processes of violence, racism, and human rights abuses within the country. It could be argued, however, that there were understandable reasons for that: the international community may have feared hurting the poor by halting its development projects, or it may have thought that continuing to promote economic development would be the best path to peace and democracy. In short, it may have judged that negative conditionality would not have achieved the goal of stopping the racism, violence, and human rights abuses.

Each of these propositions is debatable but cannot be said a priori to be without truth. We will never know what could have been. What we do know is that when credible threats were made in early 1991 and mid-1993, there was a clear impact on government behavior. It is equally clear, however, that these occurrences did not stop the processes that led to genocide. Thus, all in all, negative conditionality is an unsure, double-edged sword: it was not used in Rwanda in the early 1990s the way it might have been, but it is unclear whether it would have made any difference.

I also made another argument in this chapter that goes beyond the usual debates about the merits and feasibility of negative conditionality. I argued that, while one can accept that development agencies may have had good reasons to remain present in Rwanda during the 1990s, they could have shown much more flexibility and imagination in defining their mission in the face of the visible and dramatic disintegration of Rwandese society. After the genocide, it became possible to devote millions of dollars to peace building, justice support, civil society strengthening, human rights monitoring, and conflict resolution. There are good reasons for this: no development will take place in Rwanda without addressing these matters. Did it really take a genocide to learn this? What does it take for the development enterprise to sit down and reorient its projects? Was the fear in the eyes of Tutsi colleagues and employees, the genocidal rhetoric and its wide acceptance, or the thousands of people killed with government complicity not enough? There lies the crucial, but too little discussed, area for reflection in the development community: When societies disintegrate into violence, racism, and hatred, what does development mean? Under what conditions should repairing roads and vaccinating people—important things in their own right—take a backseat to more social, psychological, educational, or outright political work? Can projects be modified to deal with such processes? Or more generally, does development aid have a role in conflict prevention and de-escalation? And what does this mean for relations with the state? Do NGOs have a special role to play? And what do they have to change in order to play that role (which they did not do in Rwanda)? These are questions that all development agencies face, not only in Rwanda, but throughout Africa.

Notes

This chapter greatly benefited from the assistance of Elise Keppler, senior at Brown University. She did much of the work on the tables and provided excellent feedback and discussion. John Gould of USAID was very helpful in providing data. I also greatly appreciate feedback from James Boyce at the University of Massachusetts.

1. At the time of completing this manuscript, this position also seemed to be the one taken by a Belgian senate committee on Rwanda.
2. Even Paul Kagame stated in a recent interview (Gourevitch 1997, 185) that "the feeling was certainly that something was terribly wrong. But we were still figuring out exactly what. [Gourevitch: So it really took you by surprise?] Sure. But more the monumental size of it than the fact that it happened."
3. These amounts come from various sources, including *Africa Research Bulletin*; AGCD, GTZ, SDC, and USAID annual reports; and various issues of *Africa Confidential*. The figures often differ between sources.
4. Production and Marketing Policy Reform abstract, USAID database project no. 696-0135.
5. These amounts are still small compared with what was spent after the genocide, primarily on the Rwandans who fled the country. In 1994, international aid to Rwanda totaled US$708 million, of which 41 percent (that is, $291 million, more than all aid Rwanda received until the early 1990s) went to emergency aid, and 26 percent to program aid.
6. *Africa Research Bulletin*, March 16–April 15, 1993.
7. The total cost was approximately US$1 million. See OECD Creditor Reporting System on-line at www.oecd.org/dac/htm/sooncomn.htm. Note that these data reflect commitments and not actual disbursements. In 1992, USAID developed a US$900,000 Democratic Initiatives and Governance Project that was to establish a Center for Civil Action and Democratic Initiatives, enhance the capacity of the free press, and establish a Democratic Initiatives Support Fund. As far as I know, this project never took off. See USAID database project no. 696-0133.

8. Project data sheet, Democratic Intiatives and Governance Project, no. 696-0133, September 1992.
9. It must be noted that the aid community spent considerable amounts of money on NGOs, both foreign and local. A significant share of the aid from the United States, the Netherlands, the EC, and Switzerland, to mention but a few, went to NGOs, and except for program aid, that proportion increased in the 1990s. This aid was by and large given within a "development as usual" framework, however, not within a civil society framework and even less a human rights one. NGOs were subcontractors of ordinary development projects that were supposedly more participatory, more flexible, and cheaper, but they were not a response to the disintegration of Rwandese society. See also data in Brusten and Bindariye 1997 and Chapter 8 of this book.
10. OECD on-line Creditor Reporting System; the same is true of the Development Assistance Information CD-ROM of USAID.
11. Most IMF funds are not technically development aid but are often discussed in that context.
12. According to Braeckman 1997, the Belgian senate committee on Rwanda writes that article 17 of the rules of engagement stipulate that UNAMIR was allowed to intervene using all means in the case of "ethnically motivated criminal acts."

PART III

THE CONDITION OF STRUCTURAL VIOLENCE

The Concept of Structural Violence

Almost three decades ago, Johan Galtung (1969) and later Pierre Spitz (1978) wrote about the condition of structural violence, in which the poor are denied decent and dignified lives because their basic physical and mental capacities are constrained by hunger, poverty, inequality, and exclusion. Galtung (1969, 168) defined violence as "those factors that cause people's actual physical and mental realizations to be below their potential realizations." As such, violence of this type can be built into the structure of a society, "showing up as . . . unequal life chances." For example: "in a society where life expectancy is twice as high in the upper class as in the lower classes, violence is exercised even if there are no concrete actors one can point to directly attacking others, as when one person kills another" (Galtung 1969, 169, 171). According to Khan (1978, 836), structural violence can take four forms: "(a) classical, or direct, violence; (b) poverty—deprivation of basic material needs; (c) repression—deprivation of human rights; (d) alienation—deprivation of higher needs." The latter category includes such intangibles as mental and emotional harm, denial of dignity and integrity, and the "destruction of the individual in a psychological or spiritual sense"—all issues that scholars of violence have studied over the ages and often included in their definitions of violence (Hoffmann and McKendrick 1990, 4–5). Two decades later, Galtung (1990, 292) defined violence as "avoidable insults to basic human needs, and more generally to life, lowering the real level of needs satisfaction below what is potentially possible," referring to survival, well-being, freedom, and identity as the four basic needs categories diminished by structural violence.

In the scientific literature, the term *structural violence* is still occasionally used to describe situations that are characterized by a combination of inequality, repression, and racism. As such, the term can pertain to living conditions in Brazil, apartheid South Africa, and inner-city America, where high degrees of acute violence also exist. Mamdani (1996, 59) also used the term to indicate colonialism's impact on native people in Africa.

Researchers studying poor black adolescents' perceptions of violence within their communities in the United States were presented with structural violence, as manifested in a lack of employment opportunities and social facilities, as well as in the racial stereotypes faced by black inner-city youngsters (Kaljee and others 1995). Many of the youngsters and their parents saw an explicit link between structural and acute violence. Earl Shorris (1997, 37–39, 97), following his belief that "when anyone other than the poor defines poverty, the definition itself becomes a force against them," asked hundreds of poor people in the United States to describe what poverty meant to them. In that discussion, factors such as lack of communication, unsatisfactory social life, exclusion from duties and rewards of citizenship, racism, and isolation turned out to be as important as hunger and lack of adequate housing. Poverty, then, is about privation as much as about oppression, the latter including "being despised (not hated) by the powerful" and "responses limited to passivity or violence." Without using the term, Shorris is describing important elements of the concept of structural violence.

In writing about South Africa, Hoffmann and McKendrick (1990, 20) defined structural violence as "institutionalized inequalities of statuses, rights, and power," adding that "these inequalities are not the result of freedom of choice by the individuals and groups who are victimized, but rather are the consequence of the more powerful group's use of coercion, which has become institutionalized into legal systems, and justified through mythology, religion, philosophy, ideology and history" (see also Van der Merwe 1989; Gil 1970). In the next chapters, I argue that the development ideology and practice constituted part of the superstructure of structural violence in Rwanda.

Nancy Scheper-Hughes's 1992 book about Brazil, *Death without Weeping: The Violence of Everyday Life in Brazil*, also discusses structural violence as observed in extremely high and widely accepted infant mortality among slum inhabitants. Talking about "unrecognized, gratuitous and useless social suffering," and describing such situations as "invisible genocides and small holocausts," she rightly observes that "the paradox is that they are not invisible because they are secreted away and hidden from view, but quite the reverse. As Wittgenstein noted, the things that are hardest to perceive are often those which are right before our eyes and therefore simply taken for granted" (Scheper-Hughes 1996, 889).

What can be learned from this overview, then, is that the concept of structural violence draws our attention to unequal life chances, usually caused by great inequality, injustice, discrimination, and exclusion and needlessly limiting people's physical, social, and psychological well-being. In the rest of this part, I argue that in Rwanda, the majority of the population lived a life characterized by great structural violence in its physical, social, and psychological forms. But before I do so, it may be useful to take a brief look at the notion of human development, which helps us further operationalize the concept of structural violence and links it with current development debates.

Human Development

In many ways, the concept of structural violence can be seen as the inverse of that of human development, which is now moving up on the development community's agenda, drawing attention to oft-neglected issues of empowerment, social cooperation, equity, dignity, security, and sustainability.[1] Probably the most visible work is that of the United Nations Development Programme (UNDP), which in 1990 began publishing its annual *Human Development Report*. Designed as an explicit alternative to the World Bank's *World Development Report*, this series has generated much debate over the years, regarding both the factors to be included and the way to measure them. In its first year, human development was defined as "the process of enabling people to have wider choices." Much attention was devoted to health, education, and nutrition, which had been neglected, if not negatively affected, during the structural adjustment decade of the 1980s. Unlike the World Bank, the UNDP treated health, nutrition, and education not as means of promoting economic growth—in the Bank's parlance, investment in human resources—but as part of a much larger process of holistic improvement in people's capacities to live free, dignified lives in the way they saw fit.

With each successive year, the team in charge of the *Human Development Report* has refined and redefined the concept, based on criticisms and suggestions received. By 1996, the definition of human development had become much more comprehensive, including:

> —empowerment: basic empowerment depends on the expansion of people's capabilities—expansion that involves an enlargement of choices and thus an increase in freedom. But people can exercise few choices without freedom from hunger, want and deprivation. . . . Empowerment carries an additional connotation—that in the course of their daily lives people are able to participate in, or endorse, the decision-making that affects their lives. . . . People should not be passive beneficiaries of a process engineered by others. They should be active agents in their own development.
> —cooperation: people live within a complex web of social structures—from the family to the state, from local self-help groups to multinational corporations. They are social beings who value participation in the life of their community. This sense of belonging is an important source of well-being. It gives enjoyment and direction, a sense of purpose and meaning. . . . If people live together well, if they cooperate in a mutually enriching way, this enlarges their individual choices. . . .
> —equity: equity is usually thought of in terms of wealth or income. But human development takes a much broader view—seeking equity in basic capabilities and opportunities. . . . This applies in particular to women. . . .
> —sustainability: sustainable human development meets the needs of the present generation without compromising the ability of future generations to meet their needs. . . . What needs to be sustained are people's opportunities to freely exercise their basic capabilities.
> —security: for too long the idea of security has referred to military security or the security of states. One of the most basic needs is security of livelihood, but people also want to be free from chronic threats, such as disease or oppression, as well as from sudden and hurtful disruptions in their daily lives. Human development insists that everyone should enjoy a minimal level of security. (UNDP 1996, 55–56)

Coming from a different perspective, Robert Chambers (1995), father of the rapid, participatory, rural appraisal approach to development research, synthesized decades of work with local communities throughout the world. He argues that, from the point of view of the poor, what he calls the condition of "deprivation" reaches far beyond a lack of income and can not be solved by simple economic growth. Deprivation is characterized by "social inferiority, isolation, physical weakness, vulnerability, seasonal deprivation, powerlessness and humiliation." For the poor, actions that target only one of these aspects—usually lack of income—are too limited and often self-defeating, to the extent that progress on one characteristic (for example, increases in income) often goes hand in hand with setbacks in the other characteristics (such as increases in vulnerability and instability).

In short, it seems that the same elements appear over and over again: for poor people, meaningful development is not simply about increases in income but also about improved access to the means of production; reduction in insecurity and vulnerability, and the creation of a sustainable and hopeful future; empowerment through participation, justice, freedom, and access to information and education; overcoming physical weakness through access to health and nutrition; and social relations characterized by human dignity, cooperation, and a sense of equity. All these processes are not reducible to economic growth, nor do they automatically follow from it. Their systematic absence for certain groups, especially under conditions of macroeconomic growth, can be called structural violence.

Structural Violence in Rwanda: A Preview of the Argument

I argue that, notwithstanding positive macroeconomic indicators, a high degree of structural violence existed in Rwanda. This situation began long before 1990. Rwandan society—as well as many other African societies—is violent not only when massive physical harm is being done with arms by one group against another, as was the case from 1990 onward. The violence is continuous and structural and is exerted against the majority of the poor. It manifests itself in a deep and widening inequality of life chances; corruption, arbitrariness, and impunity; the permanence of social and economic exclusion; lack of access to information, education, health, and minimal basic needs; and an authoritarian and condescending state and aid system.

Structural violence, I further argue, provokes frustration, anger, ignorance, despair, and cynicism, all of which greatly increase the potential for acute violence. In the case of Rwanda, from the 1990s onward, the economic and political crises described in Chapter 4 combined with this basis of structural violence to push society over the brink of destruction.

As an aside, I believe that the same processes are taking place in other African countries, leading to similar results. To be sure, the occurrence of genocide is likely to remain unique to Rwanda, as it displayed certain features that are not shared by most other African countries. For example, in most other African countries, there is no tradition of institutionalized, state-sponsored, racism. Similarly, in most countries, there are more than two ethnic groups, and the balance of power among them is much less unequal. However, in many African countries, the same processes of structural violence as in Rwanda are leading to instances of communal violence. The specific form this violence takes depends on each country's historical, political, and cultural circumstances, but the basic processes underlying it are similar.

In Chapter 6, I analyze the presence of structural violence by examining development from three important perspectives that are rarely, if ever, on the agenda of any development institution (or, for that matter, of social scientists studying Rwanda). They are equity/inequality, inclusion/exclusion, and dignity/humiliation. For each of them, I present data drawn from project evaluations, conversations, surveys, and articles. The resulting diagnostic contrasts singularly with the almost idyllic dominant image of Rwanda as a nicely developing country. It shows that, for decades, Rwandan society was characterized by rising inequality; exclusion along social, regional, and ethnic lines; and structural humiliation. The conclusion analyzes the social impact of structural violence on society, describing how it leads to anger, cynicism, despair, and normlessness—factors that provide the fertile ground in which the seeds of hatred are sown. Chapter 7 then pays particular attention to foreign aid, seeking to tease out its role and its place in the processes observed and asking why development aid practitioners are so rarely aware of the condition of structural violence and their own role in it.

Note

1. Galtung himself, twenty years ago, spent much time on creating better indicators for development (see, for example, Galtung and others n.d.). He was working on a ten-dimensional concept of development that includes personal growth, diversity, socioeconomic growth, equality, social justice, equity, autonomy, solidarity, participation, and ecological balance.

6

FROM STRUCTURAL TO
ACUTE VIOLENCE

The first section of this chapter discusses poverty and inequality in Rwanda. According to 1994 World Bank data, Rwanda was the most egalitarian country among all low-income and middle-income countries in the world. These data are wrong and greatly underestimate the problems in Rwanda. In actuality, poverty and inequality were high and rising dramatically from the mid-1980s onward. I demonstrate this by analyzing data on food expenditures and undernutrition and by looking in greater detail at a number of local studies on trends in land and income inequality in the 1980s.

In the next section, I demonstrate that this rising inequality resulted not so much from differences in natural resource endowments or individual dynamism but from the functioning of a sociopolitical system based on multiple exclusions. I document this assertion through an in-depth analysis of the functioning and impact of rural development projects—the main path of development for the masses in a poor rural country like Rwanda.

The third section of this chapter analyzes the processes of humiliation and disempowerment that characterize the interactions between the state/aid system and the large majority of poor Rwandans. I show that the system of top-down extension, and the associated imagery of development and the good life, deprives people of their self-respect and creativity, making them vulnerable to manipulation and simplistic ideas.

The picture that emerges, then, is very different from the one presented in Chapter 3. For the large mass of poor Rwandans, life was characterized by a constant reduction of life chances and increase of socioeconomic vulnerability; the absence of opportunities to acquire information and education; oppressive, authoritarian, and condescending treatment by the development system; growing social, ethnic, and regional inequality; and a history of impunity, corruption, and abuse of power by local and national elites, often committed in the name of development.

Drawing on earlier work by Johan Galtung and others, I identify this condition as one of "structural violence," thus drawing attention to the fact that such structures and processes are violent because they needlessly and brutally limit people's physical and psychological capacities. The notion of structural violence allows us to focus on the "little people" who perpetrate the (acute) violence: the adolescents who—everywhere from Rwanda to Liberia—are the first to do the killing and to be killed, the ordinary farmers who take up arms against their neighbors, and the women who attack other women (Schoepf 1995). In the fourth section of this chapter, I discuss in some detail the mechanisms that link structural and acute violence.

Structural violence was a key component of the social basis on which the edifice of genocide was built. The condition of structural violence is intimately linked to impunity. Together, they undermine the legitimacy of the state and the normative structures that hold societies and states together. Structural violence also reduces the effectiveness of development interventions and makes it likely that any economic progress made will be ill distributed. As such, it creates anger, resentment, and frustration, which contribute to the erosion of social capital and norms in society. A population that is cynical, angry, and frustrated is predisposed to scapegoating and projection, vulnerable to manipulation, deeply afraid of the future, and desperate for change. It is this population that bought into racist prejudice in the 1990s and was willing to kill out of fear, anger, resentment, and greed. Although they do not take the form of genocide, similar processes, with similar outcomes, are taking place throughout Africa.

Poverty and Inequality

There are few nationwide data on poverty and inequality in Rwanda. The main data come from a 1994 World Bank report (1994b, i, 10) prepared before the genocide on poverty reduction and sustainable growth, which states that the proportion of the population living in poverty grew from 40 percent in 1985 to 53 percent in 1992. The same report

(1994b, 5, 60, 25) adds that "land is less unequally divided than else-where, . . . household expenditure is relatively evenly distributed in Rwanda, and . . . government expenditure and tax policies are income neutral." Moreover, the Bank's 1993 *World Development Report* indi-cates that the percentage share of consumption of the poorest 2 deciles of the population was 9.7 percent, and of the richest decile it was 24.6 percent. One has to move up to the level of Hungary to find a more egalitarian country (World Bank 1993, table 20).

These data greatly underestimate the extent of poverty and inequality in Rwanda. They are largely statistical constructs, part of the image that the development community liked to maintain for Rwanda. A closer look at both data on undernutrition and local-level studies suggests that the extent of poverty and inequality and their recent trends were much more dramatic.

UNDERNUTRITION AND ULTRA-POVERTY

The above-mentioned World Bank (1994b, 5) figures on poverty in 1985 and 1992 are based on a 1983–85 census, in which the category of the poor was defined as "the bottom 40 percent of the sample in terms of expenditures per capita." In other words, poverty in 1983–85 was *by definition* set at 40 percent, while the nonpoor automatically constituted 60 percent of society. Although this kind of artificial cutoff may be useful for statistical purposes, especially for monitoring trends, it does not reflect the real conditions of life for Rwanda's inhabitants. Specifically, I argue that the extent of poverty in Rwanda was much higher than 40 or 53 percent.

In recalculating the extent of poverty, it is useful to start from Michael Lipton's (1988) definition of the "poorest of the poor" as those households that spend 75 percent or more of their income on food. For people to spend that much on food—to the neglect of other important things such as clothes, health care, education, investment, and leisure—implies that they are likely to be malnourished and, as a result, weak and often sick. For those people, life is likely to be a constant fight for survival—they can hardly invest in productive assets or take risks. This, in turn, means that they are typically unable to benefit from those poli-cies and projects that may aid the "ordinary" poor.

The World Bank report (1994b, 6) tells us that "expenditures on food were 88 percent of total for the poor and 74 percent for the non-poor."

Another study in 1991 found that rural households spent, on average, 80 percent of their incomes on food; in urban areas, that figure was 54 percent (Inter-Ministerial Committee 1991, 11). These data suggest that a very large proportion of the so-called nonpoor were in fact extremely poor. If we use Lipton's cutoff point, it seems that the incidence of ultra-poverty may well have been higher than 50 percent, and beyond that, another significant part of the population was poor as well.

Data on childhood malnutrition support this assertion. Although data on this topic have been inconsistent and incompatible due to different survey designs, researchers recently created a cleaned-up data series for Rwanda (Grosse and others 1995). These data on child undernutrition, an indicator that is often used as a proxy for general undernutrition (Mason, Jonsson and Csete 1996), indicate that approximately half of all children were stunted. Other World Bank data (1991c, 57) show that the average caloric intake of half of society was below 2,000 calories per person per day; they also demonstrate that the availability of calories was perfectly correlated with income and almost perfectly with farm size. Vis, Goyens, and Brasseur (1995, 374) argue that at least 50 percent of the population must be considered malnourished. Therefore, it seems that even though half of all households were spending more than three-quarters of their incomes on food, they were not getting enough food to feed their children. This seems to indicate that, following Lipton, up to half of Rwanda's population must be categorized as belonging to the poorest of the poor. Local-level data on land and income inequality confirm this picture and add more precision on recent trends.

TRENDS IN LAND AND INCOME INEQUALITY

From the 1980s onward, a process of land concentration began in Rwanda, in which wealthy farmers—usually people who earned their primary income in the administration—bought land from the poorest farmers. Although Rwanda has a policy that forbids the purchase of land by those with three or more hectares (and all land sales require authorization by the government), farmers were able to circumvent the law through long-term leases or by buying and selling in black markets (World Bank 1991b, 61; Ministére de l'Intérieur n.d., 10). In fact, Willame (1995a, 140) found that in one commune in 1988, 21 percent of the fields had been bought (mostly the result of distress sales by their previous owners), but the official data were much lower. Also, André and Platteau (1995, 22) found that land sales were prevalent in the region they studied (in fact, they were the highest for any of the sixteen African countries for which data exist). According to them, the large majority of these land sales were distress sales, often being a matter of survival for the families concerned. And Uwizeyimana (1996, 20) reported that, on average, 15 percent of the cultivated land had been bought, but in some regions, the proportion of all cultivated land bought or rented was as high as 45 percent.

This suggests that real land inequality as well as landlessness were in all likelihood much higher than the official figures indicate (André and Platteau 1995, 7 ff). According to the World Bank (1991c, 3, 57), "there is an emerging group of landowners with 5 or more hectares, while the number of landless farmers is increasing apace." According to data in the 1984 National Agricultural Survey, approximately 15 percent of the farmers owned half of the land, especially in the provinces of rural Kigali, Gitarama, and Gikongoro. The Rwandan NGO IWACU (1991, 51) stated that 26 percent of the population had become landless (see also United Nations 1991, 51). André and Platteau (1995, 7–19) also document a greatly increasing rate of landlessness in the late 1980s, adding that land sales contributed to half of all the land inequality observed by 1993.

According to the National Agricultural Commission, the minimum farm size required to feed an average family of five persons is 0.7 hectare. Using that criterion, a UN seminar on poverty concluded that 43 percent of the farm households lacked the minimum land for survival and lived in a situation of chronic undernutrition (United Nations 1991, 29). The International Fund for Agricultural Development (IFAD 1990, 8), using a similar methodology, argues that in 1990 in the province of Byumba, 50 percent of the farmers had insufficient land—or no land at all—to produce the income required to meet essential nutritional requirements; for the region of the Buberuka highlands, this figure was an astonishing 75 percent (IFAD 1992, 8). These data, then, also confirm the observation made in the previous section that up to half of Rwandan households lived in extreme poverty.

Like elsewhere in Africa, the majority of these land purchases were not by small farmers who, through sheer hard work, managed to buy a few acres more but rather by "big men" with money earned as government or aid agency wages or in commerce (IWACU 1991, 41; United Nations 1991, 30; Reyntjens 1994, 223; Seruvumba 1992, 10;

Voyame and others 1996, 127; for the situation elsewhere, see Downs and Reyna 1988, 3–9, 15). Erny (1994, 80) and many others describe the population as "extremely unhappy with the accumulation of land by the privileged of the regime and the constitution of large pastoral domains." Catharine Newbury (interviewed by Pace and Schoetzau 1995) adds:

> In a country like Rwanda, where 90 percent of the population are very poor, and of those, the majority live under the poverty line, it is a zero sum situation. So you had the spectacle of people associated with the government becoming very rich and building big villas and driving around in fancy cars and a huge influx of expatriates coming in to manage various projects. . . . The unraveling of the economy left a new generation of Rwandans who were jobless, landless, and angry—in other words, fertile for recruitment into extremist militias that attacked the Tutsis in Rwanda.

In one of the few documents that present a farmer's opinion about the causes of the genocide, asset and income inequality figure in first and second place (Mugwaneza 1994, 26).

Similar processes took place in the urban and periurban regions. It is widely known that the control of urban real estate provided great opportunities for personal gain to the well-connected (Pabanel 1995, 115). As Kigali and other cities grew, they consumed land from the surrounding farmers, often at extremely low prices, thus creating a growing army of mendacity (IWACU 1991, 10). These lands were covered with housing, often for a small upper class of technical assistants and local high cadres, providing enormous windfall profits to those owning the lands.

In addition, the state could and did expropriate land regularly, with very little, if any, compensation, causing extreme resentment and destitution among farmers. As a World Bank (1994b, 35) expert wrote on this subject with uncharacteristic bluntness, "these laws are not unusual in the world, but are carried to a rather severe extent in Rwanda. For example, if a local government decides to zone an area for industrial development or middle-class housing, peasants will have their land confiscated. As practiced, this policy is strongly anti-poor." Yet almost all development projects are characterized by the construction of offices, houses for the staff, demonstration fields, access roads, and reforestation areas on lands that were similarly expropriated (IWACU 1991, 8; de la Masselière 1992, 112).

Not surprisingly, the available data indicate that income inequality was high and growing quickly in the 1980s. Data for rural areas are rare, but it is known that rural incomes are strongly correlated with land distribution, which was discussed in the preceding paragraphs (Clay and McAllister 1991). Data are much better for people with formal jobs, earning wages. According to 1986 Ministry of the Plan data, the lowest-paid 49 percent of all salaried people in Rwanda earned 7.6 percent of the total salary mass, while the best-paid 1.1 percent earned 27.8 percent (Ministère du Plan 1988, 83). By 1988, the lowest-paid 65 percent earned less than 4 percent of all salaries, while the top 1 percent had increased its share to 45.8 percent (Ministère du Plan 1989, 95). According to Maton's (1994) nationwide analysis, the income share of the richest decile in Rwanda increased from 22 percent in 1982 to 52 percent in 1994, vastly higher than the World Bank data suggest. And according to data by Marysse, De Herdt, and Ndayambaje (1995, 46–47), in a rural region in the province of Butare, the richest 10 percent earned 66.4 percent of that region's income in 1992. The same team documented that the lowest eight deciles saw their incomes decrease, while the highest two deciles experienced increases between 1990 and 1992; the most severe income losses, approximately 60 percent, were found in the lowest groups. Average income of the lowest decile was RF 388 per month, and of the highest decile, RF 188,900 per month—in other words, 487 times more (the gap was "only" 185 times more in 1990) (Marysse, De Herdt, and Ndayambaje 1995, 46).

None of this takes into account the revenues of expatriates. Already in 1982, Marysse (1982, table 6) calculated that the average expatriate income was 114 times higher than that of one-third of the farmers (meaning more or less one-third of society, given that up to 95 percent of society is rural). By 1992, this gap had certainly risen. Caviezel and Fouga (1989), in the Burundian context, calculated that expatriate incomes were 600 times higher than those of average farmers in the early 1990s; the situation in Rwanda was probably similar.

FORCED IMMOBILITY

One factor that contributed to poverty was particular to Rwanda: the existence and systematic enforcement of a multitude of limitations on people's mobility and initiative. Through residence permits, zoning regulations, restrictive labor practices, copious taxes, and police harassment, the state was always present in the life of any person who sought to produce or sell a product—and it often discouraged that person from doing so (World Bank 1994b, 37). Internal migration was made all but impossible through deliberate government policy. Residence permits were required for any stay anywhere, travel permits were needed to move, and "trading licenses are required even for those wishing to sell a basket of vegetables" (World Bank 1994b, viii; Guichaoua 1989). As the U.S. Department of State's 1993 human rights report stated:

> Freedom of movement and residence are restricted by laws and regulations which require all residents to hold national identity cards and residence and work permits. Police conduct periodic checks, especially in urban areas, and return all those not registered in the locality to their own commune. Property owners who do not require tenants to show valid documentation are subject to fines and even imprisonment. Undocumented tenants are subject to expulsion.

Guichaoua (1995, 3–4) adds:

> The umuganda card [noting participation in the obligatory communal labor] was kept up to date by the communal authorities (or in many cases by the staff of development projects of the major foreign donors) and had to be presented at all police controls. Travel permits were required for all non-residents (and especially young, uneducated kids from the countryside) to come to Kigali.

The official justification for many of these policies was to combat urban poverty and slum creation—goals that were accomplished. After Bhutan, Rwanda was the least urbanized country on earth, with 95 percent of the population living in rural areas. Note that, like so much else about Rwanda, this is partly a colonial legacy: in 1953–54, the urbanization rate of Rwanda was 0.9 percent; the policies restricting internal population movements already existed; and the capital, Kigali, had a total population of no more than 3,000 (Voyame and others 1996, 50).

However, these policies had negative repercussions. According to the World Bank (1994b, vii), "restrictions on population movement and on urbanization have impeded the development of market centers essential for developing a market economy. . . . This has increased poverty by limiting options for the poor and reduced the potential for economic growth." More generally, since opportunities for education, health care, small enterprise and commerce, and social mobility were highest in urban areas, the policies contributed to the further exclusion of the majority of Rwandans. Imagine the frustration of the tens of thousands of semieducated youth spawned by the education system each year when they were forbidden to leave the countryside, forced to stay on their meager plots, without hope for the future.

These data paint a very different picture from the one drawn by the World Bank, which suggested that inequality in Rwanda was low and government policies income-neutral. Poverty in Rwanda has always been higher than these data suggest, although it is impossible to know by how much. Moreover, trends over the last decade have worsened the situation. From my analysis, I can conclude that, by the early 1990s, approximately 50 percent of Rwanda's society was extremely poor (incapable of feeding itself decently or investing productively), up to 40 percent poor, 9 percent nonpoor, and perhaps 1 percent positively rich (consisting of a small elite of local "big men" at the highest levels of the state and in the business sector, as well as a few thousand mostly foreign technical assistants and experts). This distribution is confirmed by U.S. Agency for International Development (USAID) data that put 90 percent of Rwanda's rural population (and 86 percent of the total population) below the poverty line—the highest poverty figure for the whole world.[1] If Lipton's observation that the ultra-poor do not benefit from projects and economic trends that may benefit the poor holds true in Rwanda, up to half of society has not benefited from whatever progress has been observed in the macroeconomic data presented in Chapter 3. Data on the widespread nature of the famine at the end of the 1980s (IWACU 1991, 6) and the growing landlessness suggest that this may well be the case. This is admitted by some people, both in writing (United Nations 1991, 34–40) and in policy: I encountered one major European nongovernmental organization (NGO) in Rwanda that explicitly indicated that it did not seek to work with the poorest 30 percent of the people because they were beyond help.

Inequality greatly increased from the 1980s onward for a variety of reasons: the economic crisis brought increased hardship to the majority, but also new opportunities to a minority (through the purchase of land from distress sales, for example); the extent of corruption and clientelism increased; and the number of people at the top—technical assistants and the big men of the state—increased. This coincided with the dramatic reduction in life chances for the majority of the poor and created significant frustration and discontent in Rwanda.

Thus, long before the 1990s, life in Rwanda had become devoid of hope and dreams for the large majority of people: the future looked worse than the already bad present (Bagiramenshi and Bazihizina 1985, 87; Willame 1995a, 137). Peasant life was perceived as a prison without escape in which poverty, infantilization, social inferiority, and powerlessness combined to create a sense of personal failure. One could occasionally glimpse this pervasive sense of failure and hopelessness in direct interviews with farmers. In 1982, for example, a team evaluating an agricultural development program in Kibuye asked farmers if they wanted their children to be farmers; 77 percent of them answered no (Corrèze, Gentil, and Barnaud 1982b, 81; also personal observations and de Ravignan 1980, 16). Similarly, a 1985 reflection workshop with farmers in Gitarama, a widespread feeling that life was devoid of a future, both economically and socially, surfaced (Hétier 1985, 18; Groupe de Labeaume 1985, 81, 86). In both cases, a majority of respondents stated that only those who could not escape would remain on the farm—in other words, they equated their own occupation and lifestyle with failure and humiliation. Note that these interviews occurred before the mid-1980s; the economic crisis that lasted until 1994 worsened this situation. It is also in this light that one must understand the impact of the long-standing policies forbidding migration and rendering self-employment costly. These policies pleased many experts who appreciated the lack of shantytowns in Rwanda. For the rural population, however, they signified one more damper on hope for escape. Young men were hit especially hard: they had far less land than their fathers and were incapable of supporting families or even marrying. The number of the landless was increasing rapidly. By the early 1980s, according to one source, hundreds of thousands of young men could neither attain education nor inherit land and were in a permanent search for low-paid, temporary jobs, mostly in vain (CIDSE and CARITAS Internationalis 1995, 9). They were blocked in their educational advancement, were limited in their employment and migration options, and lacked the resources to make a decent life in agriculture.

The Forces of Exclusion

In Rwanda, like elsewhere in Africa, exclusion was embedded in the functioning of society. In Rwanda, this exclusion was social, regional, and ethnic in character. In a society where the development enterprise has been so central, in both ideological and financial terms, it comes as no surprise that exclusion was deeply ingrained in the processes of so-called development. In this section, I study rural development projects—the primary destination of aid money, and the central focus of the development discourse. I demonstrate how such projects act as mechanisms for exclusion and for reproduction of the privileges of a small elite.

THE MUTARA AGRICULTURAL
DEVELOPMENT PROJECTS (1974–87)

A rare insight into a particular development project's complicated social effects is afforded by combining an analysis by René Lemarchand, one of the world's foremost African scholars and an expert in the Great Lakes region, and the official World Bank reports on a rural development project sponsored by the International Development Association (IDA) that began in 1974 and ended, after two phases, twelve years later. The first Mutara agricultural development project began in 1974, after six years of identification studies and difficult negotiations. Its goal was to install 7,000 families on *paysannats*, government-sponsored farms started by the colonizer in 1953 and continued by the independent government, located in so-called underpopulated areas. Farmers were to be given fixed quantities of land with contracts that specified the agricultural techniques to be employed. A major innovation was the creation of ranches following a similar pattern: grazing rights as well as small plots of land would be given to 3,000 pastoralist (Tutsi and Hima) households in return for certain behaviors (destocking, payments, and so forth). A parastatal organization, OVAPAM, was created to manage the project.

The audit of the first phase observed that most physical targets of the project had been met. Indeed, 750 kilometers of roads had been constructed, and OVAPAM's own elaborate infrastructure had been built: forty-seven houses, two warehouses, offices, and other structures. Cars and office supplies had also been bought. The experts and employees could sleep safely, although the Rwandan director of OVAPAM never spent a night in the rural headquarters.

The rest of the project was a complete failure. A water supply scheme that was part of the original project was dropped because the cost of the above-mentioned constructions had greatly exceeded planned budgets. No social infrastructure for the population was built at all. According to the audit, this was "deeply resented by the population" (World Bank 1979, 10; 1981, 4). The crucial extension component of the project also failed: neither farmers nor ranchers adopted the proposed techniques.

Thus, after six years of study, five years of work, and $4.5 million (to be reimbursed, albeit on soft terms), the project's sole output was an enormous infrastructure for itself (84 percent of total project cost; World Bank 1981, 6) and the creation of some 160 jobs (60 were evaluated as necessary). Its economic rate of return was negative, its management was poor and conflict-ridden, cost overruns plagued the whole project, and consultants had not managed to train anyone because they hardly spoke French. The audit report also mentioned in passing that many pastoralists from the region had left for Uganda out of fear of the project and the intentions behind it (World Bank 1979, 14; 1981, 35; 1991a, 2) and that the rules on land distribution had been violated consistently. The so-called beneficiary committees set up to oversee the process of distribution never functioned; people from outside the zone (from Ruhengeri, the president's region) had in all likelihood benefited disproportionately.

Nevertheless, the audit report managed to conclude on an optimistic note: the project had created dialogue between the Bank and the government (World Bank 1979, 18; 1981, 44). As a result, a second phase was proposed, with the same institutional setup and an extension of the zone, as well as slightly adapted objectives: a primary focus on the creation of social infrastructures (water supply, schools, health centers), and improvements in the extension messages to farmers and pastoralists (World Bank 1979, 26).

The 1991 completion report, covering phase II of the project (1979–86), announced that the physical targets had been met, although with substantial cost overruns and a two-year delay (the water system was finally built in 1986, twenty years after the first mission, and twelve years after the project began). The bad news was that the "technical extension package had little to offer" to the farmers, and the research station did not create any outputs of relevance to them (World Bank 1991a, iii, 5). Most of the innovations proposed were either not adopted or abandoned after the project ended. The group ranches still were not sustainable; in fact, the ecological situation probably became worse during the project's life (World Bank 1991a, iv). Project management remained as conflicted and unclear as before.

Until now, the story has been essentially one of mismanagement, ineffectiveness, and ignorance—qualities often encountered in the development business. They produce dramatic consequences, furthering inequality, waste, and possibly even poverty. But a closer sociological analysis shows that these outcomes are not the result of bad luck or particular incompetence, but rather the result of profound forces of politics, exclusion, and maldevelopment that existed in Rwanda. According to Lemarchand, the above-described results of the Mutara project are not accidents but are directly related to the forces of exclusion that characterized the project zone and Rwanda in general. Lemarchand documents a "more or less deliberate policy of ethnic favoritism on the part of influential Hutu politicians at the regional and national levels," directed primarily against Tutsi but also against the Burundian refugees who lived in the region. He demonstrates that this policy primarily favored people from Ruhengeri and a select number of other "clients," mainly Hutu (Lemarchand 1982, 25–26).

But the forces of exclusion were not solely ethnic; they also operated between the small urban, well-connected, educated sector and the peasant masses (Lemarchand 1982, 23). "Pre-existing differences have been further accentuated by the ability of the wealthier and better-educated recipients to supplement their income through a variety of jobs within and outside the project parameter" (traders, OVAPAM employees, workers in Kigali) (Lemarchand 1982, 59). These same people are the ones who managed to obtain much of the land distributed during these ten years; indeed, according to Lemarchand, up to 40 percent of the land was awarded to absentee ranchers, that is, people who do not cultivate the land but rent it to others. These absentee ranchers were mainly politicians, civil servants, and OVAPAM project employees themselves (Lemarchand 1982, 45, 58–59).

The final result of this project, then, was a great increase in inequality between regions, social classes, groups, and individuals (Lemarchand 1982, 27, 41, 58, 63; see also Newbury in Pace and Schoetzau 1995). It was a system in which a small group of people managed to obtain most of the advantages of the multi-million-dollar project: jobs inside and outside the project; free land to be cultivated by family members, renters, or political clients; and large herds overgrazing at the expense of the original Tutsi and Hima herdsmen. It is no accident that those who benefited were often from the president's region, nor that almost all of them belonged to the usual class of *evolués*, urban people in the loop, with connections to the right people. These people also received most of the access to cars, foreign training, and the forty-seven new buildings. They, in return, fueled a system of clientelism, through which ordinary Hutu could get access to land, salaried jobs, agricultural inputs, and so forth.

In conclusion, Lemarchand (1982, 1, 4–5) writes about

the gap which inevitably separates intentions from results when, by accident or by design (in this case the latter), the sociopolitical dimension of rural development is left out of the accounting. . . . To view the OVAPAM project simply as an effort to improve the material conditions of the "poor" thus leaves out at least two major intervening variables: the manner in which ethnicity affects the definition of the "poor" and how traditional forms of social organization [Lemarchand refers here to clientelism, which he considers a traditional social phenomenon] operate to incorporate the poor into the social matrix of the Mutara. . . . The social dynamics operating in the project area proved largely incompatible with the very objective of rural development as defined by the Bank, in effect denying the poor access to the resources, services and institutional support structure that might have allowed them to move up the economic and social ladder.

BEYOND MUTARA

The above description is particularly worrisome if one looks beyond the specific project to uncover the persistent pattern behind decades of "failed" projects. To be sure, some projects created useful social infrastructures, albeit typically at great cost overruns and with low sustainability. They sometimes brought real benefits to a number of poor people. However, I argue that most projects—even those deemed successful by their promoters (and, rhetoric notwithstanding, there are probably few people in the World Bank who truly believed that the Mutara project was a success)—have results similar to those of the Mutara project. This outcome is more than unfortunate, more than "bad luck." It is structural and relates to the pattern of interaction between the aid system and the state, the primary locus of the forces of exclusion. This repeated practice is the norm, the result expected both by the population at large and by the real beneficiaries, which partly explains the latter's desire to repeat the same type of inefficient projects over and over again.

These assertions are not easy to document. Objective information about projects—especially if negative—is difficult to come by. Evaluations are rarely made and are usually limited in scope, excluding any assessments of the social and political aspects of projects. In most cases, those conducting the evaluations have built-in biases, blindness, time constraints, and mechanisms of self-censorship that make truly critical work all but impossible; in the worst cases, bad news is simply censored out, as Lemarchand's evaluation shows.[2] Needless to say, the poor and the farmers are not the ones writing project evaluations or, for that matter, project identifications. Even when farmers are addressed more or less directly, their opinions are typically asked only about technical subjects related to project goals, and their responses are heavily filtered by the evaluator's own biases, as well as farmers' strategies and perceptions about what can be said without risk. Finally, apart from the Swiss Development Cooperation agency, no major aid agency has published an independent, public, and critical review of its operations in Rwanda.

It is often said that the main positive impact of development projects is the creation of jobs. Indeed, those with paid jobs, no matter how insignificant, earn incomes much higher than what they could ever make in agriculture. In the early 1980s, for example, when the average farm income was approximately RF 15,000 a year and the average artisanal income around RF 25,000 a year, the *monthly* salary for drivers was RF 15,000, for secretaries and teachers RF 20,000, and for low-level military people RF 30,000. High-level project managers could make more than RF 1 million a year. Most of these jobs were part of the civil service, and people were assigned to them by central decision.

Virtually all major projects in rural areas[3] begin their life with the construction of big and expensive houses—the biggest ones for the foreign technical assistants, so they can live in conditions at least equal to those in their home countries, and smaller ones for the Rwandan cadres working for the project—followed by garages, storage places, meeting rooms, offices, and, in most rural development programs, countless demonstration fields. The cost of these constructions, as well as the space they take up, is enormous, and the case of OVAPAM is by no means unique. As a matter of fact, resentment about the space taken up by development projects often comes up in discussions with farmers (Bugingo and others 1992, 35; CIDSE and CARITAS Internationalis 1995, 9; Godding 1983, 76; Michel 1984, 33 ff.; Nzisabira 1992).[4] Plus there is the cost of the cars, many of which are used solely to drive a lucky few to and from the capital; others are abused for purposes other than their official ones. In most rural development projects, the purchase and maintenance of vehicles consume more than 20 percent of the total local funds. All in all, more than two-thirds of all project costs, especially in the first phase (if there is more than one phase), tends to go to technical assistant salaries, construction of project infrastructure, and cars. This situation prevails in most of Africa. Thus, quite remarkably—although usually unremarked—and contradictory to stated intentions, most of the development aid funds ends up in the hands of the richest 1 percent of people in society (Voyame and others 1996, 512; Godding 1983). No wonder Ngwabije (1995, 39) observes that, to farmers, most projects "benefit only those who promote them and those who work for them."

Apart from aiding their own employees, many development projects end up supplying services primarily to the wealthy stratum of society. Many of the cattle-ranching projects of the World Bank, for example, had this effect. Thus a USAID study mentions, without any negative connotation, "the eagerness with which wealthy individuals are setting up cattle ranches to take advantage of new pastures and milk-processing facilities established under a World Bank project in Gishwati forest" (USAID 1991, chap. 2).

More broadly, clientelism, corruption, and abuse of power constantly intervene in project execution, determining much of the project's impact on poverty, inequality, and exclusion. This starts at the drawing board of the project, when decisions are made on where to locate it. According to some data, from 1982 to 1984, nine-tenths of all public investment—the main proportion of it financed by development aid—was in the four provinces of Kigali, Ruhengeri, Gisenyi, and Cyangugu (the first is the capital; the others are provinces in the north); Gitarama, the most populous province after Kigali, received 0.16 percent, and Kibuye 0.84 percent (World Bank 1987, 12; Reyntjens 1994, 222). This is the same pattern of regional inequality observed by Reyntjens (1994, 33), who found that more than a third of the eighty-five most important government positions, as well as the quasi-totality of direction functions in the army and the security apparatus, were held by people from Gisenyi, the president's native province.

The wheels of the machinery of social exclusion are further oiled when project-related jobs are allocated to the well-connected (Braeckman 1994, 87);[5] when project employees use project cars, buildings, and work time for personal purposes; when farmers are required to pay kickbacks to get credits, and these credits go to the family members and friends of the project employees; and when significant proportions of the improved or reclaimed lands end up in the hands of local administrators, political cadres, provincial civil servants, military men, or traders (Kabirigi 1994; Nkubito 1995, 286; Nshimiyunurenyi 1993, 23; Ntezilyayo 1995, 324–25). The wheels turn further when such abuses are discovered and no sanction follows. The number of corrupt administrators promoted to better jobs and unprofessional or unethical managers protected against all evidence and eventually given better-paid positions, for example, is much larger than the number of those who are punished.

In this respect, it is instructive to look at the population's attitude toward development projects. Anyone who has worked in Rwanda will agree that distrust is probably the predominant attitude, combined with lack of involvement if not outright resistance. Thus another team of World Bank experts (1987, 12–3, 27) writes with a straight face:

> The local population does not, in general, question the nature of the projects to be carried out, provided, i) they participate as paid labor (thereby earning extra cash income); ii) land developments do not affect their farm holdings (requisition of land or encroachment for infrastructure or other works); iii) the works can be reversed (erosion control measures); and iv) most of all the projects do not involve compulsory participation in the form of labor or result in heavy financial charges.

This paragraph should provoke some serious thinking: it states quite correctly that most poor people manage to live with and survive development projects and the associated administration as long as these projects do not hurt them or force them to participate. The main merit of projects for poor people seems to be that they create a plethora of (temporary) salaried jobs. This is a far cry from the original intentions of the development mission.

On occasion, people's sense of alienation and discontent with the way the development system works goes beyond passivity and distrust and moves into active resistance. Indeed, there are many documented cases of farmers destroying project realizations that were supposed to benefit them, such as wells, electricity generators, reforestation areas, and other project-created infrastructures (Nshimiyunurenyi 1993, 21). Other documents report farmers invading uncultivated lands owned by churches or dignitaries of the regime (Seruvumba 1992, 12). Some technical assistants have told me of stones being thrown at their vehicles by angry farmers. As a former student of mine wrote, "this resistance denotes a sense of disapproval, of indignation by people against the humiliation that is inflicted upon them in the treatment of 'their problems' and in the satisfaction of 'their needs' . . . and denounces the derailment of the integrated rural development programs" (Nshimiyunurenyi 1993, 22). From the moment in mid-1990 that multiple political parties were allowed and control by the single party (MRDN) was relaxed, peasants increased their acts of vandalism, defiantly pulling out coffee plants, destroying antierosion structures on their own lands, and invading communal and project demonstration areas as well as reforestation areas (Ntezilyayo 1995, 319, 323, 324). *Umuganda* (compulsory community labor) had to be abandoned totally, since nobody wished to participate in it anymore, and many of the infrastructures fell into disrepair. As USAID's 1992 annual report notes:

In the last 2 years, . . . people have attacked local authorities for launching development projects that brought little or no benefit to the community, for being personally corrupt, and for being inaccessible to and scornful of citizens in general. . . . Those who felt themselves injured by past communal decisions on such matters as land-holding are taking matters into their own hands to reclaim their rights. People are refusing to do compulsory community labor and to pay taxes. They are refusing to listen to the burgomaster and even lock him out of his office or block the road so that he cannot get there.

During the chaotic months of the genocide, there was further vandalism, including the complete and systematic destruction of most development project housing complexes, offices, storage places, and experimentation fields (Ntezilyayo 1995, 323–24).

EXCLUSION AND THE DESTRUCTION OF SOCIETY

These processes of exclusion have important social repercussions. It is clear that they contribute to the inequality documented in the previous section. But their impact goes further, undermining the moral fabric—or social capital, to use a popular term in development circles—of society. They do so through two mechanisms: impunity, and loss of credibility and legitimacy.

If there is only one point that almost all people in Rwanda are willing to agree on, it is probably that impunity[6] was and is one of the key underlying problems in society (Groupe d'Ecoute 1995; Kabirigi 1994; Oxfam 1996, 8; Ugirashebuya 1996, 36; Guichaoua 1995a, 45–46). There were two types of impunity in Rwanda, and each contributed to violence in different ways. One was the well-known and oft-discussed impunity enjoyed by the perpetrators of violence. After the pogroms in 1963–64 and 1972–73, as well as the killings of innocent people between 1990 and 1994, the organizers and perpetrators of violence were basically never punished (not surprising, as they usually worked closely with the powers that be). It is widely felt that if this kind of impunity for grave human rights violations does not end, the cycle of violence in Rwanda will continue, for unpunished violence provokes further violence (Nkubito 1995, 285).

Further, there existed in Rwanda, as in many countries, a second kind of impunity that was a matter of daily life and worked hand in hand with the process of exclusion. When judicial procedures often see the highest bidder prevail (Nkubito 1995, 283 ff.), when entry into secondary and tertiary education is the result of money and influence rather than knowledge and perseverance, when the best jobs are allocated on the basis of not competency but connections, and when manifest incompetence or abuse of power often ends in promotion, people lose their faith in the system, become cynical, and are easily tempted to break laws themselves.

The repeated abuse propagated by development projects and the institutions that promote development has also tainted the notion of development itself, significantly decreasing its legitimacy. As stated in a document on education in Rwanda, "being successful at school or in life was not dependent on efforts made to work hard and fulfil one's role, but only on effort furnished to find a 'godfather,' in all fields of life. . . . Young people could find inspiration only in practices of clientelism, cupidity, and the cult of mediocrity" (Nayigizente 1995, 43–44). Or, as Braun (1990, 37–38), a former technical assistant from the International Labor Organization (ILO) in Kigali, admits with rare candor:

> Our projects tell the farmers and artisans that if they organize and work hard, they will develop. But what is for these people the real-life model of success? . . . Who is the person that becomes wealthier fast? . . . Most of the time, the person who becomes richer did not have to join cooperatives, did not have to attend training sessions, did not need project credit. He became richer very fast because he had "friends" in the right places, and because a little present given can always lead to a little present received. In that case, with our development model that takes so much time and effort, do we have any credibility at all?

Not surprisingly, then, besides cynicism toward the ideas of development and progress, structural violence also leads to an accumulation of anger directed at the institutions and representatives of the state and the aid system—for it is they who embody the development discourse that has lost its meaning, who transmit the humiliation, and who benefit from the processes of exclusion.

Prejudice and Humiliation

In this section, I deal with the third component of structural violence, focusing on processes that are more or less on the sociopsychological level. I argue that the mode of interaction between the state (backed up by the aid system) and the people was characterized by prejudicial and humiliating attitudes and structures. Following Avishai Margalit in his

fascinating book *The Decent Society* (1996, 1, 9), we can define humiliation as "any sort of behavior that constitutes a sound reason for a person to consider his or her self-respect injured." Such humiliation,
Margalit goes on to explain in a way that resembles our discussion of
structural violence (to which he does not refer), can be institutional,
resulting from the structures, laws, and practices of society. John Rawls,
in his *A Theory of Justice* (1971), adds the social bases of self-respect as
one of the primary goods of a just society. Together, these concepts refer
to the sociopsychological aspects of structural violence: the disregard for
people's knowledge, abilities, creativity, self-respect, and, ultimately,
humanity; and their exclusion from the basic norms of civility and
respect. Again, I believe that these processes are crucial (although by
themselves not sufficient) to understanding the structural basis on which
genocide grew.

THE SECOND PREJUDICE

Prejudice existed in Rwanda in not one but two forms. One was the
already discussed official Hutu ideology, which was quite different from
the more usual African state ideology of national unity. The other was
the prejudice of those called the *evolués*—the urban, educated, modern,
"developed" people—toward their rural, illiterate, "underdeveloped"
brothers. Through that prejudice, which is widespread in Africa and the
rest of the Third World, the poor were considered backward, ignorant,
and passive—almost subhuman—and were treated in a condescending,
paternalistic, and humiliating manner.

A few authors have made passing reference to this concept. Destexhe
(1994, 68; see also Vidal 1991) writes about a "'fourth ethnic group,'
that incorporates those Hutu and Tutsi who have acquired an education
and a European knowledge (savoir-faire). . . . All these people denigrate
the rural way of living." This group's lifestyle was radically different
from that of the majority of the population, inspired almost exclusively
by the Europeans. Its members had a different language (in every conversation with ordinary people, they would make sure to use French
words, incomprehensible to the latter, to remind them of the difference),
were literate, traveled broadly, had access to cars (pens and paper, as
well as car keys, casually displayed, were important symbols of the
evolués), ate different food and drank different beer, and wore different
clothes. The lifestyle, culture, language, and dress code of this group

were upheld as the only desirable, modern ones. In turn, the lifestyle, culture, and modes of expression of the large majority of the people were considered inferior and given no recognition or space. Some have spoken in this context of a kind of social apartheid with invisible boundaries.

At the individual level, this image usually goes hand in hand with a condescending and rude attitude toward "the masses." As Ntamahungiro (1988, 12–13) writes:

> A bad habit has installed itself in our mores, in which the rich, the power-ful, the civil servant, the educated person always has priority over the poor, the weak, the non-educated, the "non-civil servant." This can be observed in court, at the doctor, in the administration and even in taxis. . . . This lack of respect towards peasants manifests itself amongst others in the way they are addressed. They are spoken to in a commandeering tone, often with disdain. They are required to behave as inferiors, to make themselves very small. (See also Willame 1995a, 147.)

A large part of the population internalized these values, accepting this lifestyle as the only "good" one, and judged its own fate as primitive, inferior, and extremely undesirable. Little was left of the "traditional" pride of the African farmer in his culture, in Rwanda as elsewhere. Most farmers, especially the young, considered the need to farm a demonstra-tion of failure and lowliness and would give up farming immediately to become a sentry, a cook, or especially a driver in any development pro-ject and to live in the city. The above-mentioned data indicating that most farmers hoped that none of their children would become farmers must be interpreted in that light. To a certain extent, this attitude was based on a realistic assessment of their chances of prospering with agri-culture; yet it was also the result of a widespread sociocultural change that began under colonization (Willame 1995a, 137).

As Franz von Benda-Beckman (1993, 122) writes, "villagers resent the arrogance of bureaucratic power, which is not based on knowledge and skill but on power of the state and what state officials consider to be the law. They resent the arrogance of people who will not work with their hands anymore, who won't lift a finger when work is to be done, yet exhort them to work harder; who ride around on scooters or cars and have villagers come to their offices on foot in vain." This intellec-tual and social arrogance humiliates people and undermines the credi-bility of the development enterprise. What exactly do ordinary people think when they see employees of the development enterprise with their finely polished shoes and crisp white shirts coming out of their air-conditioned cars to tell them how to develop? What unspoken yet loud messages are the habits, clothes, and attitudes of these people sending to Rwandan youth about their own lives (see Cart 1995, 469)? How credible are the slogans of development coming from foreigners with their foreign travel, nice houses, and drinks at the poolside of the Hotel des Milles Collines that cost more than the monthly income of farmers? It may well be that part of the answer to the eternal question of why they do not listen to our intelligent advice lies in the messengers' lack of credibility.

THE HUMILIATION OF
TOP-DOWN DEVELOPMENT

Attitudes of disdain toward farming and farmers went hand in hand with a top-down, authoritarian mode of interaction between the state and aid systems and the majority of the people. The authoritarian, vertical nature of social relations was most noticeable in the agricultural extension system. Most critical observers describe the role of the farmers as mere executors in programs conceived without asking their opinion (Cart 1995; Derrier 1985, 613–4; IFAD 1990, 10; IRAM 1985; Netherlands Development Cooperation 1992, 53; Ntamahungiro 1988; United Nations 1991, 36; World Bank 1987, 86–7; 1989a, 7). But the problem extended beyond agricultural development to encompass the public administration system, the health system, and others. The previously quoted USAID report (1992) describes how people perceived communal personnel as "being inaccessible to and scornful of citizens in general." A quote from a UN report (1991, 39) gives an apt example of the imbrication of vertical institutions: "without prior consultation, the authorities do not hesitate to communicate, during Sunday mass, the weekly calendar: reception of important visitors, meetings of the sectoral or the cell committee [local subdivisions of the single party], work in the coffee plantations, obligatory labor on roads, etc." The Rwandan peasant, silent and hardworking, often resembled more an unpaid employee of a public enterprise than an independent farmer.

At the same time, the contents of the messages being forced on the farmers, and the competencies of those doing the forcing, were often unadapted to local needs. Most agricultural extension evolved from the promotion of a few export crops, foremost coffee, and not the food crops of prime interest to farmers (Little and Horowitz 1987). The obligatory nature of coffee production is well documented: in many ways, it consumed the overwhelming part of the energy of the extension system, and it was the area where force and pressure were most used. Yet it was not limited to coffee; others document that farmers' adoption of compost pits, for example, was done more because of fear of fines than out of a desire to use them (USAID 1991, chap. 3.3).

In short, "the system is very vertical and authoritarian. . . . There is an enormous loss of content between the top and the bottom of the system. . . . Only some simplified messages arrive at the level of the farmer. Moreover, the extension agents tend to situate themselves hierarchically towards the farmers, and abuse their position" (Erpicum 1986, 22; Nkeshimana 1987, 85). As one of my Rwandese students, an agronomist with a Belgian-funded project, put it uncomprehendingly: "in our project, I asked myself the question why we always had to 'force' the farmers to listen to us, to adopt the new techniques proposed by the Ministry via the project."

The system of obligatory community labor (*umuganda*) was part of Rwanda's much-vaunted development machinery. Every Saturday, one adult male per family had to participate in community labor on projects chosen by the state: campaigns to construct primary schools, offices for the communal administration and its personnel, roads, markets, or antierosion structures. Even though absence could lead to fines and even imprisonment, discontent with and resistance to these obligatory work programs were strong, for people often saw no benefit in these works (sometimes they saw a clear loss) and resented their obligatory nature. There were many instances of abuses whereby *umuganda* works served the private interests of local authorities; also, the *evolués* usually managed to escape *umuganda* altogether (Derrier 1985, 618; Voyame and others 1996, 99). As most communal administrators chose not to risk further lowering their legitimacy, they rarely fined absentees, and participation was low (Guichaoua 1991; Willame 1995a, 142). When democratization began, *umuganda* stopped altogether.

The technical assistants in the country, even if they were ideologically predisposed to working in a bottom-up, participatory manner with farmers, more often than not found themselves trapped in the structures they worked in. Linguistically and socially handicapped, and caught in systems of expectations and misunderstanding, they found themselves unable to forge any meaningful contact with farmers (Nzisabira 1992). From the 1980s onward, following the realization in the wider international development community of the unsustainability of many development projects, a desire to increase the beneficiaries' participation in the design and implementation of projects and policies became an increasingly regular part of the rhetoric of all development agencies, including in Rwanda. It is fascinating to trace that rhetoric—and its largely failed implementation—through a case study of one rural development program in the remote region of Kibuye.

The project,[7] started in 1974, was limited to traditional extension, focusing primarily on coffee. Already, the word *participation* had the positive ring that it does today, and it was widely used. A 1981 credit request, reflecting on past experience, observed happily that "our system of training-extension that is based on true popular participation has produced very positive results." A first major evaluation in 1982, however, extensively documented the low level of farmer participation in the project and suggested a reorientation as a capacity-building project. Yet by the end of the 1980s, a major reflection seminar still discussed at length the "weak participation" of farmers in the extension system, the "lack of farmer participation in research," and the "absence of beneficiary implication in the fight against erosion." In the 1990s, a new approach was launched, focusing on the commune, the so-called motor of development. In 1991, after fundamentally reorganizing (and renaming) the project, the agency managing the project wrote that "it is crucial for the success of the project that the peasants be the owners of the project, and not simply the executors of more or less constraining obligations emanating from above." Yet in a report after the genocide, the same agency informed the world that a decision had just been made to continue the project while restructuring it along participatory lines.

The goal of this (admittedly brief) example is not to ridicule technical assistants or their superiors in Western capitals. Most of them (and this particular project had up to a hundred technical assistants living in Rwanda, plus a few hundred more experts on short-term missions) sincerely wished to involve farmers. Rather, it is to demonstrate the difficulties that well-meaning foreigners encountered in attempting to modify the nature of the interactions between Rwanda's peasant majority and the state system designed to "develop" them. As these people discovered, increasing participation in projects is not an easy matter, for it has a history and a context. The history is more than half a century old and includes forced labor to combat erosion and increase food security, obligatory contributions to "community development" projects, *umuganda*, and fines and punishments for cash crops not maintained according to central directives.

In this respect, it is fascinating to read a discussion of participation as defined by a high-ranking Rwandan civil servant in charge of communal development. After repeatedly stating the great importance attached to farmer participation by the government and the donors, he went on to outline that beneficiary participation had greatly increased and discussed the forms it took: *umuganda*, the dreaded obligatory communal labor; and *umusanzu*, obligatory financial participation in the construction and maintenance of infrastructures (Niyibizi 1986, 56). This is the same mind-set that allowed some of Rwanda's top development experts to write in a study on the role of the communes: "the key question is to create the conditions that ensure that development is not spontaneous and anarchic, but rather rational and systematic" (Bugingo and others 1992).

Under such an authoritarian and vertical system, even good-looking, progressive ideas on paper soon degenerate. In the 1980s, for example, a lot was said and done about an extension model working through "model farmers," in which supposedly dynamic farmers received intense support by extension services, the aim being that their highly visible (and hopefully successful) innovations would spread to their neighbors by example and imitation. However, many of these innovative farmers were the wealthier ones, and the exclusive attention paid to them basically equaled neglect of most of the other, poorer farmers. Moreover, the quality of the support that even the model farmers received was weak; their success was often due more to better access to inputs (improved seeds, for example, or fertilizer as a result of possessing livestock) than to advice and support (Michel 1984, 189).

A similar practice was to award prizes to those farmers who most faithfully adopted the agricultural packages being promoted by the extension services. This, too, was based on the idea of promoting spontaneous adoption of innovations by neighboring farmers impressed by the success of the innovators. Here again, the idea was deemed to be a progressive one. As a brochure for field-workers explained it:

> The most common form of encouragement [to adopt the agricultural practices recommended by the extension system] in Rwanda is negative: farmers are punished if they do not obey the authorities. . . . Positive encouragement addresses itself to farmers who improve their cultivating methods. Its elements are various compensations for the efforts undertaken: prizes, visits by the local authorities to the fields of the farmers, publication of the names and pictures of the progressive farmers at the communal office, etc. Together with this, it is necessary to sensibilize and train the farmers so as to render them capable of understanding and applying the new techniques. (PAK 1980)

This practice, too, suffered from a combination of authoritarian imposition of preconceived packages and corruption and clientelism among those who received the prizes. As the above quote illustrates, the notion that certain technical packages that had been preestablished by the specialists needed to be adopted by all farmers (who were not smart enough to do so by themselves) was never questioned; only the method to achieve this goal was changed. Practice has shown that the prizes often went to the same people year after year and that their impact on the social environment was small. As one person described it, "without seeking to understand why a certain recommended practice had not been implemented, sanction replaced dialogue. The award system thus became a nightmare for the farmer who, without the least conviction, worked to obtain points for the awards" (Kayitesi 1993, 51).

One of the effects of all this is the inconsequential impact that most development projects eventually had on their target groups. On the rare occasions when data are given, one is always struck by the extreme insignificance of the results, especially when compared with the magnitude of the resources invested. IFAD (1991, 91), for example, mentions that out of the 50,000 farmers targeted by one of its projects since 1970, "4,000 were participating in the implementation of the methods developed by the project, although only 70 had adopted the full package." We have already seen how, in the Mutara project, whatever adoption there was of innovative farming or livestock practices disappeared a few years after completion of the project. An evaluation of another World Bank–funded project—the agricultural production project in Gitarama—explains that after two years of work costing $12.7 million, about 10 percent of the farmers were reached by the new extension, and 5 to 6 percent adopted some of the themes; only 3 percent of them, however, received the vegetable seeds required, and 1 percent received the cuttings (sweet potatoes) (World Bank 1989a, 7). An evaluation of the Swiss-funded Programme Agricole Kibuye in 1982 (seventeen years after its inception, at more than $1 million a year) observes that only 2 percent of the farmers entirely adopted the antierosion techniques proposed by the project—the cornerstone of its work (Corrèze, Gentil, and Barnaud 1982a, 42). As a matter of fact, an evaluation team observed that in this region, innovations *did* take place, but without the support of the project, and sometimes against the explicit wishes of the government (Voyame and others 1996, 87). A World Bank report on the matter concluded that "there are only a few examples of specific government interventions which can clearly be shown to have had a significant impact on productivity to date" (World Bank 1983; 1989b, 30). Note that all these statements were written by professional aid evaluators, often employed by the very agencies that managed the projects being judged—in other words, people with a strong inclination to overestimate impact and put a positive spin on whatever trends they encountered.[8]

Much of what has been said about the top-down, vertical nature of the relations between the state and its citizens has been observed all over Africa. What is specific about Rwanda, however, are the omnipresence and strength of the state and the development machinery. Thus, paradoxically, it is in the "best" country—the developers' dream location, where things were implemented the way they were stated on paper by a strong, well-endowed state committed to development—that life most resembled a forced labor camp, with questionable benefits.[9]

To sum up, relations between the administrative and technical state system and the population in Rwanda were vertical and authoritarian, making it almost impossible for ordinary people's voices to be heard— assuming that anyone was interested in listening. A set of social attitudes, behaviors, and lifestyles daily brought home the distinction between the failure of the farmers and the success of the *evolués*. Most of the development aid system also continued to function along topdown, externally defined lines, bypassing people's own creativity, capacities, histories, and senses of value (Rader 1990, 229). Observers have noted how development in Rwanda infantilizes poor people, depriving them of their self-respect and their creativity (Hanssen 1989, 34; Braeckman 1994, 88; Guichaoua 1995a, 3–4; Willame 1995a). Thus the ideological tenets of the "developers" and the political requirements of the powers that be join in defining development largely without people's input, without much respect for poor people, and often without much benefit to them (see also CIDSE and CARITAS Internationalis 1995).

It is uncommon for analyses of development to dwell at length on the factors discussed here: prejudice, humiliation, and infantilization. Questions related to these phenomena are not asked of farmers, and evaluators do not examine them. They are largely invisible and, at those rare moments when we may be aware of them, they tend to look unchangeable. However, harm is done by treating people in an infantilizing, condescending manner, by limiting their options, and by stripping them of their dignity and creativity. Disempowering people, even in the name of development, is not neutral: it has impacts on their minds and bodies.

When people are denied the realization of their full human and intellectual potential, when they are deprived of choices and information, they are more easily manipulated. When people are treated in a humiliating and prejudicial manner, when they are made to lose their self-respect, the result is frustration and anger, as well as a strong need to regain self-respect and dignity. As Willame (1995b, 445) writes, "the population, who slid unnoticed from poverty to misery, is easily manipulable by forms of ethnicity in which the 'other,' the 'stranger,' or the 'invader,' becomes the scapegoat." Recourse to ethnic identity, scapegoating, and the projection of hostility onto weaker groups constitute important effects of structural violence. According to Lindiro Kabirigi (1994, 2–3), "the lack of popular expression constituted a solid ground for violence. When people cannot express themselves in words or deeds within society because there always is an 'intellectual' to do it for them and to tell them what they should do, it is normal they accumulate a sense of resentment and demands which end up by exploding in an uncontrollable manner as soon as opportunity presents." As Soedjatmoko, late rector of the United Nations University, wrote, "without freedom to dissent, responsibility for creative developmental impulses of a society disappears" (quoted in Tomasevski 1989, 155). Imprisoned in a system in which they were not free to choose their own development, devoid of information and choices, constantly at the receiving end of political and technical messages, people became unable—and indeed unwilling—to resist reductionist schemes and were tempted to be passive, fundamentalist, cynical, racist, or violent (Godding 1983, 82).

From Structural Violence to Genocide

For most of us, it is hard to imagine how tense and frustration-ridden a society must be when every day the large majority of the population is shown the lifestyle of the "developed" and exhorted to achieve it but is at the same time structurally excluded from this "good life," with very little chance of achieving it. This can only have a profound impact on people's attitudes, beliefs, and behavior. Many social scientists, particularly sociologists such as Robert Merton and Ted Gurr, have argued that such situations are major causes of resentment and, through that, violence. Similarly, others have shown how impunity, the flip side of inequality and usually occurring in tandem with it, creates frustration and a sense of loss that lead to scapegoating and facilitate violence (Oxfam 1996, 8; Guichaoua 1995a, 38).

For many people, hatred of "the other" served to combat the low self-esteem caused by chronic unemployment and squelched aspirations; these young, frustrated men were the ones most vulnerable to the kind of ethnic appeals that led to genocide. It is generally suggested that they were the ones who made up the radical militia (Willame 1995a, 127, 154, 160; Kabirigi 1994, 10). Everywhere in the world, these men are the recruits for urban gangs and extremist militias. As Galtung (1990, 294) writes, "a violent structure leaves marks not only on the body but also on the mind and the spirit." There is a profound need to make sense of life, to reestablish self-respect. And as Simpson and Yinger (1953, 61) wrote long ago:

> Prejudice is an attempt to find meaning, to explain. . . . Prejudice may be an attempt to enhance one's self-esteem or to remove a threat to self-esteem. In a culture that stresses the opportunities each person has for success but prevents success (by its own definition) for a great number, it is not surprising to find a great many people creating a shadowy image of success by placing themselves, categorically, above all members of inferior groups.

I hold that anti-Tutsi racism fulfilled this psychological function for many of the poor Hutu, which is why the regime was so successful in using racism for decades to legitimize its hold on power. To understand the crisis in Rwanda, we thus need to see how the two types of prejudice worked together: the prejudice against the large majority of the poor that caused mass frustration, loss of self-respect, and a need for compensation through externalization; and the official, state-sponsored racism against Tutsi that provided a convenient, institutionalized scapegoat (and diverted attention away from the privileges enjoyed by a few in the name of the masses). As Staub (1990, 56) writes, "under such conditions [difficult life circumstances and a culturally established devaluation of a social group] scapegoating can diminish feelings of personal and group responsibility for problems, protecting self-concept." Or as explained by Simpson and Yinger (1953, 51) in their seminal work on prejudice, "a person who is brought up in a culture that is rich with traditions of prejudice, . . . and who is insecure or frustrated will have a high probability for prejudice." The benefits of joining in scapegoating include renewed comprehension of the world, hope, and feelings of purpose (Staub 1990). Anywhere in the world, this applies foremost to young men, who tend to suffer most from the contradiction between their self-images and the opportunities offered by society.

Furthermore, structural violence lowers the barriers against the use of violence. As the norms of society lose legitimacy, as people's knowledge base is reduced to slogans, as progress becomes a meaningless concept, as communities are riveted by conflict and jealousy, as people's sense of self-respect is reduced, and as segments of society show their contempt for the rules of decency as well as for farmers, people become increasingly unhampered by constraints on the use of violence to deal with problems.

To conclude, the physical (ill health, malnutrition) and psychological harm done through structural violence may not be as visible as the mass graves that sporadically fill our television screens, but its effects are equally profound and debilitating. If one recognizes the condition of structural violence, one can understand that profound racist prejudice and outbursts of murderous violence are part of a continuum of ever-present violence in which violence is the answer to violence, and in which victims temporarily become perpetrators and then victims again. The differences between structural and acute violence parallel those between public/indirect and private/direct violence, with the former referring to the system of oppression and exclusion operating through the mechanisms of the state, and the latter to individual acts of aggression, opportunism, and self-protection that result in part from the former. Typically, the violence of individuals—black youngsters in the U.S. inner city, street children in Brazil, shantytown dwellers in South Africa, and others—tends to be widely perceived, while the violent acts of the state are not recognized (Scheper-Hughes 1996, 894 ff.).

In many ways, then, structural violence lays the groundwork for acute violence. Under conditions of structural violence, acute violence can serve different functions: it is a tool for temporary personal gain, as culturally acceptable as it is common and necessary for survival; it is a pressure release from the frustration and lack of self-respect, as acceptable as it is encouraged by the political leadership; and it is a job opportunity for the lucky few who join militias and mobs, its gain potential vastly bigger than any legal opportunity available.

In Rwanda in the 1990s, the interaction between structural violence and racism created the conditions necessary for genocidal manipulation by the elites to be successful. Structural violence provoked a need for scapegoating among ordinary people; the existence of long-standing racism allowed parts of the elite to use this need to build a genocidal movement. Without the profound racism, we would find not genocide but "ordinary" communal violence, of which there is so much in Africa;

without elite manipulation, structural violence would lead to more diffuse, anomic modes of violence such as petty criminality, sorcery, or domestic abuse—all of which are on the rise in most of Africa.

Notes

1. USAID database, 1993 USAID proposition, subsection on poverty reduction. The countries that are close are Bangladesh, the Sudan, and Bolivia.
2. Lemarchand was originally part of the team that evaluated the first phase of the Mutara project. His report was deemed undesirable, though, and was not included in the final evaluation. He waited three years and then published it as a working paper.
3. In urban areas, technical assistants usually rented nice houses at exorbitant prices, which created an extremely lucrative market for the well-connected people who controlled urban real estate and construction.
4. A former student of mine wrote angrily about "the technical assistants . . . who transform the region in a veritable holiday colony and delect themselves in an insolent tourism on project funds under the angry looks of the hungry farmers." Having done it myself—and always having felt uncomfortable under the scrutinizing looks of the locals who passed the high, guarded metal fence around my Swiss chalet in the middle of the *collines* (with hot shower, refrigerator, CD collection, garden, parking for my car)—I must admit that this description is not too far from reality.
5. Note that, among the people directly hired by the foreign aid agencies themselves, Tutsi were often highly represented. In many ways, in times of peace, the dominant form of exclusion in Rwanda was social rather than ethnic.
6. Defined by the on-line version of *Merriam Webster's Collegiate Dictionary* as "exemption or freedom from punishment."
7. I do not wish to identify the project by name and thereby single it out for criticism that it does not deserve. For that reason, there are no citations for the applicable quotations.
8. I have been guilty of the same. During the early 1990s, for example, I evaluated a rural development project in Burundi after more than a decade of existence. Although none of its central objectives had been adopted by more than 2 percent of the target group, I tried to convince myself that I could somehow write down something like 5 percent to at least give a slightly better impression of a project that I appreciated very much and had invested quite a bit of time in. I eventually dropped the entire issue from the final report, contenting myself with vague statements, taken from project employees, about positive trends of increased adoption. I presume that the previous evaluators had done the same, for I could never find any serious figures about adoption rates anywhere—only the same vague statements. Note that I was not afraid of losing my job if I did not report positive results. The people managing the project were open, committed, intelligent people. Rather, I was motivated by a spontaneous desire to see good things and block out doubt, to be a good team player, a positive, not-too-judgmental white person—in short, an ideal development professional. This is an aspect of the "normal professionalism" that Robert Chambers has not written about, although it is as dangerous as the tendency toward top-down, technology-driven development he criticizes: the

lowering of expectations, the fear of judgment, the desire to be liked by the locals and the superiors, the ignorance about what really goes on, and so forth.

9. This most clearly applies to the *umuganda*, as well as to the approach to coffee (Guichaoua 1991; Willame 1995a, 142).

7

AID AND STRUCTURAL VIOLENCE

In this chapter, I seek to clarify the multiple interactions between development aid and the processes of exclusion and structural violence.

The first part analyzes the relationship between development aid and structural violence. It focuses on both the direct and the indirect ways in which this interaction takes place. It concludes that development aid is symbiotic to the processes of exclusion and structural violence. The second part of this chapter deals with a different but related question: why have aid practitioners, usually people committed to social change and improvements in the lives of the poor, not seen these effects of aid? What are the political, institutional, ideological, and psychological factors that render the development aid system blind to its own effects? The case of Rwanda is a fascinating one, given the enormous gap between the image of Rwanda as a model developing country and the reality of structural violence and the eventual genocide.

The Impact of Development Aid on Structural Violence

In the preceding chapter, I was critical of the impact of development projects. However, as a rule, development projects in Rwanda provided some benefits to the general population, albeit usually much less than expected or perceived. Even the Mutara projects eventually constructed water supplies, as well as a few health and education infrastructures—all much-needed services. Hence, much of the aid did benefit the population at large and can be said to have contributed to some generalized

141

national "development." Note, however, that important issues of sustainability and distribution typically remain unresolved: How long did these infrastructures function? What happened when they needed repair? Did the government make available other necessary resources for these infrastructures to function optimally, such as medicines or teachers? Were the benefits of the project sustained after the withdrawal of the foreign aid? There are also trickier issues of distribution that are typically unanswered: Who received access to the schooling, especially post-primary education? Were the medical supplies used equitably, based on need? How did political interference affect the project's social impact?

Some projects may have contributed to increasing poor people's incomes. Artisans may have learned new techniques and, especially as long as the foreign-funded project was present, may have found a market for their products; some farmers may have become organized in order to buy supplies or sell their products at better prices; a few other farmers may have received credits or opportunities to deposit money safely; other farmers probably managed to adopt some of the proposed agricultural techniques and may have seen the productivity of their lands increase, or at least stop falling. Unfortunately, such positive impacts usually involve no more than a small proportion of the population. This is the case either because the projects are small to begin with (such as most NGO projects) or because the projects, even when large, fail to reach most of the people they seek to help. Moreover, I suspect that, most of the time, those who benefit from development project interventions do not belong to the half of the population categorized as the poorest of the poor. All in all, the nature, size, cost, and sustainability of project benefits vary greatly—and in the worst cases, approach nil—as do the proportion and representativeness of people who benefit from them. Usually, these positive outcomes are far below expectations, and this is quite well recognized.

Table 7.1 presents an example of the impact of thirty years of development cooperation by one of the most progressive donors with extensive involvement in Rwanda, the Swiss Development Cooperation agency. The main conclusion is that, for the more than $200 million spent, the results are remarkably few, uncertain, and unsustained. I chose this example for the sole reason that Switzerland is the only country that has evaluated its official development aid to Rwanda critically and publicly. My personal observation is that the quality of Swiss aid is superior to that of the average bilateral and multilateral aid. Its aid is almost totally untied to political or economic considerations in the donor country, and it is managed within a framework that puts great emphasis on assistance to the poorest people, strengthening of local institutions, long-term relationships, and transfer of knowledge. Hence, the negative outcomes shown here are likely to be much stronger for many other agencies.

Unfortunately, the development aid system is not simply ineffective, unsustainable, limited, and uncertain in its impact—unsatisfactory as that may be. It also contributes to processes of structural violence in many ways. It does so directly, through its own behavior, whether unintended (as in the case of growing income inequality and land concentration) or intended (as in its condescending attitude toward poor people). It also does so indirectly, by strengthening systems of exclusion and elite building through massive financial transfers, accompanied by self-imposed political and social blindness. Once more, most of what I discuss here applies to all of Africa, and not solely to Rwanda.

THE DIRECT IMPACT ON
STRUCTURAL VIOLENCE

The development enterprise directly and actively contributes to inequality and humiliation. The material advantages accorded to a small group of people and the lifestyles of the foreigners living in Rwanda contribute to greater economic inequality and the devaluation of the life of the majority (Cart 1995, 469; Schürings 1995, 499). The spending patterns of most development projects are disproportionately in favor of the smallest groups in society, that is, the richest 1 pecent or so, composed of technical assistants and their "homologues," plus merchants and high-level government officials. The more one moves down the social ladder, the fewer the resources that projects provide to people. This is the case for almost all projects, even the relatively successful ones, and it helps explain the popularity of donor-funded development projects with the powers that be.

It has often been said—and I largely concur—that the prime impact of development projects is to create jobs for the lucky few who manage to obtain them. These benefits are distributed very unequally: the income gain of the extension agent, who receives a RF 3,000 supplement over his meager official salary, is small compared with the gains awarded to high-level project staff, for whom access to cars, housing, foreign travel,

Table 7.1 Thirty Years of Swiss Aid to Rwanda

Name	Period	Swiss Francs (Million)	Project Description	Comments
TRAFIPRO	1963–86	32	Support to Rwanda's largest complex of consumer and producer cooperatives	Longtime successful enterprise, providing important services to the population; however, repeated financial misuse, overly expensive construction of large buildings, and heavy political interference led to its bankruptcy
Banques Populaires Rwanda	1973–93	30	Creation and support of savings and credit cooperatives based on Raiffaisen model	Very successful project, fully independent of government; fast growth, showing it responded to a popular need; increasingly dependent on donor funding, however; has been criticized because large majority of deposits were from farmers, while large majority of credits went to urban people
Centre IWACU	1980–93	8	Creation and support of cooperative training agency	Important and successful grassroots support agency; too much money spent on construction of building in Kigali; contrary to rhetoric, no farmer involvement in management and policy
Programme Agricole Kibuye	1964–93	34	Integrated rural development program	Constantly seeking, always unsuccessfully, to increase farmer involvement; in the end, remarkably little real impact
Forest Projects	1969–93	39	Forest management programs	It was observed in 1993 that "such projects can not be implemented against the wishes of the adjacent population"; great success in becoming basis for government policy

(cont.)

Table 7.1 Thirty Years of Swiss Aid to Rwanda (cont.)

Name	Period	Swiss Francs (Million)	Project Description	Comments
Infrastructure	1978–93	27	Electrification, telephone, water, roads	Often weak impact and bad management; doubts about relevancy
Construction materials	1983–93	16	Creation of brick and roofing enterprises	Financial abuse by manager; highly foreign aid dependent
Artisanal support	1989–93		Transformation of soybeans into tofu; support to informal sector in Kigali	Successful by themselves, but relevance for the population questionable; political and financial mismanagement of the latter project
Official College of Kigali	1964–78	6		Highly aid dependent
Macro-economic support	1983–92	19	Included cofinancing of structural adjustment programs	Almost no impact; policies hardly implemented
Presidential adviser	1963–92	4		Unsure impact (interrupted for some years in mid-1970s)

Source: Joseph Voyame, Richard Friedli, Jean-Pierre Gern, and Anton Keller, *La coopération suisse au Rwanda* (Berne: Département Fédéral des Affaires Étrangères, 1996); Henri-Phillipe Cart, La coopération suisse au Rwanda ou les limites de l'aide extérieure, in *Les crises politiques au Burundi et au Rwanda (1993–1994)*, edited by A. Guichaoua (Lille, France: Karthala and Université des Sciences et Technologies de Lille, 1995); Jean Nzisabira, *Participation populaire au processus de développement du Rwanda. Les idées et les faits* (Louvain-la-Neuve: Cahiers du CIDEP vol. 13, 1992).

and salaries in the hundreds of thousands of francs per month are reserved; the advantages of technical assistants are usually much greater still, with salaries in the millions of Rwandese francs. Usually, one-third of all project costs goes to a handful of technical assistants, experts, and consultants.[1] Of the remainder, around a quarter is spent on cars, and in the early phases of a project, up to 50 percent more is spent on the actual installation of the project, including nice houses for its top employees. These spending patterns, then, are the primary and unrecognized direct results of the development aid system: they are heavily weighted in favor of the wealthiest and the well-connected.

Yet all evaluations of development projects and programs, as well as all analyses of economic and social trends in Rwanda and other African countries, tend to leave the development aid system out of the picture—as if it were not a permanent part of local society, consumption patterns, social stratification, and many people's aspirations. All data on income distribution in Africa, for example, fail to include the well-known salaries and lifestyles of most technical assistants, foreign consultants, and the few lucky locals working with them. In other words, income inequality is calculated by leaving out the wealthiest, most visible segment of society. This is the segment of a thousand or so foreigners and maybe as many nationals who own almost all the beautiful houses, primarily in the capital, but also scattered throughout the countryside; who buy up most of the land from destitute farmers; who travel abroad and share the French culture. Most of these people work for the development enterprise and derive their wealth from it. Their salaries are hundreds of times higher than the incomes of farmers.

How would we react if such inequalities existed in our own society? Do we expect people of all walks of life to be unaware of this situation? To not adopt expectations and lifestyles that reflect this extreme inequality? The lifestyles and consumption patterns of those in the aid business are thus not neutral facts but generate social exclusion. As someone wrote, "some aspects of consumption inequality are themselves causes of exclusion. The visible growth of mass consumption among affluent minorities . . . clearly intensifies the sense of exclusion among other groups even if absolute poverty does not increase" (International Institute for Labour Studies and UNDP 1994, 3).

This social fact becomes more worrisome when access to these coveted positions is determined by ethnic, regional, or other arbitrary criteria, as it is in most African countries. When the large majority of high-level civil servants and project managers in Burundi are Tutsi;

when there are legal limits on the number of Tutsi that can enter civil service in Rwanda; when the top positions go disproportionately to people from the president's region and assorted other friends; when the best-paid jobs are always reserved for Bazungu, regardless of competence; when many of the people with well-paid positions in the private aid sector are Tutsi; in other words, when ethnic and regional criteria intervene so crucially in the distribution of the direct benefits of development projects, is the aid system neutral? Or does it create skewed structures and incentives that often work directly against its stated objectives and are highly charged politically?

In the case of Rwanda, with its high rural population density, there was one more profoundly unequalizing direct impact of many development projects: land grabbing. Most rural projects conduct themselves as if land were not scarce, liberally sprinkling offices, homes, storage buildings, demonstration and multiplication fields, and access roads across the countryside. If one understands the manner in which these lands were made available for the projects, sometimes involving land expropriation with little or no compensation, one can imagine the misery this sometimes created.

The humiliation created by the functioning of much of the development aid system constitutes another direct and profound impact. In many ways, what underlies the ideology and practice of development is a vision of basic needs based on the model of Maslow's needs hierarchy (from physiological to self-actualization). The strength of this vision, and the reason for its widespread adoption, is its secular, humanistic, and seemingly neutral (culturally unbound) nature. Its important weakness, however, is that it posits a hierarchy between "basic" and "less basic" needs that brings about a skewed and dangerous sense of priorities for development aid. As Fisher (1990, 90–91; see also Mitchell 1990, 160) states it: "the normative specification that lower needs must be satisfied before attention is given to higher needs could be used to justify deliberate inattention to non-material needs and for preserving an unacceptable status quo." This leads to a privileging of material goals over social ones and causes a widespread sense of material urgency, which reinforces the neglect of social factors. But development, as we know by now, is much more than simply income: it is a process of social change in which different aspects of people's lives cannot be separated— the economic from the social, the cultural from the political and the religious (Hiebert and Hiebert-Crape 1995, 284). People need much more than bread or income alone, and it is quite possible that even with more bread, they can be worse off. They need recognition and capabilities to act as full human beings.[2]

Another problem with this top-down, "basic needs" definition is that it tends to favor rapid, technical, externally defined "fixes" for what are considered to be urgent basic needs, and thus bypasses people's creativity and knowledge. Indeed, the basic needs orientation considers that issues of creativity, self-actualization, respect, or sense of community are less important or urgent than those of food production, jobs, and economic trends. Tomasevski (1989, 155) synthesizes the problem well when she writes that "the human needs approach—which mainly states that in priority people should be fed, clothed and housed well and that the other things come afterwards—treats people as recipients of aid, rather than as agents of their own development." As a result, it tends to become top-down and limited, bypassing people's own creativity, capacity, history, culture, and sense of value and community (Rader 1990, 229). This approach also ignores politics; it is capable of working with repressive governments as long as they seem to be capable of promoting development as defined by technocrats.[3]

In many countries, this approach mirrors and strengthens the state system, which, for the same ideological and attitudinal reasons, as well as for reasons of political control, is also highly top-down, authoritarian, and ignorant of local dynamics. The ideological tenets of the "developers" and the political requirements of the powers that be join in defining development largely without people's input, without respect for poor people, and, often, without benefit to them (CIDSE and CARITAS Internationalis 1995).

THE INDIRECT RELATIONSHIP BETWEEN
DEVELOPMENT AID AND STRUCTURAL VIOLENCE

In a country like Rwanda, it is difficult to separate the aid system from the state system. To begin with, the lion's share of all aid, upward of 80 percent, goes to the government; the rest is subject to its approval (Bugingo and Ntampaka 1991, 9). A Swiss evaluation of the impact of development aid states that "the development of policy-making and administrative activities and of the public service (foremost education and health) in Rwanda is done as far as investment goes through the flows of development aid and as far as functioning goes through fiscal receipts" (Voyame and others 1996, 56). This is an understatement:

Many projects actually covered significant portions of the current budgets of some ministries, most notably by paying the full or partial salaries of their local agents, providing them with means of transportation, training them, and so forth. Moreover, many of the local funds the government spent originated with foreign aid also—counterpart funds from food aid or balance-of-payment support, for example.

To understand the imbrication between foreign aid and state policy, let us return to the sector of rural development. Every economic and social development plan and every speech of the president repeated the centrality of food self-sufficiency and rural development as the government's foremost objective (World Bank 1989c, 1; IFAD 1990, 3; Voyame and others 1996, 52). Yet a closer analysis of the government budget shows that, all through the 1970s and the 1980s, only between 4 and 6 percent of current expenditures was devoted to rural development, with more than half of that going to salaries (Marysse 1982, 43; Voyame and others 1996, 58; see also tables on government expenditure by functional classification in the UN's annual *African Statistical Yearbook*). Agriculture never accounted for more than 5 percent of the government's own capital expenditures. To put these figures into context: urban infrastructure took up 40 percent of the Rwandan capital expenditures, and higher education 5 percent, while 7 percent of state revenues was spent on massive subsidies to a small and inefficient parastatal industrial sector (Voyame and others 1996, 55, 58). COOPIBO, a major Belgian nongovernmental organization (NGO), observed in 1980 that agriculture came in tenth place in the government budget. Clearly, small-scale agriculture was not a priority of the government, and the portion of state expenditures that went to the large majority of the Rwandan farmers was minimal—a far cry from the rhetoric.

Most of the resources spent on rural development went to promoting export crops (World Bank 1983, 39; 1994b, 32; COOPIBO 1980). While 34 percent of all bank credits went to agriculture, 90 percent of these went solely to coffee. Of the credits extended by the famous Banques Populaires du Rwanda, more than two-thirds went to the cities, although 80 percent of the savings were rural.

The aid system partly compensated for the neglect of agriculture by the Rwandan government. Between 25 and 35 percent of all aid was allocated to agriculture (World Bank 1989c, 8–9; Voyame and others 1996, 53). There were over sixty major donor-financed agricultural projects covering more than 100 of the 143 communes (World Bank 1989a, 3). Up to 200 local and foreign NGOs, with a few thousand employees, added approximately 740 more small projects in rural development (Seruvumba 1992). These projects together had significantly more money and personnel than the Ministry of Agriculture (UNDP 1987). Through the payment of either "primes"—important salary complements to public-sector employees working with development projects—or full salaries, the development aid system funded a significant part of the current budget devoted to agriculture (World Bank 1989c, 3). To get an idea of the extent of aid's importance: in the second half of the 1980s, government funding to the agricultural sector amounted to US$16 million, compulsory community labor was (highly) estimated to be the equivalent of US$14 million, and foreign aid provided US$39 million (World Bank 1989a, 14). The same report estimated that there were 177 foreign technical assistants in the agricultural sector, compared with 122 cadres in the Ministry of Agriculture.

These hundreds of projects—largely acting without coordination, each according to its own (often conflicting) objectives, modes of functioning, and procedures—ended up largely constituting what passes for "national development policy" (Nzisabira 1992). In the case of agriculture, the World Bank (1989a, 11) observed that the Ministry of Agriculture had basically no control over the projects: "extension and in general agricultural development projects have been largely donor-driven." Other studies show that the same holds true, even more so, for the NGO projects (Bugingo and others 1992, 83). As another Bank consultant observed (World Bank 1989c, 1–2; see also Bugingo and Ntampaka 1991):

> Most of its [the government's] activities are geared to projects and focus on defining terms of reference for studies of specific projects to be carried out by outside consulting firms. . . . Most of the agricultural strategy of the government is implemented through specific projects which cover more than 70 percent of the existing 143 communes. Yet, the mission could not get consistent, reliable information from MINAGRI staff on (i) the number of on-going projects, (ii) their costs and implementation schedule, (iii) their financing sources, (iv) the current state of funds disbursement, and (v) any feedback on how implementation is proceeding.

In other words, Rwanda's rural development policy, like most if its other sectoral policies—and like most government policies throughout Africa—more or less equals the sum of hundreds of aid-financed and -controlled interventions, almost all directed by foreign employees, plus whatever government agents could add to them.

To sum up: the aid system was very involved in the rural development sector in Rwanda, financing the largest part of it, and managing literally hundreds of projects. This means two things: first, that the aid system compensated for some of the weaknesses of the Rwandan state and thus may have positively influenced development for the rural majority; and second, that the processes of social, regional, and ethnic exclusion documented in the previous chapter took place under the eyes and the (predominant) presence of the aid system. The problem is determining to what extent the aid system can be held accountable for the processes of exclusion or whether it is a victim of processes it cannot control.

At first sight, given the enormous importance of development aid, one would expect donors to have a profound impact on national policies and local outcomes. The aid donors control the planning and execution of projects and hold the purse strings; they always have their own man (rarely a woman) to head projects and control the finances. Yet the reality is a far more ambiguous situation in which neither the donors nor the government control the outcome, but both acquiesce with whatever emerges because it suits their interests.

To understand this better, it may be useful to begin by observing that the development enterprise is carried out at two levels. One is the level of general development policy of the recipient country in domains such as agriculture, health, education, and the like. As we saw earlier, in many highly aid-dependent African countries, these policies amount to little more than the sum of all the projects that donors are willing to finance, plus some ideological and administrative packaging by the government. Recipient governments hardly control their policies, and often their top staff does not feel much of a sense of ownership of and hence commitment to these so-called policies.

Individual donors do not usually control these policies either, however. The projects of each donor tend to be too small and regionally concentrated to determine national policy, and, contrary to rhetoric, donors generally do not coordinate their projects in the field. Finally, sovereignty obliging, donors act as if the government is in charge and create a variety of mechanisms to uphold that impression. Thus, the recipient government has quite a lot of leeway to play donors against one another and to get some of its key interests funded. At the end of the day, then, there is really nobody who sets the national policy in these areas: it simply emerges out of a set of behaviors by different players that are sometimes interacting, sometimes competing, and sometimes indifferent to one another.

The second level is that of individual projects and their implementation. Here again, it is the donor agencies that control the purse, through both their technical assistants and their headquarters in donor countries. Negotiations are part of the game, but ultimately, decisions about over-all budgets and strategies, new project phases, and what to do with the lessons from evaluations (or even whether to evaluate) are made by the donors and not by recipient-country personnel.

But this does not mean that the government, or specific people within the government, have no ability to influence projects in specific direc-tions, or that all rural development outcomes are directly traceable to the intentions of their designers or managers in aid offices—far from it. Government desires—or, more specifically, the desires of the president, specific ministers, or high-ranking civil servants and politicians—inter-vene significantly in the unfolding of projects. They typically play a cru-cial role in deciding where specific projects will take place and in the allocation of contracts, benefits, and jobs. The recipient government can refuse to accredit technical assistants, delay negotiations and signatures, modify administrative structures, propose new projects to other donors, and so forth. Specific people in government and the administration can seek to obtain credits, travel, and kickbacks for construction; they can award jobs, contracts, and project benefits to family members and allies, especially if the aid managers (who are usually unfamiliar with the local language, power relations, and customs), barely realize what is going on.

Thus, altogether, the specific outcomes of specific projects result from an unclear, usually unspoken mixture of behaviors in which it is difficult to attribute full (or even consciously shared) responsibility to any one party. High-ranking civil servants, national and local politicians, foreign experts and managers, and even ordinary project employees can and do seek to use specific projects for a variety of purposes—the result being that the implementation of a coherent, pro-poor development strategy often ends up being the last concern.

At the heart of this ambiguous outcome lie two of the cornerstones of relations between rich and poor countries at the end of the twentieth century. One is the principle of sovereignty as defined since World War II, that is, the basic prohibition against foreign intervention in domestic matters, regardless of the behaviors and capacities of governments (Jackson 1990, 6, 27). The other is the ideology of development and its institutional, psychological, and political manifestations.

It is the interplay of these two factors that creates the ambiguous out-come of the development game, in which the donors partially abandon control of their projects and programs and the recipients partially take control, particularly of specific project benefits, which interest many people much more than general policies. Neither side takes responsibility, and neither side can do what it does without at least the acquiescence of the other. Thus the game of development cooperation is played in a twilight zone of ambiguities, politically correct statements, lofty declarations, voluntary blindness, and mutual reproach—a game in which the forces of sovereignty, power, and ideology confront one another incompletely. No one side stands for a clear position; there are no good guys versus bad guys, only muddling through and outcomes that are systematically suboptimal and unexpected, except for the powerful and well-connected.

To sum up, I have argued that the development outcomes in Rwanda— including the processes of exclusion documented earlier—cannot be understood in isolation from the development enterprise, which underwrote and legitimized them. Both the development aid system and the state are imbricated in manifold ways, and eventual outcomes are an ambiguous, misunderstood, uncontrolled, hybrid mixture of both. The relationship between development aid and the processes of exclusion and structural violence is symbiotic, with both sides existing through each other, and the outcome the result of this interplay. The latter assertion can be interpreted to mean that development aid has no importance, for it is not in control of outcomes. That would be wrong. Although the nature of the development game may be one of muddling through and ambiguity, that does not mean that there is no potential for drawing lines. Development outcomes are not under the full control of the donor, but neither is the latter without power to act—to stop, cut, refuse, renegotiate, pay attention, suspend, rethink, clarify, speak out. The fact that donors usually choose not to do so does not mean that the possibility does not exist. The constraints are man-made, not natural.

In myriad ways, the development aid system becomes part of societies' stakes, conflicts, expectations, myths, structures of oppression, and channels of gain. Development aid strengthens processes of exclusion both directly, through its own behaviors, and indirectly, through its acquiescence and implication in other actors' behaviors. We ourselves become creators of expectations and myths of development and desirable consumption patterns; we ourselves become exploiters when implementing government policies that discriminate against ethnic or social groups or when condoning corruption and abuse of power; we ourselves are the channels of personal gain for those who manage to ingratiate themselves with us; we ourselves often reinforce the take-it-or-leave-it position toward poor people treated as recipients of top-down charity and orders.

Why the Blindness?

The existence of structural violence and the role of the development aid system in it usually go largely unnoticed and unsanctioned. The reasons for this are multiple and often work in tandem; they range from the institutional to the individual. These factors touch on the profound core of the ideology and practice of development; it is thus worth discussing them in some detail.

To begin, in identifying and evaluating development interventions, too much attention is still focused on aggregate outcomes, and not enough on micro-level distributions. Project goals are usually expressed in large-scale, overall terms, typically applied to entire regions, and projects are considered good (or acceptable, or subpar) if they achieve these aggregate goals, regardless of their other effects. Thus, in the Mutara project, the evaluators could conclude by pointing to the social benefits from the project: land had been allocated, cattle had been distributed, and wells had been built. Were these not the objectives of the project?[4]

Yet the same actions that promote positive aggregate outcomes may coincide with increased clientelism, corruption, inequality, exclusion, or insecurity for certain groups. Hence, it is important to consider the micro-level distribution of benefits. Who exactly obtained the jobs, the land, the credits, or the training? What criteria were used to select these people? What happened to the poorest, to women, to minorities? These questions are rarely addressed directly, for two closely related reasons: the widespread but usually unspoken acceptance of an assumption of community (Amselle 1988), and the existence of a series of operational biases that Chambers (1983) documented more than a decade ago and that render the poor all but invisible to the majority of development specialists.

Another explanation for the blindness of the aid community is that development is defined in apolitical terms by all involved. The social and political are outside of the game of development (Lemarchand 1982, 1, 6, 43, 65; Ferguson 1990). Development is done through projects, that is, well-defined technical/financial packages with limited time frames as well as functional and regional scopes. Scant attention is paid to the national or international context or to the political background against which these projects occur (Brusten and Bindariye 1997, 29). This is more than appreciated by the powers that be in recipient countries, for whom the development ideology precisely serves the function of legitimation and distraction from inequalities. However, this blindness to politics by project planners and managers does not make their political effects disappear; it just renders them unrecognized and undiscussed, to the pleasure of those who stand to benefit.

At another level, the presence and the functioning of the project itself—and, more broadly, of the development community—are usually excluded from the picture. Yet the internal functioning of projects may well be among the most important impacts they have on society. Who was hired by the project, on the basis of what criteria? What was the ethnic and social composition of its employees? What kind of wages did it pay compared with the other economic opportunities available? On what basis were its employees promoted or demoted? What lands were confiscated, and were people reimbursed? Did the project stand tall against human rights abuses, clientelism, and mismanagement, whether from its own employees or from its partners? Did it treat its employees and clients fairly, without any bias, and refuse to condone such bias from its partner institutions? Or did it close its eyes and look the other way? In short, did it apply basic human rights standards to its own behavior?

One other aspect of the same problem is the mental trick of eliminating one's own presence from the picture of local society (Escobar 1995, 7). The more than hundred-year presence of the Bazungu, with assets and interests of their own, is almost entirely neglected in any analysis of the social dynamics in society. We saw how income inequality data, for example, do not include the salaries and assets of foreigners, as if they were invisible, not there. Yet every African I ever met knew those salaries (or thought he or she knew) and had seen that lifestyle; a great many sought to emulate it at all costs. The decades-long presence of Bazungu in Rwanda profoundly influenced its economic trends, its political constellations, its cultural-ideological processes, yet almost no literature and no data at all exist on this matter. This trick permits the outsiders' community never to have to question itself; it also permits the maintenance of the conceptual separation between "them" and "us," underdeveloped and developed, poor and rich, inside and outside, recipient and donor. In the end, it allows the maintenance of the purity and impermeability of the usual hierarchical binaries in which the foreigners stand on top and have superior knowledge and assets.

The problems mentioned above are structural and quite independent of the characteristics of the individuals working in the development world. But there are some personal factors that add to the bias. First, the training and knowledge of those designing, managing, and evaluating development projects and programs are usually economic or technical, neglecting social and political factors. For almost all these people, issues of ethnicity are rather distasteful and incomprehensible—easier to ignore (Stavenhagen 1990, 6, 88; Rupesinghe 1988, 38–39).

Another closely related factor is that most experts, technical assistants, and evaluators have little, if any, in-depth knowledge of the social, political, and historical background of the countries they work in; training in these matters is not usually considered a major issue by the agencies that send them, nor is knowledge of the local language. They know little before arriving, never learn *kinyarwanda* (a very difficult language), and leave after a short time (Voyame and others 1996, 187). As a result, most (though not all) of the people in the foreign aid system are incapable of even noticing the political stakes and abuses of their actions. Rwandans in all positions (like many Africans in general) have become extremely adept at keeping these foreigners' blindfolds in place; foreigners often seem to wish for little more than hearing their development rhetoric repeated to themselves.

In a country like Rwanda, where the culture and the language are very different from those of almost all technical assistants, and where intermediaries of all kinds are always present, it is hard to hear the voices of poor farmers, women, Twa, and so on. I cannot count the number of foreigners working for rural development projects who have told me that after years in Rwanda, they had no idea what the peasants thought of the project; all they knew about the peasants was what they heard from the mouths of civil servants.

To the extent that some people at some point do realize the political and social stakes and abuses that surround development aid and its projects, they often choose not to react. This has various causes, including fear of rocking the boat, of making enemies, of losing jobs (governments, after all, can and do refuse to renew visas); a desire to get on with the job of development (defined as independent from political and social processes); a sense of powerlessness and incapacity to promote the kind of change required; and a complacent, racist attitude of low expectations. In colloquial terms: many people know, or have a strong suspicion, that serious problems exist and that development is not taking place for the large majority of the people, but they do not act on this because it is too difficult to do something about it, or acting might jeopardize the nice development project they are managing, or it might make life too difficult—and anyway, that's how things go in Africa.[5]

On a more fundamental level, as many social scientists have noticed, it is often that which is most blatant that goes unnoticed, for it has acquired the quality of "normalcy." It is "normal" that technical assistants maintain their home lifestyles while living in rural Africa; otherwise, most of them supposedly would not take these jobs, which would be bad for development. It is also "normal" that local counterparts interact with farmers in a manner that is condescending, unreliable, and unadapted; that's the way things are done, and development surely cannot come about without local cadres. It is "normal" that projects, after years of functioning, fall far short of their goals, touching no more than a few percent of the population in their area of intervention; after all, the previous project did the same. It is "normal" that farmers' opinions are not asked, their language not known, their desires and hopes reduced to those of crop producer; there is little time to waste fighting poverty, and beneficiary participation will be increased in the next phase. It is "normal" that ethnic and regional quotas are applied in education and that clientelism and corruption determine who advances; these are the ways of Rwanda, and we cannot intervene in internal politics (Ford 1996, 13).

But maybe the most profound reason underlying all of the above resides in the very nature of the development mission. The development enterprise shares two fundamental assumptions that are so basic that I hesitate to discuss them for fear of sounding simplistic: first, that "they" are underdeveloped and "we" are not; and second, that we have the stuff that will help them become more developed (Hobart 1993, 2 ff.). If either of these assumptions were not accepted, there would be no reason to engage in the development cooperation enterprise, either because there is no "development problem" or because there is nothing we can do about it. Every person in the development world shares these assumptions, although he or she may resist their apparent simplicity when spelled out.

These assumptions exclude, or at least create strong barriers against, two things. First, they make it very difficult to put "underdeveloped" people at the heart of the development enterprise, to start from their talents, knowledge, aspirations, dynamics, and resources. Indeed, in my years of working in the development world, I have learned countless techniques for defining problems in more or less expensive, detailed, participatory, or scientific manners. I also know of and have taught many methods of identifying, designing, managing, and evaluating projects, ranging from the complicated to the simple, from the technocratic to the more or less participatory. Yet I know of almost no project planning method that resolutely starts from poor people's resources, few well-developed and widely used methodologies that favor poor people's own perspectives and dreams, and almost no project that began by analyzing local dynamics rather than constraints. This bias is fundamental to the development world and is even widely shared by those who claim to be closer to the people and more participatory (Hobart 1993, 15; Quarles von Ufford 1993). It creates a constant pressure for top-down, often authoritarian interventions that disregard people's moral, social, and intellectual qualities (and weaknesses). It renders the externally defined, humiliating nature of most development aid unrecognized and unproblematic.

In addition, these assumptions, by definition, produce ignorance; they create a tendency to think of developing countries as places that happen to need exactly the kind of resources that outsiders think they can provide. The image of Rwanda as a country where development will proceed if it is injected with development professionals' agronomic, financial, and intellectual resources is no aberration; it is essential to the development mission, for it justifies its presence. Transferring money, machines, and expertise is what development agencies are supposedly competent at. Understanding how to keep communities together, how to fight racism, how to involve the poor in the decisions that affect them, how to combat alienation and anomie, and how to wage political struggles against the powerful and the strong is not something they have much to say about; even in their own societies, these issues are far from resolved.[6]

Hence, as I described in Chapter 3, an image of Rwanda was created in the development literature that was, long before the 1990s, false and reductionist; yet it prevailed until the society fell apart in hatred and violence. This image was a deliberately apolitical construction made out of repetitions of government propaganda, supposedly universally applicable ideas, feel-good catchphrases, and unspoken assumptions. Note that this process is not unique to Rwanda.

This almost willful ignorance, this systemic blindness to reality, is not the result of stupidity or accident; rather, it is profoundly linked to the ideology and functioning of the development system. As Louvel (1994, 18) says:

These decisions that cannot be implemented, these projects begun knowing that they will never succeed, do not necessarily reflect incompetence, machiavelism, manipulation or cynicism ([phenomena] that do prosper, however, in these troubled waters). Rather, they reflect the symptoms of a collective neurosis that seeks to reinforce an image of Africa . . . that is necessary for our social imagery, our interests, the metabolism of our culture.

Ferguson is more specific and discusses two closely related functions of this ignorance. One is that, for the agents of external intervention, this discourse allows for the creation of an object of underdevelopment that is in need of development aid and external expertise (Ferguson 1990, 70). The other is that, for the local powers that be, this discourse fulfills the function of depoliticizing social reality and expanding bureaucratic state power (Ferguson 1990, xv). Quarles von Ufford (1993, 157) adds, "ignorance is a defensive construct against the false assumptions which, for cultural and political reasons, underpin development policy-making." Thus the simplistic image and the associated blindness fulfill a dual mandate in favor of powerful interests—the bureaucracy and the foreign aid system—and to the detriment of the poor in whose name the game is played. As Louvel (1994, 21) states it beautifully: the "common imagery [is] in certain ways a co-illusion synonymous with collusion." This collusion, then, is both ideological, related to foreigners' need to create a place that requires their competencies and their presence; and political, related to the need to accommodate the powers that be, who, in a world system based on sovereignty (no matter how much of a myth that sovereignty may be) must be placated, involved, deferred to. This collusion is more often than not detrimental to the majority of the poor.

Notes

1. According to a recent study, 47 percent of all funds for technical cooperation go to international experts (Bugingo and Ntampaka 1991, 9).
2. I am reminded here of an interesting presentation given recently by Mr. Jolly, now director of the team in charge of the UNDP's *Human Development Report*, and previously coeditor of *Development with a Human Face*, the important book that, more than any other in the 1980s, successfully advanced a discourse that went beyond economic growth as development. In his talk, he began with the definition of human development provided by UNDP. The rest of his presentation was, in his words, a positive picture of the progress made in Africa in that respect. It consisted exclusively of evidence of the greatly increased rates of immunization achieved through UNICEF's efforts in Africa—in my eyes, a major and unjustifiable reduction of the concept of human development to a technical matter. A final slide, intended to show that UNICEF's expenditures on vaccination had greatly decreased, with governments having taken up the slack (thus demonstrating sustainability), also showed another point: a quintupling of UNICEF's

expenditures on emergencies in Africa. That was the other side of so-called human development in Africa—the one of despair, conflict, violence, hatred, and abuse. Cynically, one can point out that 85 percent of the Tutsi who were slaughtered and 85 percent of those who did the killing in Rwanda were vaccinated.

3. This also helps explain long-standing debates about whether autocratic regimes are better at promoting development than others—the longtime consensus having been yes. One can have such debates only if one has excluded most issues that are related to political freedom, personal empowerment, and social pluralism from the realm of development.

4. Conversely, criticism of the project was based solely on the same aggregate criteria: the fact that the internal rate of return was lower than planned, that calendars had not been respected, that certain physical outputs had not been achieved.

5. The same attitude can be said to have existed, at least in part, in the Catholic Church and, more specifically, among the many foreign missionaries in Rwanda (Theunis 1993).

6. This explains why there are so few development specialists who are deeply engaged in the struggle for development in their home countries, so few trainers in participatory methods who went to inner-city youth and applied these methods there, and so few development NGOs that work both abroad and at home. Although it is politically correct to affirm that underdevelopment also exists at home, I know of few organizations or persons that take this seriously in practice. The reason is simple: at home, we realize how difficult it is to overcome apathy, fear, racism, poverty, distrust, alienation, violence, bureaucratic inertia, and so forth. We know about the historical legacies of problems, the way they are deeply ingrained in relations of power, in ideologies, and in social systems. In far-away places, about which we know little, we can pretend that these problems do not exist and that we can promote development through some simple actions. Ignorance is truly what allows us to act. Note that Albert Hirschman (1967) saw some positive aspect to that, to the extent that it allows us to take risks we would otherwise not have taken and sometimes achieve success.

PART IV

TWO ISSUES:
THE ROLE OF CIVIL SOCIETY
AND ECOLOGICAL
RESOURCE SCARCITY

8

AND WHERE WAS CIVIL SOCIETY?

Most specialists and observers considered Rwanda's civil society to be highly developed—one of the most advanced cases in Africa, and certainly a highly visible contrast with neighboring Burundi, for example.[1] Most people also agreed that this development of a Rwandan civil society was the major and most promising trend to take place in the 1980s (Brusten and Bindariye 1997, 30). Thus, a World Bank (1987, 28) team happily commented that "social life in the rural areas is intense and numerous forms of association give concrete shape to mutual solidarity and community actions. The widespread presence of cooperative, associative and risk-sharing groups, which is considered to be one of the distinguishing features of the Rwandese countryside, is largely responsible for the vitality of local communities." Yet since the beginning of the 1990s, Rwanda has seen increasing racism, violence, and hatred, culminating in a genocide in which up to one million defenseless children, women, and men were slaughtered, followed by the fleeing of more than two million people. In other words, this dense associational network notwithstanding, Rwanda self-destructed in a matter of months.

This self-destruction of society, state, and economy cannot help but present some fundamental questions to all those involved with or interested in Rwanda's civil society and in the democratizing and empowering promise of nongovernmental organizations (NGOs) in general. In the words of a group remembering the first anniversary of the genocide: "often presented as better than the others, . . . the NGOs have to question themselves with regards to the Rwandan drama. . . . Incapable of avoiding the worst, should they not more than ever reflect on the meaning of their actions? Is not the genocide in Rwanda also a condemnation, a recognition of their failure? A trial of their practice, if not of their ideological basis? And then we are not speaking of their objective complicity, whether through naivety or by choice for some of them" (CNDC 1995, 10–11).

This chapter is the result of the apparent contradiction between these two realities—of a dense associational fabric on the one hand, and a total and rapid destruction of a whole society on the other. Scholars and development practitioners alike think that dense associational fabrics—often called civil societies—promote pluralism, stability, tolerance, and economic progress. Why have these expectations been so falsified in Rwanda? What does this mean for our understanding of both development strategies and political theory?

Overview of the Associative Sector in Rwanda

The associative sector in Rwanda can be divided in five categories: cooperatives, farmers' organizations, tontines and informal associations, foreign and local development NGOs, and the churches. Data on these organizations—their numbers, memberships, activities—are scarce and contradictory, but I present an overview of what is known about them here.

Cooperatives are the oldest organizations with development mandates, promoted during the colonial period primarily to facilitate the production and commercialization of export crops; they are formally registered and have capital, boards of administration, elaborate rules, and so forth. The first cooperative was created in 1943—a milk cooperative in Nyanza. At independence, there were eight cooperatives, linked to specific state offices for the extraction of natural resources (coffee, minerals) or to the church. The latter included TRAFIPRO, a large consumption and commercialization cooperative whose secretary, Gregoire Kayibanda, became Rwanda's first president. Apart from TRAFIPRO, all these cooperatives floundered at or soon after independence. TRAFIPRO itself, heavily subsidized by Swiss aid, folded by the early 1980s because of overextension, mismanagement, and debts (Voyame and others 1996).

Notwithstanding the failures of the older cooperatives, from 1975 onward, following a policy change by the new Habyarimana regime,[2] the number of cooperatives greatly increased: by 1985, 297 were registered (Mugesera 1987, 69–72; Nzisabira 1992 mentions 223 cooperatives). Among them, we find the famous Banques Populaires du Rwanda (BPR), a network of savings and credit cooperatives supported by a Swiss NGO. The associative sector remained high on the government agenda: 1989, for example, was "the year of the self-organization of the rural world." A special presidential fund was also created to provide credits to new cooperatives.

Farmers' organizations are essentially less formal and smaller versions of cooperatives, which is why they are often called "pre-cooperatives," as if they are on the way to becoming the real, full-fledged, thing. Nearly all of them are in close relation with the state and the aid system, which are usually at the basis of their creation. Subsidized credits, access to communal land, and the catalyzing work of NGO and government agents are the prime means of promoting farmers' organizations. In a 1985 study, IWACU, a prominent local support NGO, counted approximately 3,000 so-called pre-cooperatives in Rwanda (Munyantwari 1992; Nzisabira 1992 mentions 3,015 pre-cooperatives). The World Bank reported these data with a small change, writing that "there are an estimated 3,240 registered cooperatives and farmer groups in Rwanda. . . . The cooperative and mutual help movement is strong in Rwanda and is an important ingredient of local communities" (World Bank 1989a, 15; 1987, 28).

The term *tontine* is originally from West Africa, where it refers to rotating savings and credit associations. More broadly, there exist in Rwanda many associations sharing labor, savings, or materials for construction; they are small, informal, usually temporary, and related to traditional mechanisms of mutual help.

Nzisabira (1992) counts 9,243 tontines, with approximately 200,000 members. They often exist for only a limited time (as long as it takes for three to four young men to build their houses, for example). According to him, they are built on traditional mechanisms of mutual help adapted to modern times. They typically receive no external support (Corrèze, Gentil, and Barnaud 1982b, 107). According to a survey conducted in Kibuye, these mutualist organizations involve primarily midlevel and wealthy farmers, but not the poorest (Corrèze, Gentil, and Barnaud 1982b, 108–9). In addition, the number of informal groups has been estimated at 30,000 by both the World Bank (1989a, 15) and the Netherlands Development Cooperation (1992, 51), which wrote of "more than 30,000 spontaneous cooperatives and savings groups of small farmers." The rapid growth in these small local associations during the 1980s was primarily the result of economic distress and the simultaneous decrease in state-provided services (USAID 1992). Such organizations were promoted by the international aid agencies as part of their structural adjustment–inspired policies.

Development NGOs are organizations of professionals, foreign and local, who seek to promote grassroots development by supporting all the previously mentioned types of organizations. In 1985, there were at least 268 of them, mostly of religious inspiration, and many foreign (Godding 1985, 15). INADES, an African support NGO with an office in Kigali, counted 143 registered NGOs in Rwanda in 1987: 42 of these were nonconfessional, 68 Catholic, 10 Protestant, and 1 Muslim (INADES 1987; Nzisabira 1992). Major local NGOs such as the Bureau Episcopal du Développement (BED) or IWACU (Centre de Formation et de Recherche Coopératives) had more than 100 employees and multi-million-dollar budgets. The NGOs were organized in various federations, such as ACOR (Association for the Coordination of NGOs in Rwanda, born in 1983) and CCOAIB (Concertation Council of Local Support Organizations, created in 1987). Together, these NGOs spent RF 1.7 billion, managed 730 projects, and employed more than 4,000 staff members, 370 of whom were foreign technical assistants (Seruvumba 1992; Nzisabira 1992). Note that, like in most other countries, the NGO sector is highly unequal: of the forty-eight NGOs for which data were available, two had budgets above RF 400 million, and twenty-one had budgets below RF 10 million (Nzisabira 1992, table 6.4).[3]

Thus, Rwanda had an extremely high civil society density. Surely there are few countries in the world where there is approximately one farmers' organization per 35 households, one cooperative per 350 households, and one NGO per 3,500 households—and these are conservative calculations. According to one source, more than 12 percent of the Rwandan active population belonged to peasant organizations (Ntavyohanyuma 1987).

Finally, the church—foremost the Catholic Church, but also a variety of Protestant denominations—is Rwanda's largest nonstate actor, with enormous resources and social clout. As Longman (1995a) has argued, it is both a vertically integrated, hierarchically managed (and conservative) bloc and a set of local, often critical and spontaneous initiatives. It has been active in what is now called "development" for over a century; its primary mission, evidently, lies elsewhere.

It suffices to be in Rwanda's countryside on a Sunday morning—or in the Rwandan refugee camps any day—to observe the strength of

Christianity. Everywhere one goes in Rwanda, one can see the red-brown churches surrounded by schools, health care centers, and extension centers of all kinds: agriculture, handicrafts, and so forth. After the state, the church is, and has been for decades, Rwanda's prime employer, landowner, and investor and is very well connected with European aid agencies and political parties (Guichaoua 1995a, 18). The church was a key player in education, health, charity, professional training, spiritual well-being, and community development. Even the Protestant churches, a minority in Rwanda, possessed more than 300 primary school centers with 173,000 pupils, 20 secondary schools with approximately 4,700 students, 480 centers for adult literacy, and a multitude of hospitals (Gatwa 1996, 39). Local church groups, NGOs associated with the church, and parish priests are all important elements of civil society (Longman 1995a).

The Puzzle of Civil Society in Rwanda

There is a long-standing tradition in Western political thought, dating from de Tocqueville, in which the presence of voluntary associations (organizations below the state and above the family, and sometimes including the for-profit sector) is considered to promote pluralism, democracy, rapid economic growth, effective public service, and resilience against external shocks. Recently, this tradition has been revived by a widely discussed work by Robert Putnam (1993) on Italy, in which the author (re)develops the notion of social capital. In his analysis, the existence of social capital, caused by participation in voluntary associations, was the main determinant of the performance of local governments in Italy in the 1980s.

For Putnam, as for many political theorists and sociologists, it is unimportant whether third-sector organizations are concerned with public affairs or not; bowling clubs, singing associations, and neighborhood improvement associations all have the potential to "foster civic engagement in cooperative problem-solving," to "reinforce democratic principles and practices," even to teach "leadership and action skills," which all in all contribute to create "social trust, cooperation, reciprocity, and inclusion" (Brown and Ashman 1996, 3; Fox 1996; Fukuyama 1996, 26; Heilbrunn 1993; Putnam 1993). Michael Cernea, the foremost social scientist working for the World Bank, echoes this approach when he writes that "whatever the purpose at hand of one or another kind of organization, whatever the specific activity for which it was established (economic, political, religious, recreational, etc.), organizations are apt to amplify social energy and render social action more, rather than less, effective. . . . Creating organizations is equal to creating social capital" (Cernea 1993, 24). This social capital and this habit of compromise, then, are widely expected to provide the pillars of a democratic, pluralistic society (Rueschemeyer forthcoming) and lay the foundations for an effective government and rapid economic growth (Putnam 1993; Fukuyama 1996).

Certain processes can explain this positive relation between civil society and democracy, pluralism, and government effectiveness: more NGOs means that more voices can be heard in the process of making and implementing policy, and participation in voluntary associations fosters attitudes and practices of civility and compromise (Rueschemeyer forthcoming). The international development aid community justifies its increasing interest in (and funding of) NGOs by referring to many of the same reasons (Brusten and Bindariye 1997, 24, 30). During the last months before the genocide, there was an increase in funding for civil society organizations motivated explicitly by such concerns.

My analysis of the case of Rwanda, however, cautions against excessive, mechanistic optimism about the democratizing and stabilizing impact of NGOs. Rwanda seems to be a strong rebuttal of Cernea's dramatic statement that "creating organizations is equal to creating social capital." The point I wish to make here has been well formulated by Stephen Ndegwa (1996, 7), writing about neighboring Kenya: "civil society cannot be assumed to be congenial or supportive of democratic pluralism by its mere existence, expansion or level of activity." In the next pages, I make three arguments. First, it is doubtful that a civil society truly existed in Rwanda; the emergence of a civil society is a qualitative matter, not a quantitative one, and the factors required for this qualitative change to take place were not present in Rwanda. Second, NGOs do not promote pluralism and tolerance in society if they do not seek to do so. In other words, civil society organizations' positive effects do not follow automatically from their existence but must be targeted. By and large, this did not happen in Rwanda. Third, for civil society organizations to have an impact, there must exist a social and political space or margin for maneuver. Such space did not exist in Rwanda prior to 1990; when it slowly emerged after 1990, this space was rapidly filled by the loud and well-organized voices of radicalism and ethnic division that effectively drowned the weak alternative voices that came from some parts of civil society.

Civil Society: Quantity versus Quality

According to some scholars, there is little basis on which to build a civil society in Rwanda; there is neither a historical tradition of it, nor are the current economic, social, and political conditions present for it to emerge. Lemarchand talks about the scarcity of social capital in Rwanda: the fact that there is little tradition of associationalism and little local-level leadership, that "the social environment remains thoroughly fragmented" and "neither the clan nor the extended family have retained enough vitality to provide a meaningful basis for cooperation" (Lemarchand 1982, 17, 60). Jean Nzisabira (1992, 1) makes essentially the same argument when he writes that "beyond ad-hoc exchanges between households linked by blood and matrimonial ties or between neighbors, traditionally, Rwanda does not have economic or social mutual help practices of a horizontal nature." And Lemarchand, speaking about the present, adds that "as long as the main form of social organization remains clientelistic in character, there is little incentive for people to organize themselves horizontally and on a more or less equal basis for the performance of common tasks."

In the African context, as elsewhere, arguments that explain social phenomena by referring to the "traditional mentalities" of people should always be taken with a grain of salt. They are made too often, and in contradictory fashion, to be taken at face value (see Chapter 10 on Rwanda's "traditional" deference to authority to explain mass participation in the genocide). Yet, there is no doubt that the present builds on the past and that the historical roots of social phenomena tell us much about their nature and functioning. Hence, it pays to look more closely at questions such as: Where did these civil society organizations come from? What do they build on?

Rwanda's civil society organizations were mostly of recent creation. They were also strongly externally inspired and driven, truly products of the development aid machinery. The cooperatives were all created in the decade after 1975, as a result of a government policy change. Most of the more than 100 Rwandan NGOs were created after 1985, as were the pre-cooperatives and the farmers' organizations. As the already mentioned World Bank (1987, 28–29) study observed, "the large majority [of these groups] were set up quite recently. They are small. . . . The more structured groups have not, however, been able to grow to any size except where the staff of outside agencies have taken on positions of responsibility within the groups. . . . In most cases, the actual producers do not occupy the responsible positions that ought to be theirs, these posts generally being held by government officials, technicians, members of the clergy or members of foreign aid agencies." Someone with years of experience observed that Rwandan NGOs suffer from too much money, too rapid creation, imposed structures, and little internal information or accountability (Braun 1990). For many of them, the possibility of obtaining external gifts—land, money, access—may have been the prime reason for their creation.

Hence, this multitude of NGOs is not so much the reflection of the presence of a civic space conquered by people going beyond the boundaries of family, ethnic group, and location as the reflection of externally defined policies by government and foreign aid agencies, backed up by significant external resources and social pressure—all within a context of a profoundly authoritarian and vertical system, with an omnipresent state. Or, as a former student of mine and employee of IWACU put it, "the state turned even self-help into an obligation and the concept lost its meaning" (Seruvumba 1992). Chrétien and his colleagues (1995, 91) speak about "l'organisation du volontariat contraint du paysan."

This is nothing unique or special: the same observations have been made throughout Africa by other well-meaning people. It also does not mean that these organizations cannot fulfill important functions for development. The fact that all Rwandan NGOs are recent creations and closely linked to the functioning of the aid system does not signify that they cannot be useful and effective subcontractors to international aid agencies or service providers to their clients. The fact that all farmers' groups are recent creations of the aid machinery does not take away their real potential strengths in such fields as agricultural extension or the maintenance of collective infrastructures. The fact that the major cooperative systems such as TRAFIPRO or the Banques Populaires were created, funded, and managed largely by the foreign aid system does not take away the fact that they provided important services for the community, including some of the poor.

What it *does* mean, though, is that the addition of growing numbers of such organizations does not automatically equal a civil society (see Kabirigi 1994). For the total to be more than the sum of the parts, social learning and social change are required, and these things take time. In his analysis of Italy, Putnam (1993) goes all the way back to the Middle Ages and traces a vicious circle of low civil society organization followed by bad, corrupt, and clientelistic public-sector management, which discourages people from organizing, and so on. Heilbrunn (1993) traces the different histories of civil society organizations in Benin and Togo back to the end of the previous century, looking at the different colonial paths taken by both societies. Not surprisingly, it is only Cernea, the development aid expert, for whom social capital seems to be something that can rapidly be engineered ex nihilo, through some fine project management.[4] Social scientists see social capital accumulation as a slow, long-term, internal process of gradual accumulation of the capacity and the willingness to negotiate, compromise, and shape the political arena. Without this, the addition of individual small organizations will never be more than the sum of the parts.

In other words, the move from a multitude of local-level agricultural nongovernmental projects to a vibrant civil society that is a factor in promoting pluralism and democracy requires more than a process of quantitative change (addition of numbers); foremost, it involves a qualitative change (a change in nature). In this process, people of all walks of life gain confidence in their capacity to undertake initiatives in the public sphere; networks of contacts and collaboration are built, both within communities and between them; boundaries and divisions of region, ethnicity, sex, and clan are transcended or crosscut; and attitudes and knowledge about politics, policies, management, negotiation, and compromise are acquired. At the very least, such change takes time and learning space. Both these factors were absent in Rwanda.

I just argued that civil society is a slow historical construct that cannot be created ex nihilo from abroad. Its emergence is probably hurt, rather than helped, by excessive external intervention. Learning of the kind described above must be done by the people concerned; it cannot be imported based on outsiders' knowledge of what works (even if this knowledge were somehow objectively "true"). Any attempt to rapidly create a civil society through development aid (and with the tools of the typical development project) will lead to fake, superficial results. In the next section, I analyze the claims made by development workers and scholars alike as to the democratizing, civil society–strengthening nature of NGOs, arguing that these claims, too, are simplistic if not outright false.

On the Democratizing
Impact of Civil Society

In his stimulating book, Stephen Ndegwa (1996; see also Rueschemeyer forthcoming) specifies two conditions that are required for NGOs and civil society organizations to have a democratizing impact: first, they must actively seek to promote democratization, and second, they must have an opportunity to do so. These two conditions seem perfectly relevant—and absent—in the case of Rwanda. The first point—which essentially states that NGOs cannot contribute to democracy if they do not seek to do so—can be made through two arguments. First, Rwandan NGOs were as divided by ethnic conflict, exclusion, and hatred as society at large; and second, in the image of the international development community from which they emanated (and by which virtually all are funded), they defined their mandate in strictly apolitical terms.

It is perfectly possible for civil society organizations, whether grass-roots organizations or intermediary ones, to have goals and values that are exclusionary, antidemocratic, regressive, or racist (see ACORD 1995, 64). The fact that organizations claim to have developmental goals does not render them immune to particularistic interests or racist values, nor does it mean that they automatically contribute to democracy and equality (Lemarchand 1992; Rueschemeyer forthcoming).

In Rwanda, there were many organizations and leaders who subscribed to the dominant racism and eventually took active part in the genocide. Every Rwandan knows the names of certain NGO leaders—including the first president of IWACU—who were members of extremist "Hutu power" parties, who participated in the genocide, who even joined the "provisional government" in ministerial positions (Kabirigi 1994). African Rights has begun documenting troubling cases of members of Rwanda's few human rights NGOs playing roles as instigators, leaders, and participants in the genocide and of other members of these organizations covering up these acts, even afterwards. All the opposition parties—supposedly the source of renewal for Rwanda—were divided into extremist-racist and moderate wings. At the same time, other NGO leaders and members acted with great courage, risking their own lives; many were killed. Others stood by, uncomprehending, fearful, or passively complicit. In so doing, they all reflected broader social trends.

It is in the church that this may be most visible. Many authors have documented that the divisions in society also reigned within the Catholic Church. At independence, there were more Tutsi than Hutu in official positions in the church. After independence, Tutsi youth, whose avenues for high-level jobs in the state or the army were closed off, had even stronger incentives to make careers in the church. Thus, among the rank and file of the church, the proportion of Tutsi remained high. Simultaneously, however, the top levels of the church were gradually and deliberately purged of Tutsi, and by the 1970s, all high officeholders were Hutu (Longman 1995a). All observers agree that this power structure was very close to the Habyarimana regime. The most visible sign of this was the fact that, until 1990, Rwanda's archbishop was a member of the executive bureau of Habyarimana's party.

At the same time, inside religious orders and denominations, conflicts between Tutsi and Hutu were common. Nominations to important positions within the church hierarchy tended to lead to conflicts with ethnic undercurrents (Linguyeneza 1996, 4). And at the grassroots, there were people who actively promoted social change and spoke out in favor of minorities, including Tutsi. On the ethnic question, the Catholic Church reflected society—some leaned this way, some the other way, and the powers that be favored the status quo.

This means that one cannot simply say that the church backed up the genocide. Rather, the church was divided on the genocide, as was society. It was from the church that some of the strongest voices in favor of political and social change were heard by the early 1990s. It is also there that some of the few initiatives to stop the spiral of violence and hatred were taken: a "week for tolerance" with a local human rights NGO in December 1992, culminating in a march for peace on December 13; pastoral letters calling for peace and tolerance; attempts to broker negotiations between opposition parties; a few democracy information workshops in 1993; and some marches for peace in January 1994, as well as some sessions on nonviolent conflict resolution (CIM 1994). Finally, the genocide reached perhaps its worst horror in churches: thousands were slaughtered while seeking refuge in churches, and hundreds of priests were killed with them.

There are also many well-documented cases of priests, ministers, nuns, and brothers participating in the genocide, and bishops who did not speak out against it or even tacitly encouraged it.[5] Most observers agree that the statements of the church in the year before the genocide were too little, too late; they were certainly characterized by ambiguity and halfheartednesss (Longman 1995a). This is also reflected in the number of pastoral letters written afterward that flatly deny the genocide or accuse the Rwandan Patriotic Front (FPR) of organizing the genocide.

In short, the church was divided along the same lines and into the same camps as society at large. As Linguyeneza (1996, 4; see also Archer n.d., 17, for Burundi) observed: "l'Eglise au Rwanda est à l'image de la société rwandaise." The same holds for all civil society organizations (ACORD 1995, 39). They are all part of the society they exist in (contrary to much development literature, which treats them as existing in a social vacuum) and, as such, reflect its divisions, attitudes, and ideologies.

As an aside, there is another argument regarding the church's role in the genocide. It essentially states that the reason Christians (lay members and religious professionals) were so involved in the genocide is that Catholicism never became deeply ingrained in the Rwandan mind and culture. Prunier (1995, 34), for example, writes that "the reasons for converting to Christianity were fundamentally social and political. Christian values did not penetrate deeply, even if Christian prejudices and social attitudes were adopted as protective covering. . . . [The church] was a legitimizing factor, a banner, a source of profit, a way of becoming educated, a club, a matrimonial agency and even at times a religion." This argument conveniently solves the riddle by denying its existence and attributing violence, racism, intolerance, and so forth to non-Catholic (supposedly traditional or local) factors. As such, it is a simple circular argument, saying, in effect, that if people did un-Catholic things—despite professing to be Catholics and generally behaving like it—it must be because they were not really Catholics.

The same argument has been made regarding civil society organizations in general. It has been suggested that they were simply emanations of central power, but that would be wrong: both the church and the NGOs did exist as independent actors. Yet both were riddled by contradictions and conflicts, as society itself was (Karemera 1995, 24). This may disappoint our (overly high?) expectations, leading us to find simple solutions, but as social scientists, it should not really surprise us.

A second point is that most NGOs defined their role in nonpolitical terms. Whatever their effectiveness in promoting agricultural and rural development—and it must be said that a significant proportion of the NGOs did provide services of use to the population, probably more so (but on a smaller scale) than most bilateral or multilateral development aid agencies—the large majority of NGOs were not actively seeking to achieve mass empowerment or democratization or the overcoming of racism. Almost all of them were in the business of small-scale development, sometimes in a fashion almost as authoritarian and top-down as the government's. Like the international aid system with which they shared their ideology and their funding, "the Rwandan NGOs refused to take into account certain factors, although they were very present in society (ethnicity, regionalism, exclusion . . .) under the pretext that they were a-political" (Kabirigi 1994, 33; see also ACORD 1995, 73; Brusten and Bindariye 1997, 24). The list of sectoral engagement of NGOs in Rwanda is an almost perfect reflection of the same for the official aid community: education and training, agriculture, health, hydraulics, family planning, and the like—not a single political category (Ntavyohanyuma 1987). By more or less voluntarily restricting their domain of activity, NGOs did not become vectors for challenging the multiple exclusions in Rwandese society.

For example, in a self-critical reflection by religious professionals with long field experience in Rwanda, it was observed that "despite the extensive assistance, not one aid agency has ever analyzed and addressed openly and seriously the Hutu/Tutsi problematic, instead, they have reinforced it" (CIDSE and CARITAS Internationalis 1995, 10).

The aid community, especially in the United States, tends to assign a crucial role to NGOs in the construction of a democratic society. Starting from that position, aid to NGOs is often justified on the basis of its contribution to democratic change. The idea is then to use development aid to "enhance the role of citizen participation in promoting democratic governance in Rwanda by strengthening Rwandan NGOs as civil society instrumentalities engaged in civic education, information dissemination and political advocacy" (USAID 1992). However, the fact that the majority of NGOs define their mandate in traditional, apolitical terms and have no experience or inclination to do otherwise means that this may be more of a dream than a reality.

To a certain extent, it is foreign aid itself that is responsible for this. It is from decades of foreign aid, its discourses, and its modes of functioning that local middle-class professionals throughout Africa, including in Rwanda, have learned how to play the game of development. Foreign donors reward local NGOs for their mastery of the language and for adopting the goals of what they themselves adhere to and discourage organizations with political goals or with nonstandard projects (ACORD 1995, 62). The standard relationship between rich country funding agencies and Third World NGOs remains one of project funding, which leaves no space for the kind of broad-based, unplannable, contingent work that NGOs should engage in if they are to play a role in shaping democratic societies rather than vulgarizing seeds and distributing vaccines. As all NGOs, with few exceptions, are totally dependent on foreign aid for their survival—indeed, their existence and their ideological basis—it is expected that they would talk the talk and walk the walk of the development community's big players.

It was only at the very end, in 1992–93, that part of the aid system tentatively enlarged its mandate to include political factors, human rights, racism, and democracy on its agenda. The CCOAIB developed and carried out a series of training programs on democracy and nonviolence. In 1993, a few Belgian NGOs, with funding from the Belgian bilateral aid agency,[6] created human rights programs, while the Belgian NGO community cofinanced the major human rights NGO study of 1993. Oxfam funded a set of reconciliation workshops with church organs (Mukene 1993). And as we saw, the U.S. and Swiss bilateral aid agencies set aside money for democracy and human rights. This was too little too late, though, and had little or no impact on the forces of violence and radicalism.

The final point Ndegwa made that I wish to discuss here concerns the role of the state. Indeed, the Rwandese state, as already described, was a very controlling, authoritarian, omnipresent one in which little or no space was available for truly independent political action. After independence, through intimidation, legislation, and negotiation with their foreign supporters, the state managed to bring all cooperatives more or less directly under its control.[7]

From the 1970s onward, in line with the great capacity of the Habyarimana regime to play the development game, the policy increasingly became to allow NGOs, all of them funded from abroad, to take up part of the slack, within tight political constraints, while taking much of the credit through a discourse of self-help. Hence, NGOs were allowed to flourish, provided they were willing to "program and coordinate . . . development actions . . . within the framework of the national development priorities" (Godding 1985, 13) and abstain from politics. All this forced most NGOs into defining themselves along the restrictive lines of the development ideology to which the government, the donors, and, in all likelihood, most of their personnel adhered.

In a survey of ninety-one NGOs in the late 1980s, 73 percent said that they had close relations with government ministries, 71 percent with communal authorities, 56 percent with prefectoral authorities, 56 percent with church structures, 36 percent with peasant groups, and 15 percent with other NGOs (Seruvumba 1992). This bias in favor of close relations with state authorities should not surprise anyone, since many NGOs were created by these same state authorities and had government employees as their managers (Willame 1995a, 149). Yet it must be observed that the NGOs were probably the most mixed institutions in Rwanda, in terms of being founded and staffed by both Hutu and Tutsi together. Those people founding and leading NGOs belonged to the class of *evolués*; many of them had public jobs or had taken leave from them. As such, the apolitical development rhetoric suited them well, for it was in their personal interests not to bite the hand that fed them. In the late 1980s, the state also embarked on a campaign of co-optation, giving high positions in the civil service and the political party to NGO leaders or visiting their organizations with presents and great pomp (Karemera 1995, 26–27; Seruvumba 1992–93). Hence, in the end, the NGOs were too embedded in a state-dependent development rhetoric that, for reasons of pressure, convenience, and belief, neglected the political in favor of the usual service delivery. This precluded them from moving beyond a collection of semiprivatized public service providers to becoming an autonomous civil society.

It is only from 1990 onward that some space became available for new voices to be heard, under the pressure of a slowly advancing democratization and multipartisanism. Part of the NGO community attempted to move forward along more political lines, seeking to build peasant unions and political structures (van Hoof 1994). These attempts all failed, however, due to a combination of factors: weakness in management and support, government pressure (including co-optation), and lack of farmer interest (Brusten and Bindariye 1997; Karemera 1995). Other NGO leaders allied themselves with opposition parties. A number of human rights NGOs were created, involving mainly intellectuals; some of them were truly independent and did excellent work (USAID 1992). However, this period was too short and too rapidly filled by the much better organized and stronger forces of ethnic radicalism (newspapers, radios) for any genuine grassroots counterforces to emerge.

With a few courageous exceptions during the 1990s, foreign NGOs largely took the same position as the official aid system—maybe closer to the people (but not always), and maybe with some alternative techniques, but still the same definition of the role of aid and the same definition of development. Like elsewhere, international NGOs adhered to the common view that "development and human rights work constitute two distinct areas, where development is devoted to the promotion of economic growth and the satisfaction of basic needs, while human rights work exposes abuses of power" (Tomasevski 1989, 113–14). This is also the easiest position for most development NGOs.

To sum up, in his 1994 presidential address to the American Sociological Association, William Gamson (1995, 4) discussed the politics of exclusion, in which certain groups of people are not considered part of the moral universe of a society. He added that "in most societies, the boundaries of some of the universes of obligation are often hotly contested and changing. Social movements that challenge cultural codes . . . typically challenge these boundaries of obligation." In Rwanda during the 1990s, the boundaries of obligation changed toward further and deeper exclusion and, ultimately, genocide. I documented these processes in previous chapters; here, I discussed the fact that civil society did not manage to stop these processes, let alone move them in the opposite direction. I distinguished a number of reasons for this state of affairs.

One reason is that certain parts of civil society, often well-organized ones, backed the genocidal ideology or were at least ambivalent about it. In other words, to the extent that social movements existed, they often sought nonemancipatory, racist, exclusionary goals. Significant sections of NGOs, political parties, the Catholic Church, and farmers' organizations joined extremist parties and participated in the genocide, sometimes in positions of leadership.

Moreover, it is doubtful whether Rwanda really had a civil society or "social movements" that deserved that appellation. There were a large number of organizations in Rwanda; thousands of them were active in the development sector, and many more for prayer, soccer, or mutual help. However, these organizations existed within a narrow field, restricted both by the omnipresent, authoritarian state and by a self-imposed exclusion of the political and social realm from their scope. In so doing, the NGOs by and large followed, if not reproduced, the behavior and ideology of the dominant section of society.

Another factor that was not discussed in this chapter but emerges from the rest of the book is that structural preconditions were hardly met. Extreme poverty and inequality in life chances, coupled with a political system of clientelism, a profound lack of access to information, and a long tradition of infantilization of the rural population, create conditions that render the establishment of an autonomous, progressive civil society that is truly representative of the majority of the poor extremely unlikely, if not impossible.

All in all, the picture painted is contrary to the expectations of most theorists and many practitioners, who believe that the establishment of more voluntary organizations—regardless of objective—equals more civil society and, as a result, more tolerance, democracy, and the like. It does not, however, and naive assumptions need to be revised.

Notes

1. This dense associational network was the envy of development specialists in neighboring Burundi. I was sent in June 1993 on a mission to Rwanda to learn from its example how to successfully promote grassroots initiative in Burundi.
2. Nzisabira 1992 documents that the second Five-year Economic, Social, and Cultural Development Plan "recommends to implant one multi-functional development cooperative in each commune"—which promptly happened in less than two years. He also documents the mediocre quality of these cooperatives. Corrèze, Gentil, and Barnaud (1982b, 114) document cases in which all inhabitants of a commune are obliged to become members of the local cooperative. This is not unique to Rwanda but has happened throughout Africa.
3. The same size difference can also be observed in the number of employees. Both of the two largest NGOs are religious.
4. Cernea (1993, 26) writes about "purposively increasing organizational density through development strategies."
5. For some examples, which must be treated with caution, given the one-sided nature of the articles, see Rwanda: La machète 1995. See also African Rights 1994; Rwandan Churches Culpable 1994.
6. The total amount of cofinancing for human rights in 1993 was BF 5.6 million out of BF 84.2 million cofinancing for that year, and a total aid budget to Rwanda of BF 885 million. The European Community added BF 0.5 million cofinancing to the same sector between 1992 and 1994 (data from Brusten and Bindariye 1997).
7. This can be gleaned from Nzisabira 1992; Voyame and others 1996, 70, 165; and Cart 1995, 466, although it is not a conclusion they draw. Note that in all these cases, it led to the eventual destruction of these organizations.

9

THE ROLE OF ECOLOGICAL
RESOURCE SCARCITY

It is well known and oft repeated that Rwanda was the most densely populated country in Africa, with one of the world's highest population growth rates, one of the lowest amounts of arable land per person, and noted problems of erosion and land degradation. Starting from there, most observers believe that there was a causal link between these factors and the genocide. The nature of that link—if there was one—constitutes the subject of this chapter.

The relation between social conflict and ecological resource scarcity has received a lot of attention recently. The fate not only of Rwanda but also of other countries seems to have caused a feeling in both the intellectual and the foreign policy and intelligence communities that there is an important, hitherto misunderstood or at least overlooked link between these elements. Works such as Kaplan's "The Coming Anarchy" (1994) popularized this feeling and added an element of fear. This has spawned a renewed interest in better understanding the relations between natural or physical constraints and social behavior, an endeavor that has been out of vogue for quite a while. The interest by agencies such as the Central Intelligence Agency (CIA) to fund this kind of research to use in its own work appears to have strengthened the resolve of many, who appreciate the opportunity both for fresh funds and to influence policymaking.

At the most general theoretical level, one can distinguish three types of arguments about the relation between social conflict and ecological resource scarcity. The first "hard" Malthusian argument holds that social conflict and communal violence are the unavoidable results of overpopulation and ecological resource scarcity. Under conditions of severe population and land imbalance—when countries have exceeded their "carrying capacity" (that is, the number of people that can be fed using their natural resources)—the only outcome possible is famine and/or conflict. For adherents of this view, it is through these mechanisms that nature restores equilibrium—unfortunate, maybe, but unavoidable (except possibly through major progress in family planning). This point of view is most closely associated with authors such as the Ehrlichs (1990) and Garrett Hardin (1993), as well as NGOs such as Zero Population Growth and the Carrying Capacity Network.

Rwanda is considered a perfect example of this hard Malthusian argument by many African and Western scientists. For those adhering to this image, the 1994 genocide was the unavoidable outcome of over-population and environmental limitations. Following that, the millions of refugees in Zaire have been qualified as "environmental refugees" (Patterson 1995), and the whole conflict as having been caused by "demographic entrapment" (King 1994; see also Bonneux 1994; Vis, Goyens, and Brasseur 1994, 1995).

Less explicitly, this image also underlies much general writing on the subject of Rwanda, as can be seen in the following quote from the International Red Cross federation: "food production was slowing as dramatically as the population was increasing. . . . In the late 1980s Rwanda's foreign residents were speculating on a catastrophe before the end of the century. Would it be famine, which struck the Rwandan southwest in 1989, or AIDS with a 33 percent infection rate in urban areas in 1990? Bloody conflict arrived first" (IFRCRCS 1994). Ould Abdallah, for two years UN special representative to Burundi, when asked about Burundi's main problems in a Voice of America interview, mentioned first "how to address the fundamental problem of this country, which is overpopulation. The country doubles every fifteen years; the country is overcrowded" (Pace and Schoetzau 1995).

A second type of argument, which could be called the "soft" Malthusian one, is less adamant about the unavoidability of communal violence, arguing that although conditions of severe ecological resource scarcity constitute a source of social tensions, other variables intervene and cause outcomes to vary. In other words, this argument accepts that ecological resource scarcity can cause social conflict but acknowledges that this outcome is not automatic or unavoidable.

Proponents of this view begin by arguing that there is clearly no automatic link between resource scarcity and communal violence; if there were, Bangladesh, Belgium, China, Costa Rica, Egypt, Guinea,

Indonesia, Israel, Jamaica, Japan, Jordan, Kenya, Nepal, the Netherlands, South Korea, Switzerland, Tanzania, Vietnam, and others—all of which have higher (often significantly higher) population densities per square mile of arable land or cropland than Rwanda, and many of which are, or recently were, as poor as Rwanda—would all be destroyed by civil violence, while Ethiopia, Angola, Mozambique, Yugoslavia, and the former USSR would be places of great tranquility and harmony (data from Engelman and LeRoy 1995; World Resources Institute 1996, table 10.2). What makes some countries with high population-land ratios fall apart into violence and others not is the stuff of political and social analysis.

While the hard Malthusian argument sees a direct, unavoidable relation between famine and violence on the one hand, and ecological resource scarcity on the other, this school of thought focuses more on the factors and processes that mediate between these variables. Traditions of social cooperation, patterns of innovation, legitimacy and accountability of the state, networks of economic exchange, and so on all intervene in creating outcomes.

A team of researchers working under the direction of Thomas Homer-Dixon has done interesting work along these lines. Percival and Homer-Dixon (1995, 5) synthesize that work nicely in the following quote (note that the authors believe that the processes they outline did indeed take place in Rwanda):

> Environmental scarcity produces four principal social effects: decreased agricultural potential, regional economic decline, population displacement, and the disruption of legitimized and authoritative institutions and social relations. These social effects, either singly or in combination, can produce and exacerbate conflict between groups. Most such conflict is subnational, diffuse, and persistent. For conflict to break out, the societal balance of power must provide the opportunity for grievances to be expressed as challenges to authority. When grievances are articulated by groups organized around clear social cleavages, such as ethnicity or religion, the probability of civil violence is higher. Under situations of environmental scarcity, where group affiliation aids survival, intergroup competition on the basis of relative gains is likely to increase. As different ethnic and cultural groups are propelled together under circumstances of deprivation and stress, we should expect inter-group hostilities, in which a group would emphasize its own identity while denigrating, discriminating against, and attacking outsiders.

Nearly all scholars dealing with Rwanda, including the social scientists who have written the most serious studies of the genocide, align themselves with this position. Thus Prunier (1995, 4) writes that "the genocidal violence of the spring of 1994 can be partly attributed to the population density." Willame (1995a, 122) states that "the generalized land pressure that results from the population density poses the problem of . . . the violence that can break out in an environment where spatial adjustments do not take place anymore." The 1994 annual report of the Swiss Development Cooperation agency (SDC) explains that "demographic pressure is provoking population streams and conflicts within the African continent. . . . And nowhere in Africa is the population density as high as in Rwanda and Burundi." Generally, these statements are made without any proof other than a reminder that Rwanda had a high population density; typically, these authors focus entirely on political processes. In other words, implicitly, these authors can be placed within the soft Malthusian school: they agree that ecological resource scarcity is causally related to conflict, but they focus most of their attention on the intermediary, primarily political, variables.

Since 1994, a few authors—foremost Scott Grosse (1994a), Jennifer Olson (1995), Valerie Percival and Thomas Homer-Dixon (1995) Robert Ford (1995) and myself (Uvin 1996a)—have explicitly set out to analyze the relation between ecological resource scarcity and the genocide. Variations notwithstanding, all these authors end up at the soft Malthusian position, arguing that ecological resource scarcity played a role in the processes that led to the 1994 violence but that this role cannot be understood in isolation from political processes.

A third type of argument sees no relation at all between genocide and ecological resource scarcity. Some of the scholars belonging to this category are anti-Malthusian: they generally believe that more people equals more innovation, more economic activity, more knowledge, and more organization, all of which, they contend, stimulates growth and progress. These people refuse to accept the basic Malthusian tenet and sometimes end up turning it on its head (Simon 1981; Franke and Chasin 1980; Uvin 1994a). Others might not go that far but consider ecological resource scarcity the product of human agency rather than a fixed situation. If Rwanda used the technology (and had the wealth) that is prevalent in, say, Belgium, then it would easily be able to feed all its population from its land or produce enough exports to buy food. In other words, the character and impact of ecological resource scarcity in Rwanda are not dictated by nature but are the result of historical, political, and economic processes. People belonging to this category tend to treat the intervening variables of the soft Malthusians as independent variables. I know of no authors who explicitly make this argument for the case of Rwanda. However, included in this school of thought could be the large group of authors (such as Colette Braeckman, Filip Reyntjens, Jean-Pierre Chrétien, and Claudine Vidal) who have studied the Rwandan genocide without ever referring to, or considering, ecological resource scarcity. By not addressing the question, they seem to have implicitly chosen the position that there is no direct relation between ecological resource scarcity and the genocide.

In a nutshell, the three schools represent different positions on a continuum of thought regarding the relation between ecological resource scarcity and social conflict; the line of the continuum consists of the importance attached to intervening variables. The hard Malthusian school sees a direct and more or less automatic causal relation between the conditions of ecological resource scarcity that Rwanda faced and the events that took place there. Given the former, the latter was basically unavoidable; intervening variables made little difference. The softer Malthusian school adds intervening variables to the picture. It argues that ecological resource scarcity caused social tensions or (in a weaker version) played a role in the conflict, but one needs to look at the nature of social relations and the state to understand outcomes. Social and political factors mediate between ecological resource scarcity and final outcomes. The third school sees no direct relation between ecological resource scarcity and violence, for the main reason that it does not consider the former to be a natural construct but a social one, the result of human agency. Thus the intermediary variables—the history, politics, and economics of states and societies—become all-important; they become the independent variables that explain the outcome.

In this chapter, I begin by presenting a detailed overview of the nature of the ecological constraints Rwanda faced, as well as the strategies people adopted to deal with them. This will allow us to understand the nature of the crises that hit Rwanda from the mid-1980s onward, and to make a reasoned choice among these competing perspectives. To my own surprise, I end up largely accepting the third position, arguing that there is no direct causal relation between ecological resource scarcity and the genocide in Rwanda: both are largely man-made, with deep historical, political, and cultural roots.

Rwanda's Ecology: An Overview

Rwanda can be divided into three main agricultural regions, according to topography (by adding soil quality, rainfall, and dominant economic activity, much more complex divisions have been constructed). The largest part of the country is composed of thousands of hills from about 4,900 to 6,500 feet in height, cut by rivers. The average temperature is 68°F, and average annual rainfall is between 39 and 49 inches. With the exception of the wetlands in the valley bottoms, this has always been the main agricultural region of the country, with the highest population density (in 1960, 250 persons per square kilometer or more) and the largest share of Rwanda's population. The second zone is the Zaire-Nile crest, a strip 99 miles long and 12 to 31 miles wide, located in western Rwanda; it is 6,500 to 13,100 feet high, with a cold and wet climate (average temperature 59°F; average annual rainfall above 46 inches) and a low population density (less than 150 persons per square kilometer in 1960). Eastern Rwanda constitutes the third zone. It is an almost flat plateau region below 4,900 feet, with high temperatures and low rainfall—31 to 39 inches per year. The vegetation is a tree-covered savanna type. It contains the main national parks. This climate is well-suited to animal husbandry. It used to have a low population density (in 1960, fewer than 100 persons per square kilometer) and was mainly pastoral, with a strong Tutsi presence.

Since independence, with a population growth rate consistently above 3 percent annually, Rwanda's average population density has greatly increased: from 106 persons per square kilometer in 1960 to 280 by 1992 (World Bank 1994b, 28). In almost all World Bank and many government reports, this figure is accompanied by the observation that this is "the highest population density in Africa." However, in terms of population density per square kilometer of arable land (a better indicator of real land scarcity), Rwanda's position is only sixth in Africa.[1] Yet there is no doubt that Rwanda's population density is high and has been so for a long time.

The high population densities on the hill slopes in the central plateau and the bordering regions are no accident. Neighboring regions— Burundi, Kivu, and Kigezi, for example—have similar population densities. In most of the country, the soil is very rich and fertile; rainfall is abundant; the climate is excellent for humans and animals, being neither too warm nor too cold; and the country is quite disease free (no malaria and no tsetse flies, although there is a greater prevalence of pulmonary disease than elsewhere) (World Bank 1991c, 3).

The high population density was the first thing that struck the Europeans who arrived a century ago. From the 1920s onward, the region has consistently been declared "overpopulated" (Delor-Vandueren and Degand 1991; Ford 1995; Willame 1995a, 119 ff.). This assessment was borne out by the fact that the country suffered from regular famines: according to some estimates, between 1900 and 1950, there were seventeen years of famine (Grosse 1994a, 11). Yet the population was then only between one and two million (CePeD 1994). By the beginning of the 1980s, Rwanda's population had increased to seven million. What happened in these decades?

Ecological Resource Scarcity: Challenges and Responses

Faced with these constraints, Rwandan farmers and the Rwandan government have adopted a variety of coping strategies. A distinction is usually made between processes of extensification, that is, bringing new lands under cultivation, and those of intensification, or increasing the yields on existing lands. A third, related strategy of promoting food and livelihood security is diversification, which involves decreasing household reliance on any single pattern of production or source of income. Rwandan farmers have moved along all three of these axes but have pursued extensification to the greatest extent. According to most experts, agricultural intensification in Rwanda is not far advanced, and diversification is still very limited. This is both good news and bad news. On the one hand, it means that the increase in production took place in an inefficient and unsustainable manner, trying to cultivate the last centimeter of often marginal land on steep slopes. On the other hand, this implies that there are important remaining possibilities for intensification and diversification, if the conditions that encourage them can be created. Let us look in detail at these strategies.

Historically, extensification in Rwanda has taken two forms. One is the conversion of pastures and wetlands into agricultural land. The second is internal migration, which is closely related to the former, for it often entails a move to regions in the east that were previously used primarily for pasture.

The area used for pasture declined from 487,000 hectares in 1970 to 200,000 hectares in 1986, or from 34 percent of the cultivated surface to 19 percent. In parallel, the total cultivated land area expanded from 528,000 to 826,000 hectares (Olson 1995, 326). By the late 1980s, 94 percent of all cropland was devoted to food crops, which took up 42 percent of the total land area (up from less than 25 percent in 1965;

World Bank 1991c, 4, 55). Bananas, beans, sweet potatoes, and manioc were the prime crops. The area cultivated with maize increased from 23,000 hectares in 1965 to 77,000 hectares in 1988; the same figures for sorghum were 94,000 and 170,000, respectively (Mitchell 1995, 149). During the same period, farmers (with the support of the government and the aid system) brought hundreds of small wetland areas under cultivation; the remaining ones are too difficult or too costly to modify (Ford 1993, 151).

However, the available data are often contradictory and hard to interpret. Two high-quality national agricultural surveys done in 1984 and 1990, for example, confirm that the pasture area decreased greatly (minus 50 percent, on average) but seem to suggest that fallow land and woodlots, not cropped fields, were the prime beneficiaries of this conversion (Ministère de l'Agriculture 1992). If these data are correct, that would contradict the notion of Rwanda's agriculture being in a severe crisis; it would also suggest that farmers were taking major steps to protect the environment.

The process of land conversion was accompanied by internal migration, mainly from the south and the center to the east, that is, from regions of high density to regions of low density (Cambrézy 1984; Grosse 1994a; Olson 1994a). According to Olson (1995), who has studied these matters in most detail, from 1978 to 1991, three-quarters of all rural communes experienced out-migration. There was also a significant migration into the cities, foremost Kigali. Grosse (1994a, 14) suggests that data on urbanization, which indicate that only 5 percent of Rwanda's population lived in cities, were undercounted, although it is not known by how much.

This rural internal migration was facilitated by the effects of the "social revolution." The abolition of the *ubuhake* (clientship) institution in 1961, as well as the departure, by death or flight, of more than half of Rwanda's Tutsi in the beginning of the 1960s and of more in 1972 left open vast tracts of land previously used as pasture in the east, as well as the wetlands (swampy valley bottomlands) that had been used as dry-season pasture by cattle herders. This new land was not necessarily the most appropriate for agriculture; it had less natural productivity than the fertile slopes in the center of the country. However, the available information indicates that it was less degraded, having been used for permanent agriculture for a shorter time (Clay, Reardon, and Kangasniemi 1995a; Campbell 1994, 21).

At the same time, the process of independence largely closed off the form of migration that had been the most common one—that is, migration into Zaire and Uganda. During the colonial period, migration to the Kivu region was organized by the Belgian colonizer, for the latter region was considered underpopulated (Willame 1995a, 115). Spontaneous migration within and across current borders also took place, often after famines or local conflicts.

This massive internal migration led to a homogenization of population densities in Rwanda (Campbell 1994, 17; Olson 1994a; Grosse 1994b, 12). As a result, migration is no longer an option for farmers trying to cope with land pressure. It should be noted, however, that more than 20 percent of the Rwandese land mass is still covered with national parks—the highest proportion in Africa.

Notwithstanding the widespread nature of all these simple extensification processes, Rwanda has seen a dramatic reduction in the size of farm holdings, which declined, on the average, from 3 hectares per family in 1949 to 2 hectares in the 1960s, 1.2 hectares in the early 1980s, and 0.7 hectare by the early 1990s. As discussed in Chapter 6, this average hides great divergences, with an increasing number of landless and near-landless peasants on the bottom and a growth in the size of the largest farms (World Bank 1986a, 104). What this means is that the majority of Rwandan farmers practice—and live off—some form of what has been called "gardening."

In parallel, the market for land sales and land rentals developed strongly. I presented data on land sales in Chapter 4. The 1984 national agricultural survey revealed that, throughout the country, half of all farm households rented land (Ministère de l'Agriculture 1985, 66). As with land sales, which were documented to be the result of distress, the vast majority of land rental took place not to produce a surplus but simply to satisfy nutritional needs (Willame 1995a, 139).

Cultivating ever smaller farms, most farmers have begun reducing the time that land is left fallow; that is, they resort to an increasingly permanent use of the land. This strategy may be the most long-standing intensification strategy in Rwanda, having been documented from well before independence. Ford (1993, 168, 170) states that in the province of Ruhengeri, for example, more than one-third of all land has been in constant use for more than fifty years, and most cultivation is now permanent. Between 1970 and 1986, the total fallow land declined from 200,000 to 123,900 hectares. Nationwide, only 17 percent of all land is kept fallow (Clay, Reardon, and Kangasniemi 1995a, 10). This allows for double and even triple cropping. As observed by Ford (1993, 172)

for Ruhengeri, "the frequency of cultivation, using even the most conservative estimates, is close to 100 [percent] and may be as high as 400
[percent] for many households."

Other strategies seek to increase or at least maintain the fertility of
the land. This presents major challenges in Rwanda, where the topography is very hilly, even the steepest slopes are cultivated, and cultivation
is often almost permanent. Rwandese farmers face two main challenges:
erosion and exhaustion of soil fertility.

Rwanda's high population density in combination with its hilly
topography means that even very steep slopes are cultivated: the average
slope of cultivated land in Rwanda is 17 degrees (in the United States,
farming is not advised on slopes above 5 to 10 degrees; Clay, Reardon,
and Kangasniemi 1995a, 10). Under these conditions, torrential rainfall
on steep slopes drains the topsoil down the hills to the valleys. Moreover,
human action—cultivation techniques such as tilling along vertical lines,
deforestation, or construction of infrastructures—also contributes to
erosion (Lewis 1994, 7; Lewis and Nyamulinda 1996, 54).

Estimates of the extent of erosion vary widely, depending on place,
time, and measurement technique. In the literature, I found figures from
13.3 tons to more than 200 tons per hectare per year (Ford 1993,
166–68). However, there seems to be some consensus that the annual
soil loss from erosion of *unprotected* slopes (that is, slopes not covered
by plants) is easily above 100 tons per hectare per year, which is very
high (Grosse 1994a, 36; Lewis, Clay, and Dejaegher 1988). According
to the National Agricultural Commission, half the country's farmland
suffers from moderate to severe erosion (see Clay and others 1995, 1).
There is also a consensus that erosion is worst on the steepest slopes, on
unprotected slopes, and on those with poor soil. However, land on steep
slopes represents a high proportion of total cultivated land. In the neighboring Kivu region, for example, Lewis and Nyamulinda (1989, 145)
found that 60 percent of the slopes fell in the categories of "strong" to
"prohibitive." Grosse (1994b, 32) presents data that suggest that erosion worsened in the 1980s.

The use of antierosion measures has spread widely in Rwanda, and
there is a wide variety of techniques. The construction of infiltration
ditches or terraces, obligatory under the Belgian colonizers, is not
done widely; the work is very hard and labor-intensive, and the memory of forced labor in these sectors during the Belgian colonial period
is still strong (Derenne 1989). The most popular technique is probably the planting of strips of shrubs and bushes on contour lines

around the hills—so-called living hedges, whose roots stop water and soil from flowing down the hills. Data by Lewis and Nyamulinda (1996) show that these techniques can reduce water erosion to very low levels, but they may be much less effective in addressing man-made erosion.

Other techniques to combat erosion include mulching, that is, covering the soil with a layer of branches, leaves, and the like to minimize the direct impact of raindrops; and furrowing, or creating ridges in the soil to slow down water runoff and promote its absorption. Since the 1980s, agroforestry, that is, keeping the topsoil stable by planting rows of trees whose roots break the free flow of water, has become popular with the agricultural extension system, and its adoption is slowly moving forward. All these simple, labor-intensive techniques are designed to stop runoff and minimize erosion. Many of these techniques have double uses. Tree planting, for example, serves antierosion functions while producing much-needed fuelwood or timber wood; the living hedges serve the same antierosion functions but also produce green leaves that can be fed to animals or used for green manure.

Much progress had been made in some of these fields due to incessant government campaigns, usually financed with large amounts of foreign aid. Data reveal that the proportion of land to which at least one of these techniques is applied has risen constantly. Techniques such as simple terracing through ditches or living hedges have been adopted by 30 to 50 percent of all farmers (Grosse 1994a, 38). Very few farmers apply the full package of techniques, however, and the majority of farms in Rwanda still have very little protection against erosion (see also the discussion in Chapter 6 on the low adoption of the technical packages vulgarized by rural development projects). Great progress is thus still theoretically possible.

The other crucial challenge that Rwanda's farmers face, with their small plots that are almost constantly cultivated, is to maintain soil fertility, which is threatened by overcultivation, resulting in decreased biomass. Surveys in Ruhengeri prefecture indicate that more than three-quarters of all farmers perceive soil fertility to be declining in at least one of their fields—a problem considered by many to be more severe than erosion (de la Mass>elière 1992; Grosse 1994b, 34). Olson (1994b, 26) presents data by prefecture, showing that between 26 and 56 percent of farmers perceived the fertility of their lands to have deteriorated.[2] By far the main reason for this decline is said to be the lack of manure (Grosse 1994b, 34; Olson 1994b, 25), although farmers and especially experts also argue that much of the cultivated land is fragile and of poor quality (Olson 1994b; USAID 1981, 79).

Farmers are increasingly using techniques to maintain or restore soil fertility. Although there is almost no use of chemical fertilizers in Rwanda, the use of so-called green manure (mixing leaves and other forms of biomas into the soil) is taking off. According to Ford (1993, 172), more than 40 percent of households manure their plots in Ruhengeri. Another prime technique is composting, the creation of dark pits in which organic matter is left to rot and is then applied to the field. Again, these techniques are heavily promoted by the state and the aid system, but their adoption is advancing slowly and unevenly, with extremely few farmers adopting the full packages as vulgarized by the extension services.

One of the reasons for these low adoption rates may be that there are serious doubts about the usefulness of the techniques. Many experts argue that the usual package may be uneconomical and inefficient for most small farmers. Farmers may have felt obliged to adopt certain techniques because of pressure from above, not because of their conviction that this was the best solution to their problems. This may explain why so many of the compost pits and living hedges are so poorly maintained and badly used (Grosse 1994b, 16). Bart (1993) even suggests that compost pits tend to be located close to roads, so that they can be shown to extension agents.

Others have argued that the widespread cultivation of banana trees in Rwanda constitutes an effective farmer-initiated response to erosion. It creates a permanent cover that minimizes erosion so effectively that it basically ensures the ecological sustainability of the production system. To the extent that this widespread practice was successful, this success occurred despite the explicit policies of the Rwandan state and some foreign aid agencies, which still support and encourage difficult and expensive terracing (Voyame and others 1996, 87; see also Grosse 1994a, 35). Other local practices, such as micro-terraces, ridging, micro-barrages, and traditional agroforestry, are similarly overlooked by the official extension system.

Reforestation is another crucial element in any assessment of Rwanda's ecological situation. Forests fulfill a number of crucial functions: they supply fuelwood, necessary for cooking and heating; they provide timber required for construction and handicrafts; and they have important antierosion and fertility-maintaining functions. In a country with a high population density, where farming is the prime source of income for the majority of the population, one expects forests to be under severe threat, as there are many reasons to cut them down.

As a result, reforestation has long been a priority of many aid agencies, which have published many studies on it and financed reforestation projects costing tens of millions of dollars. It is difficult to get a good idea of the extent of Rwanda's forest cover. Data differ greatly. Estimates of Rwanda's forest cover in the 1980s differed from 6 to 12 percent and up (USAID 1981, 29; Sorg n.d.) Data on trends are similarly divergent.

On the negative side, one source documents that during the period 1980–89, average annual deforestation was 5,000 hectares, while average annual reforestation was 3,000 hectares, implying a 2,000-hectares loss per year (UNDP 1995, table 17). Another source states that, according to the Forestry Department in 1986, Rwanda was annually using 2.3 million more cubic meters of wood than it was producing (Percival and Homer-Dixon 1995, 6). And a study by the University of Rwanda (1983, 110) of three supposedly representative zones showed deforestation rates of 0.4 to 15 percent between 1973 and 1979.

On the positive side, according to the World Resources Institute (1996, table 9.2), total forest cover in the decade before 1990 increased by 1.1 percent a year, largely as a result of reforestation programs. According to other experts, total forest cover in Rwanda doubled in the 1980s (Voyame and others 1996, 92). Government data suggest that the amount of communal forests rose from 27,000 hectares in 1970 to 99,500 hectares in 1986 (May 1995, 326). Ford (1993, 163–65) documents that in Ruhengeri, a highly populated prefecture, the total forested area doubled between 1980 and 1985 and in all likelihood increased more afterward. Other data from 1989 show that 66 percent of households perceived the availability of wood in the region to have increased during the last years (Olson 1994b, 24). A 1991 USAID study argued that Rwanda had more land planted with trees at the end of the 1980s than at the time of independence twenty-seven years earlier.

It may be that these divergent data reflect different periods, with the negative data dating from before 1980 and the positive data from thereafter. It may also be that the negative data come primarily from people or organizations with an interest in showing problems. It seems quite probable that, from the 1980s onward, there has been a major increase in the forest area through the actions of both small farmers and the government. Small farmers have greatly increased the use of agroforestry on their own plots: in Ruhengeri, for example, Ford (1993,

163–65) documents that small woodlots rose by a factor of five in the early 1980s. Olson (1994b, 24) shows that, on average, 47 percent of all Rwandan rural households planted trees the previous year. The progress in Rwanda's reforestation also results from government reforestation programs, backed up by massive foreign aid. All observers agree, however, that this progress is gravely compromised by the government's insistence on planting eucalyptus trees, which, though fast-growing, are of little benefit to the environment or to farmers (Grosse 1994a, 37). Many document instances of farmers ripping out freshly planted eucalyptus seedlings at night.

Farmers have also changed their land-use patterns to promote higher and more sustainable yields. Some of these practices have been well known for decades if not centuries. For example, farm households tend to cultivate five to ten small plots (gardens, really) often located miles away from one another, in different agroecological microzones. This surely produces more work and travel (one reason why many development projects long played with the idea of seeking to reduce farm fragmentation) but minimizes vulnerability to the vagaries of climate and plant diseases. Farmers have also experimented with diversifying and associating crops (Ford 1993, 166, 174). The cultivation of combinations of bananas and coffee on steep slopes, for example, is done because these crops provide high income and are also good antierosion measures. Similarly, the increased cultivation of sweet potatoes can be explained by the fact that they have a higher caloric value than other crops grown on degraded land (Marysse, De Herdt, and Ndayambaje 1993, 51). Lewis and Nyamulinda (1989, 146) also document that farmers choose their crops based on the degree of steepness of the land, with manioc—which needs little work—being cultivated on the steepest slopes.

Under the constraint of lack of land, people have decreased their usual forms of animal husbandry and replaced them with small animals—goats, chickens, rabbits—that can forage on roadsides, in forest plots, and in the front yards of houses. According to data from the World Resources Institute (1996, table 9.1, 10), between 1982–84 and 1992–94, the number of cattle declined by 4 percent and permanent pastureland by 15 percent, while the number of sheep and goats increased by 16 percent, pigs increased by 12 percent, and chickens stabilized.

It should be noted, however, that some authors have observed exactly the opposite trend for the same years. Willame (1995a, 140) writes that the number of cattle increased by 25 percent between 1982 and 1984 and was significantly higher than in 1959. Other data suggest that the number of cattle grew by 50 percent—that is, faster than population growth—between 1962 and 1973 (Mitchell 1995, 281). Grosse (1994a), having compiled data from various sources, documents that Rwanda's total cattle population in 1964, immediately after the death or fleeing of a large proportion of Tutsi, was 557,000. The figure then rose to 748,000 by 1971, fell to 626,000 in 1972 (when pogroms against Tutsi occurred again), and rose again to above 800,000 for the remainder of the 1980s.

It thus seems likely that the often-talked-about downward trend in the number of cattle did not take place, while the number of small ruminants greatly increased. However, given the great increase in Rwanda's population, as well as the rise in land and income inequality documented in Chapter 4, this still means that a large proportion of households in all likelihood have fewer cattle than before, or none at all (Grosse 1994a, 27–28). This is very important, for cattle provide farm households with organic fertilizer necessary to maintain soil fertility. Animals also provide occasional nutritional supplements and can act as a form of savings.

Hence, a variety of techniques of intensification are being adopted in Rwanda, although many of them are not yet widespread. At the same time, some of the typical ways of increasing yields are almost totally absent in Rwanda. There is still almost no use of improved seeds in Rwanda, nor of pesticides, irrigation, or chemical fertilizers. The tools employed in agriculture are few and are extremely rudimentary: the few machines found in the rural milieu, such as mills and processing equipment, are usually owned by development projects (World Resources Institute 1996, table 10.2; World Bank 1991c, 4, 33; Ministère de l'Agriculture 1985, 49). This is largely the result of general poverty and most households' lack of cash as well as the inefficiency of the state extension machinery (World Bank 1989a, 12). As a result, however, yields remain low. As a World Bank report (1991c, 11) states:

> Adoption of modern crop technologies to Rwanda circumstances . . . is at an early stage. Extension suffers from a lack of good messages; hybrid maize is unknown; other improved seeds are rare; adaptation to Rwandan circumstances of fertilizer and pesticides is limited; modern tools and equipment are seldom used. Finally, credit, processing, storage, and commerce are all at early stages of development. In general, yields remain at traditional levels because agriculture is still overwhelmingly traditional.

This is both good news and bad news. The bad news is that, after decades of efforts backed up by hundreds of millions of aid dollars, so little progress has been made, and Rwandan farming households are living so close to the edge—or have fallen off it. The data on poverty, malnutrition, famine, and the dramatic reduction in fertility described in Chapter 4 all show to what extent life for a majority of Rwandans is almost intolerably poor and insecure.

The good news is that so much more is possible. Rwanda's agricultural performance is not one of a country that has run out of space and where there is no more opportunity for progress. On the contrary, the country is still at the very early stages of progress, where yields and productivity can greatly rise through intensification. In other words, the agricultural crisis observed from the mid-1980s onward was not the result of some fixed, natural upper limit having been exceeded—the famous carrying capacity, so dear to hard Malthusians—for great progress in intensification was still possible.

Clay, Reardon, and Kangasniemi (1995) make the interesting argument that there are two types of Boserupian intensification: labor-driven and capital-driven. The former is primarily what took place in Rwanda —explaining why it still made sense, until recently, for farming households to have more children. The latter is based on increasing the quality of the land through capital investments and requires sources of cash income. This brings us to diversification and the creation of rural sources of income through off-farm employment or nonagricultural income.

Farmers have long adopted the third broad strategy of survival: diversification. Almost all farm households sell and buy goods in local markets: coffee, bananas, and other foods are their prime products for sale. Many farmers engage in pisciculture or apiculture to increase and diversify their incomes and, to a lesser extent, their diets. Most of them seek off-farm employment as farm laborers on other farms; in part-time commerce, handicrafts, or rural industry; or, most appreciated, in jobs in the public sector or in development projects. Studies show that the farmers who did best in terms of increasing their farm productivity were those whose families had significant sources of off-farm income, allowing for on-farm investments, in animals, for example (Clay and others 1995; Scherr and Hazell 1994; Reardon, Kelly, and Crawford 1995; Robins 1990). However, nobody has much of an idea where the demand for off-farm production will come from. Who will buy the artisanal or rural industrial products? The relaxation of restrictive policies against migration and urban employment seems to be a condition for progress, but it is not sufficient.

INTERMEDIATE CONCLUSION

Looking to the past, one cannot help but observe that the effects of the above-described strategies have been quite impressive. Most observers agree, often against their expectations, that, at least until the middle of the 1980s, Rwanda was able to feed its population increasingly well, had a growing forest cover, and may even have been quite effective in fighting erosion (Bart 1993; Ford 1995). This evolution resembles the trends observed in the Machakos district in Kenya or in Nepal (Tiffen, Mortimore and Gichuki 1994; see also Grosse 1994a). Small farmers were productive: one study showed that farms under 0.37 hectare produced crops worth over RF 100,000 per hectare, while farms larger than 1.91 hectares produced under RF 18,000 per hectare (World Bank 1994b, 30; the study referred to is Minot 1991).

However, from the mid-1980s onward, the picture became less rosy, primarily because trends in food production per capita became negative. As I documented in Chapter 4, between 1984 and 1991, average farm production per Rwandan farmer, expressed in kilocalories per person per day, declined by one-quarter (World Resources Institute 1996, table 10.1). Other data complicate the picture by suggesting that forest cover continued to rise, as did the possession of animals, including large ones, and that malnutrition rates remained stagnant. This makes it difficult to understand the extent of the crisis. That there was a crisis seems undeniable: the data on agricultural production are considered very reliable. However, answers to the questions who produced less? where? and of what? are not so clear-cut.

Further intensification of agriculture, combined with increased adoption of antierosion and fertility-maintaining practices, is considered by many to be the only feasible path in the short term. I have argued that there is still a large margin for improvement along these lines. However, the fact that this has not happened, despite the amount of energy and money poured into it, suggests that there are profound constraints on this strategy. The reason for that relates to the condition of structural violence as described in Chapter 6: the presence of a biased, condescending, top-down, socially exclusive, and often inefficient state and agricultural extension system—which did not change after the genocide—

may constitute the prime constraint on successful rural development in Rwanda.

Genocide and Ecological Resource Scarcity

For the purpose of this chapter, the main question of interest relates to the causes of the agricultural crisis: why did it happen? Is the crisis, to the extent that we understand its nature, a conjunctural one, due to an unfortunate succession of inclement weather conditions? Or is it a structural crisis, the result of Rwanda running out of space and exceeding its carrying capacity? Depending on the answer to that question, the puzzle that is the subject of this chapter—the relation, if any, between ecological resource scarcity and the genocide—will be solved very differently.

As stated earlier, Rwanda's agriculture is still at the most primitive stage in terms of the inputs used in the production of food and other agricultural products: no mechanization or sophisticated tools, no chemical and little organic fertilizer, very few hybrid green revolution–type seeds, no pesticides, deficient storage and transformation. It is still essentially a traditional agriculture that has slowly adapted to the changing ecological circumstances of the country. Great progress can easily be envisaged. This means that the hard Malthusian argument cannot explain the 1994 genocide. What position do we chose between the second and third explanatory models described earlier? Or, more concretely, how did ecological factors interact with political and social ones to produce the genocide?

There seem to be three concrete "transmission belts" by which resource scarcity in Rwanda could have contributed to or caused the genocide (Uvin 1996a)—that is, factors that could justify a soft Malthusian position.

First, the departure (by death or flight) of more than half of Rwanda's Tutsi in the beginning of the 1960s, and of more in 1973, left open vast tracts of land previously used as pastures in the east, as well as the wetlands that had been used for dry-season pasture by cattle herders. This provided new space for the remaining Hutu to relieve their resource constraints, and massive immigration into these regions followed. Note that both the 1959–63 and the 1973 violence occurred during a long and uninterrupted period of high growth of food production per capita and the absence of famine—hunger can not explain these conflicts.

Agronomists and economists alike have been arguing that, by the middle of the 1980s, these new lands were used up and, consequently, no more safety valves for extensification existed. In reality, extensification had not been a viable option for decades for the majority of farmers, as attested to by the constant reduction in farm size (from 2 hectares per household in 1956 to 0.7 hectare in 1990) and by the generally observed intensification of production techniques. Migration served only a minority of young households. Hence, "running out of land" was a decades-long process, not an abrupt, discrete event that took place in 1994. It had been coped with well, at least until the middle of the 1980s. By itself, it cannot explain the genocide.

A second, related argument holds that the Rwandan Patriotic Front (FPR) invasion in 1990 ignited fears among the masses—especially those in the east, but more generally all those who had taken over land vacated by fleeing Tutsi—that their lands would be reclaimed by returning Tutsi. Some suggest that Hutu extremists deliberately fueled such fears among the peasants. Moreover, the Habyarimana regime had a long-standing habit of playing that card: the argument that "there is not enough land" had been used for twenty years to justify its refusal to allow the return of the Tutsi refugees.

It is true that, with land being scarce and agriculture remaining paramount for the survival of the majority of the population, any issue related to land was crucial to families; every centimeter counted. Although hard data do not exist, it seems that local conflicts over land were omnipresent in Rwanda, clogging the courts and causing considerable conflicts between neighbors and family members (Ntagungiro 1991; André and Platteau 1995). Others have documented a general increase in rural crime. Various reports speak of farmers' need to harvest prematurely as a result of the theft of food crops while still in the field, their reluctance to grow crops in remote fields for the same reason, and the increasing theft of small animals (IWACU 1991, 8, 44; Bagiramenshi and Bazihizina 1985, 88).

Participation by some in the genocide, it has been argued, may not have been caused by ethnic hatred but by opportunism, using the occasion to appropriate someone else's land. André and Platteau's analysis of one village in the north suggests that this was the case: virtually all the people killed (with the exception of one, all were Hutu, for this village was almost exclusively Hutu) were richer or socially marginal. It must be added that, during the last decade, there had been a movement among civil servants and other wealthy people to buy land, which greatly increased land inequality in Rwanda. It does not seem, however, that these were the people killed; on the contrary, they were often leading the killing.

Third, since 1984, food production per capita had fallen by 25 percent—a very steep decline. Coupled with the free fall in coffee prices, this had brought great economic hardship to many families. Combined with the reduction in the availability of land and the general contraction of the economy, this created an almost hopeless situation for the young generation. To them, it seemed that there was no hope at all of ever improving their lives or even marrying (in Rwandese culture, it is important that a young man marry only when he has enough land or income to provide for his family; fertility data showed a rapid rise in the marriage age).

A few years later, as a result of the FPR-instigated civil war, the situation worsened. At its worst, up to one million people became refugees, living in squalid camps around the capital. At the same time, their farms produced no more food—yet this had been the biggest food-producing region of the country. Up to 40 percent of the government budget was diverted to military purposes, and social and development programs suffered (although increased development aid and military aid from some befriended regimes compensated partly). This resulted in the creation of an underclass concentrated in Kigali: thousands of young men, reduced to begging, wandered idly in the streets. This could not help but provoke frustration and a loss of self-respect. Throughout history, and not only in Rwanda, such situations have been excellent breeding grounds for radicalism and violence against minorities. It is known that the extremist militia drew strongly on these people.

Hence, there seem to be two possible links between resource scarcity and the genocide. First, severe land scarcity and limited opportunities outside of agriculture created intense feelings about land. Conflicts over land were frequent, and fears about losing land provoked profound insecurity. Such fears and intense attachments can be used to provoke violence and conflict. People can then engage in violence either as (perceived) self-defense against threats or through a process of opportunism. Second, the agricultural crisis, compounded by the FPR invasion, set in motion processes of impoverishment and marginalization that provided a fertile breeding ground for extremism and violence.

Some general observations apply to these hypotheses. For one, they are all "circumstantial," to use legal parlance. There are no smoking guns, no hard evidence, not even systematic analyses of primary sources.

These are constructions of plausibilities, probabilities, and reasonings that seem likely—not hard facts. The reason for that is simple—we have no "micro-information" about the genocide (with the exception of André and Platteau 1995; Longman 1995b): Who killed who? Why did they do so? These hypotheses could thus be wrong: history is full of plausible looking theories that proved to be misguided.

Second, neither of these hypotheses implies automaticity, that is, that the occurrence of the one factor—land scarcity or declining agricultural production—automatically leads to violent conflict and genocide. In both hypotheses, for example, external intervention is needed to move from one factor to the other. The genocidal violence began in the cities, foremost the capital, and remained confined there for a long time. It did not spontaneously erupt among those suffering from land pressure or malnutrition but spread to them slowly (Percival and Homer-Dixon 1995). The impetus for the genocide, and its spread to the countryside, was clearly urban, emanating from the ruling clique and associated extremists. Moreover, even when there are radicalized youth and the desire for scapegoating has become intense, the target of that anger is culturally defined—it does not follow from the fact of ecological resource scarcity itself. One can easily imagine the poor people's anger turned against the dignitaries of the regime; the dignitaries were, after all, the ones whose policies contributed to the crisis and who were visibly enriching themselves and buying up land. But no such thing happened. Instead, it was under the leadership of this clique that the genocide was organized. Clearly, the civil war since 1990, along with long-standing and deeply ingrained racism, explains the choice of target.

There are really two questions of importance when debating ecological resource scarcity in the Rwandan context. One is the more intellectual one involving the role of ecological resource scarcity in explaining the genocide. The other is the practically urgent one of designing a development strategy that builds a future for Rwanda's population starting from these constraints (discussed briefly earlier).

As for the former, it is easy to invalidate the hard, radical arguments presented at the beginning of this chapter. These explanations are truly monocausal, usually no more than disjointed observations that "Rwanda had a high population density" and "Rwanda passed through an episode of intense violence," thus "the violence must be due to the population density." Easy as it is to dismantle these simplistic arguments and to argue that things are more complicated, it is harder to propose a clear,

well-documented, and testable understanding of the exact role of ecological resource scarcity in Rwanda's violence and how ecological
resource scarcity interacts with other factors. I tried to uncover some
mechanisms, but they are difficult to support concretely. Part of the
problem is documentation: we know almost nothing of the micro-level
"anthropology of passions," as Claudine Vidal called it, and have no
specific data on who killed whom for what reason. Part of it, too, is
conceptual-methodological and has been the subject of long discussion
by scholars.

I was able to identify two transmission belts linking resource scarcity
to violence. Both of these, however, were strongly culturally and politically defined; they did not automatically follow from the facts of ecological resource scarcity themselves. Combined with my notion that
Rwanda had a great potential for easing the stress of its ecological
resource scarcity, this seems to force me into the third school of thought,
in which there is no relation between ecological resource scarcity and
the genocide. (This was a surprise to me, for I had expected to end up
supporting the middle position.) For the rest, I still stand behind the
conclusion of an earlier article I wrote on this subject (Uvin 1996a, 15):

> Ecological, economic, and political processes cannot be separated in the
> explanation of the crisis in Rwanda. In the same way that they do not
> form separate spheres in people's real lives, they can only be understood
> as part of a web of interactions that produces specific outcomes.
> Fundamentally, political conflicts rest on an environmental and economic
> substratum. Even though political conflicts may not be "caused" in any
> direct way by environmental issues (but rather by long-standing political
> strategies and social constructions), the dynamics related to ecological
> resource scarcity will play a role in the conflict. On the level of political
> strategy, ecological resource scarcity can be used as a tool: strategies of
> impoverishing certain groups, of destroying food and livelihood security,
> and of promoting fear, can be built on ecological resource scarcity. This is
> not automatic: discrimination and the spread of insecurity and fear can
> and do exist even in the absence of ecological resource scarcity; similarly,
> many situations of ecological resource scarcity exist that are not used to
> promote violence against other groups. Finally, under conditions of eco-
> logical resource scarcity, processes of severe political conflict and violence
> (whatever their cause) often have ecological consequences, contributing to
> the complexity of their solution. The case of Rwanda provides a perfect
> illustration of that.

Notes

1. Out of forty countries for which data exist, Rwanda is sixth behind Liberia, Ghana, Kenya, Mauritania, and Zaire (Foote, Hill, and Martin 1993, 286–87). Engelman and LeRoy (1995, 25) put Rwanda in fifth position, behind Tanzania, Guinea, Somalia, and Kenya. On a worldwide level, Rwanda is situated somewhere between the twentieth and thirtieth positions, depending on the source.
2. Note that these data indicated that between 38 and 66 percent of the farmers saw no change, and between 6 and 18 percent observed an improvement.

PART V

CONCLUSIONS

10

WHY DID PEOPLE PARTICIPATE IN GENOCIDE? A THEORETICALLY INFORMED SYNTHESIS

In this chapter, I recapitulate what we learned about the causes of genocide in Rwanda. I do so by analyzing Rwanda's case in light of the explanations derived from the study of past genocides and of communal and ethnic violence. From the differences and similarities, we can learn more about the nature of Rwanda's genocide. The next chapter draws conclusions on the role of development aid in the processes that led to genocide.

The most common explanation of the genocide in Rwanda—which was presented in detail in Part II of this book—refers to the desire of Rwanda's elite to stay in power. These analyses begin by pointing to a series of political and economic factors occurring since the middle of the 1980s that, taken together, threatened the power and privileges of Rwanda's elite. As a result, this small group of people around Habyarimana—especially his wife's family, as well as some cronies and radicals—used all means at its disposal, including racism and violence, to fend off threats to its survival and its privileges (see, from very different perspectives, Reyntjens 1994, 117–20; Kagabo and Vidal 1994, 542; Percival and Homer-Dixon 1995; Prunier 1995; Chrétien 1993a, 191; Chrétien and others 1995, 7; Human Rights Watch 1995). It is this group that spread the message of racism, organized and financed the militia, and planned the murders.

These analyses rejoin explanations of communal violence made by other scholars for other African countries, as well as studies of past genocides and the broader sociology and political science literature on social conflict (Bienen 1993; Fein 1995; Horowitz 1985). And in one of the most famous and widely quoted articles of postwar sociology, Lewis

Coser (1956) outlined the important functions of out-group conflict for in-group stability and cohesion. There is thus ample theoretical and empirical evidence that demonizing Tutsi could be a strategy for securing control over Rwanda by a small elite.

I argued that although every factor discussed in this standard explanation—the economic crisis, the rise of political discontent, the Rwandan Patriotic Front (FPR) invasion, the international pressure for democratization, the hate propaganda and the role of the *akazu*—is important, they do not tell the whole story. What this explanation fails to account for is the deeper social basis on which these processes rest. While the role of elites and the state was surely important—indeed, all genocides in history have been state instigated, organized, and legitimized (Du Preez 1994)—this explanation is limited by its exclusive focus on a small group of people. All the attention focuses on the causes and the strategies of the manipulation of ethnicity by the elites, and too little mention is given to the people who perpetrated the violence or to the social structures that allowed such processes to be set in motion.

First, it is implicitly and wrongly assumed that there is a direct, one-to-one relation between elite manipulation of ethnicity and people's behavior—in this case, the communal violence that took place. Ordinary people are conceived of as passive recipients, conforming to ethnic manipulation from above. This is at best a partial and at worst a wrong explanation. The perpetrators of communal violence are not passive instruments but active participants; the genocidal use of ethnicity by elites rests on a profound social and historical basis.

Second, even if it can be convincingly asserted that Habyarimana or his wife or the *akazu* sought to use racism as a strategy for remaining in power, the question that remains is what kind of social structures allow a handful of people to plot and successfully execute such sinister plans. Let me explain. Among Rwandans and the few specialists on that country, the question of the personality and morality of Habyarimana, as well as the nature of his involvement in the preparation of the genocide, is a hotly debated issue. Was he a decent, tolerant man, bypassed by radical people in his entourage? Or had he always been a racist, although a pragmatic one? Or had he changed his attitude at some point, and, if so, when? Similar questions can be asked about the people around Habyarimana. Yet this whole debate is of little importance for understanding the genocide and the processes that led to it. What is important in that context is a political structure in which one man's role can be so large and in which a few shadowy figures can plot mass murder; a society in which civil society is unable to stop the processes of genocide if it is not an active participant in them; a political culture in which lack of information and manipulation are realities for most people and in which racism, prejudice, and mutually exclusive histories are omnipresent; and so forth. Thus, although it is certainly of interest to understand the attitudes and objectives of the elites—from Habyarimana to the wider *akazu* to the whole "state class"—one cannot stop there: we are forced to go further and seek to understand the relations between these elites and society at large, as well as the features of that society that make it amenable to genocide.

The profound question, and the central puzzle of this book, is: how do situations come about in which people feel that they should, and may, exterminate innocent people? What kind of social and psychological processes are "so powerful that they outweigh the moral restraints that would normally inhibit unjustifiable violence" (Kelman and Hamilton 1993, 234; Du Preez 1994, 4)? Historically, Rwandans are every bit as peaceful and moral as anyone else on this planet. Yet, although cases of heroic resistance have been documented, there is little doubt that there was mass participation in this genocide. What kind of social processes have taken place that can bring societies to lose the values, restraints, and ethics that under normal circumstances make these actions impossible and abhorrent to contemplate?

Political scientists, sociologists, and psychologists have explained genocides by referring to the fact that certain social groups—Jews and Gypsies in Nazi Germany, Armenians in Turkey at the beginning of the century—are outside the "scope of justice" or the "universe of obligation" of society, meaning that the moral values that apply to other people do not apply to them and that harm to them is of no concern or even desirable (Opotow 1995; Gamson 1995; Fein 1993; Staub 1989). In the case of Rwanda, it is clear that, by 1994, Tutsi were morally excluded from the Rwandan Hutu community and that killing them was morally and socially allowed. However, this is not so much an explanation as a description of the problem. It still begs the questions: Why were people willing to morally exclude a large segment of society? And why did it take this extreme genocidal form in 1994? The rest of this chapter provides some answers to these questions.

Political Science and
Sociological Explanations

Probably the most common political science explanation for ethnic conflict is that past discrimination and oppression lead to violence; if that discrimation took place along ethnic lines (or lines that can be perceived or construed as being ethnic), the conflict will be ethnic (Gurr 1993, 59, 82, 126; Stavenhagen 1990, 16; Fein 1995; Ennals 1988, 12–13). Ted Gurr's key indicator for the risk of genocide is "the existence of systematic differential treatment by the larger society." It is a basic social science assumption that violent conflict is likely to emerge if the differences between social groups overlap rather than crosscut the superimposition of inequalities (Fein 1993; Horowitz 1985). Stavenhagen (1990, 77) synthesizes this strand of thought nicely:

> Conflicts between ethnic groups arise from a number of causes. A subordinate minority (or majority) may react to years, decades, or centuries of discrimination and oppression, and stand up to say "enough!" or it may demand rights that it has been denied by others who enjoy them. Or a dominant ethnic (whether majority or minority) may attempt to impose its own norms and standards or its own model of society on a weaker, underprivileged minority (or majority) and encounter resistance when it does so. Or the dominant majority may feel that the minority has been granted or is demanding "too much" and must be kept "in place."

A Marxist-radical variant of this model is that racial and ethnic divisions are merely smoke screens, forms of false consciousness kept alive by the elites to mask their economic and political power and to divide the forces of resistance. The true interests of the working class are in fighting the owners of the means of production, but false consciousness along ethnic or religious lines hinders it from doing so (Wetherell and Potter 1992, chap. 1; Stavenhagen 1990, 16). These theories highlight the role of the elites and the benefits of ethnicity to them; however, the general notion that below ethnic conflict lies economic and political inequality remains more or less the same. Both schools agree that more or less objective, real-world socioeconomic and political differences are ultimately responsible for ethnic conflict, while ethnicity per se is only a symptom of the problem, although a powerful one, for it is so eminently mobilizable. What are, in essence, class or economic conflicts tend to take ethnic forms because of the salience of these primordial attachments to people and the presence of ready-made institutions, symbols, leaders, and images; however, the core of the conflict is really economic or political imbalance. In its most extreme, this leads to statements such as Rupesinghe's (1988, 17, 20):

> Ethnic conflict as such does not exist. What does exist is social, political and economic conflict between groups of people who identify each other in ethnic terms: color, race, religion, language, national origin. Very often such ethnic characteristics may mask other distinguishing features, such as class interests and political power, which on analysis may turn out to be the more important elements in the conflict.

The latter statement, although popular among progressive people throughout the world, is reductionist, for it takes away the possibility of ethnicity and, more generally, identity being an independent variable. Rupesinghe acknowledges as much when he adds: "when ethnic differences are used consciously or unconsciously to distinguish the opposing actors in a conflict situation—particularly when they become powerful mobilizing symbols, as is so often the case—then ethnicity does become a determining factor in the nature and the dynamic of the conflict" (Rupesinghe 1988, 17, 39; Stavenhagen 1990, 76). Hence, the root cause of a given conflict may be economic, but ethnicity can become, over time, an independent factor in it, taking on independent dynamics and complicating its resolution.

This explanation seems to have little relevance to the Rwandan genocide. Rwanda was not a case of a small minority exploiting the masses, nor one of an exploited majority rising up to throw off the bonds of exploitation. If anything, the violence was committed by the numerically, politically, militarily, and economically dominant group against the minority.

To be sure, the historical origins of ethnicity in Rwanda are related to socioeconomic differences, and economic and social discrimination along ethnic lines in favor of Tutsi was an undisputed presence during colonization and possibly much earlier. A big part of the genocidal rhetoric consisted precisely of more or less historically accurate reminders of this past inequality and oppression. But, as stated earlier, this inequality and supposed exploitation ended decades ago—long before most of the people who did the killing were born. It hardly seems sufficient to explain why people would be willing to torture and kill their neighbors now—neighbors who, in many cases, were every bit as poor and powerless as the killers.

The Marxist-radical argument that stresses the benefits of racist and ethnic prejudice to the elites does have relevance for understanding Rwanda if one drops its overly econocentric assumptions. In line with many postmodernist authors who stress the relation between ideas and power, one can see how, in Rwanda, the ethnic ideology served as a tool for the powers that be to legitimize their dominance and to hide from the poor the injustices they were subjected to. I explained how the ideology of Hutu power, and its corollary, the ideology of the evil and foreignness of Tutsi, had served this function since independence. What is still unclear is why people were so willing to believe it and why, at some point, they were willing to set aside their human values and slaughter their neighbors.

Another basic political science explanation of ethnic conflict posits that extreme violence is likely to happen during periods of transition—from so-called traditionalism to modernization, or from poverty to development, or from authoritarianism to democracy (Fein 1995; Horowitz 1985; Moore 1987). This argument can take different forms. One version is that those who benefit from the status quo will be tempted to revert to violence to defend their privileges, while those who seek change will consequently be tempted to do the same. Another version looks at societywide processes of unfulfilled (rising) expectations, frustration, and aggression. The latter is exemplified in the following quote from Ralph Dahrendorf (1995, 2; see also Tedeschi and Nesler 1993; Gurr 1970):

> When opportunities are held out for people but are not yet there to grasp, when economic development accelerates but social and political development lags behind, a mixture of frustration and irresponsibility develops which breeds violence. Such violence can be individual and undirected, but it can also become collective and directed against apparently happier neighbours or more successful strangers in one's midst, or both.

At first, this explanation, too, seems of little relevance to Rwanda, where there has been precious little modernization, either economic or political, over the last decades. Surely, Rwanda was in the midst of a process of change, both economic and political. However, I argued that little development ever impacted most of the poor people and that the political agitation for or against democracy in the capital was rather remote to most farmers' daily concerns.

But there was certainly an element of rising expectations and associated frustration in Rwanda. It can be argued that the whole development enterprise, with its ideas of material progress, its well-paid employees (whatever the color of their skin) with their four-wheel-drive vehicles, villas, foreign travel, and hundreds of small, daily status symbols, created a permanent reminder of the life that could be but that never would be for the majority of the population. Because of their exclusion from political and military jobs, educated Tutsi were highly represented in the development enterprise, whether in the bilateral aid system or in nongovernmental organizations (NGOs). Hence, even though many of them were in the business of development and, as such, at least rhetorically committed to improving the well-being of the Hutu masses, given the great social differences between them and the masses to be developed and given the continued nonexistence of the promised development, it seems eminently reasonable to suppose that frustration among ordinary people was high and that people of Tutsi origin were considered at least part of the problem. However, closing the explanation at this point would result in only a partial view, leaving many questions unanswered. Why was the violence directed only against Tutsi, and not also against Hutu, who constituted a much larger proportion of the development enterprise? Why did people not kill those who were much more directly responsible for their poverty—corrupt politicians, land-grabbing civil servants, patronizing local party cadres, and unjust police officials—rather than their often equally poor Tutsi neighbors? And why did the genocide take place the moment it did, and with such extreme intensity and cruelty? The presence of rising but unfulfilled expectations and the frustration this engendered were necessary, but they were not sufficient to explain the genocide. Still unanswered is what determined the choice of the targets of the violence—a choice that was rather counterintuitive—and the moment of the explosion.

A different social science argument holds that ethnic violence takes place primarily in times of economic recession. Competition over scarce resources and general levels of frustration increase during economic downturns, thus causing intergroup hostilities. This argument is widely accepted in policymaking and academic circles and is used to explain communal violence almost everywhere in the world. It has also been used for the case of Rwanda and I documented, from 1985 onward, a major economic crisis did hit Rwanda, hurting almost all social groups. However, there is little strong evidence to back the argument up. Donald Green and his colleagues at Yale University's Institution for Social and Policy Studies thoroughly analyzed the data on which famous studies of hate crimes in the United States are based and added their own data on New York hate crimes. They found virtually no statistical correlations between economic indicators and racist crimes. According to them (Green, Glaser, and Rich 1996, 20; see also Green, Wong, and Strolovitch 1996), the reasons are, first, that "hate crime seems to follow in the wake of economic setbacks only when target groups are widely blamed for deteriorating economic conditions"; and second, that hate crime is primarily about "maintaining social boundaries and the relative power of one's social group." Economic insecurities play a role in this, but as Allport (1954, 60) stated decades ago, "there must also be a previous sense of in-group and out-group rivalry before the lines of competition can be perceived as ethnic, rather than individual, rivalry." Hence, we can conclude that while economic recession may play a role in increasing the frustration and alienation required for committing racist and violent acts, it is by itself an insufficient explanation of the genocide. Most notably, it begs the question of why certain groups are blamed and marginalized and others are not.

In summation, the usual political science and sociological explanations of communal violence are only partly relevant to the Rwandan genocide. Frustration with the kind of development that benefits primarily those promoting it certainly existed; elites were undoubtedly attached to their privileges and willing to use ethnicity as a tool in that struggle; the economic crisis surely exposed the fault lines in society more and increased despair. A more encompassing explanation is needed, however, that manages to bring these elements together without being reduced to them and that can ultimately account for the question: why were so many Rwandans capable of putting aside their moral principles and killing innocent people? It seems imperative to turn to (social) psychology for further illumination.

Psychological Explanations

Psychological explanations of conflict and violence have been developed since the nineteenth century. Many psychologists believe that people have invariable psychological, if not genetic, propensities that promote conflict (Staub 1989, 52–53). In this view, people need to identify with groups and naturally tend to feel hostility toward other groups and discriminate against them. Other psychologists, such as some Freudian theorists, argue that there is a certain amount of "free-floating" aggression in people that can become activated as a result of "social permission to attack a certain group," especially if that group is defenseless (Banton 1983, 82–83; Hoffmann and McKendrick 1990, 16–17). Still others develop a "state of consciousness" argument that describes the processes by which individuals exhibit more norm-violating, irrational, and violent behavior in group situations (Mummendeny and Otten 1993). In other words, violent tendencies exist in all people, and they "break through" when the social norms that keep group hostility in check break down (Stavenhagen 1988, 17–18). What unites all these theories is that they explain actual conflict by reference to the existence of aggressive tendencies in all people, especially when in groups.

The problem with this type of explanation is that it applies to everyone and thus fails to account for variations in people's behavior (Wetherell and Potter 1992, chap. 2). Although these psychological theories may provide valuable insights into the potential for out-group violence that exists in all people, they tell us little about the actual processes that make that violence happen. Again, they are more descriptive than explanatory. As a result, most psychologists and psychoanalysts have abandoned these views (Marmor 1992). We need more than general statements about human dispositions.

Another psychologically inspired school of thought seeks to explain the genocide by referring to primitive, irrational forces that are typical to Rwandans, to Africans, or to humankind. Jerome Bernstein (1995, 11), a Jungian psychoanalyst, believes that the Rwandan genocide "has deep roots in the irrational, in the collective unconscious of society"—a "psychotic force." Marc Sommers (1996) documents that, in the refugee camps around Rwanda, such explanations are common within many churches. Essentially, the explanation is that the forces of evil exist in all of us and somehow took over the Rwandan collective soul for some months. In my talks to Rwandans, many of them invoked similar arguments, often with the purpose of moving on with life after the genocide. The problem with these explanations is that they are very general and do not explain why genocide occurred at a specific time (if these dispositions are ancient and universal, why does genocide not erupt more often?). Such explanations use the mantle of irrationality to cover up the concrete, well-planned, freely chosen actions of leaders and ordinary people alike. Most scholars of the Holocaust, for example, have refused to enter such paths of reasoning and have observed that "Nazism cannot be explained as a reversion to an uncivilized or barbarian state" (Kressel 1993, 185).

Another important psychological explanation of people's participation in violence states that, with the right justification, nearly all people would be willing to obey orders to severely harm other people. This has been called the "normality thesis," for it argues that "people who would not ordinarily be decribed as unusual, deviant, sick, mentally ill, or pathological are capable of committing acts of unrestrained violence and evil" if told to do so by legitimate authorities (Miller 1986, 185). It is the almost exact opposite of the previous explanation, which attributed mass participation in violence to irrational, primitive, dark forces. The experiments on obedience by Stanley Milgram (1974; for an excellent analysis of the impact of his work, see Miller 1986) are the most famous in this area. This approach, which stresses the importance of situational factors such as social pressure, obedience to authority, compliance, and social organization, is similar to Hannah Arendt's famous "banality of evil" theory in which ordinary people participate in genocides because they are small parts in the machine controlled and organized from above (Arendt 1963; see also Kressel 1993, 29, 187; Kelman and Hamilton 1993; Miller 1986, chap. 7). Du Preez (1994, 86, 90) stated it eloquently:

> Perhaps the most extraordinary fact about the psychology of genocide is that there is no need to search for abnormality. Genocide is the work of perfectly normal and ordinary people. . . . It has never been necessary to empty the lunatic asylums in order to recruit people for pogroms or genocides or holy wars.

Arguments along these lines have often been applied to Rwanda, usually in conjunction with explanation based on elite manipulation. It is said that the monarchist, unquestioning, obedient, or conformist nature of the Rwandan traditional mentality made Rwandans especially inclined to follow orders from above, including to slaughter their neighbors (Cart 1995, 468, 473; Voyame and others 1996, 99–100). A slightly different argument states that Rwanda's farmers have not changed much over the generations, and they still crave the sense of order and security that strict vertical structures of authority have always provided. For that reason, they killed when told to do so (Erny 1994, 91, 109, 165 ff.; Gourevitch 1995, 84, 93; Prunier 1995, 57). A Human Rights Watch (1995, 17–18) study described the killings in exactly these terms: "In Kibirira they [the officials] told Hutu to kill their Tutsi neighbors to fulfill their umuganda obligation for the month. . . . Just as authorities began the violence, so they could stop it. In Kibirira they sent two policemen who halted the killings just by blowing their whistles and giving orders to disperse."

This explanation is popular, for it combines generality with expediency. It was equally popular, it should be noted, for explaining (away) the Holocaust (Goldhagen 1996, 11, 116 ff., 383). At first sight, and as seen by an outsider, the facts seem to bear this vision out: most Rwandans *do* act in a less forthright and extroverted manner than, say, most Americans; the public administration structure *is* built in a vertical and all-encompassing mold; obedience and respect for authority *do* seem to be crucial parts of Rwandans' daily lives. This allows people to present these similarities as proofs of the hypothesis that centuries-old mentalities of obedience underlay the genocide.

Yet, explaining the genocide by arguing that Rwandans are tradition-ally inclined to great obedience is fundamentally wrong. To begin with, in the context of the genocide—which was executed largely by Hutu people—this presentation of Rwandans as obedient and docile bears a dangerously close resemblence to one of the crucial elements of the mythical imagery of racism: the old myths of the Hutu as obedient and docile and the Tutsi as commandeering and cunning (Malkki 1995, 99; Chrétien and others 1995). Moreover, this type of explanation is vague and contradictory: anybody can "discover" any supposed traditional character trait to "explain" the genocide. Thus, at the same time that Rwandans are described as obedient and docile, they are also described as distrustful, lying, and dissimulating (see Cart 1995, 468, for exam-ples)—features that seem quite contradictory. In my discussions with Rwandans, I have heard many similar, and always contradictory, expla-nations: the Rwandans have a tradition of brutal regulation of conflict, there is a centuries-old tradition of father killing, and so forth. The vagueness and generality of these explanations tend to make them tan-tamount to absolutions, rather than explanations, of the genocide—and that is the context in which they are often used.

The Rwandan culture, like many other cultures in the world, values the nonexpresssion of disagreement, but that is not the same as saying that all Rwandans are obedient by nature, and it certainly does not explain mass murder. Rwandans are pefectly capable of not following orders, as the many rooted-out coffee plants, the not-adopted agricul-tural techniques, and the nonattended communal meetings attest. They are capable of protesting authority, as the rapidly growing opposition to the Habyarimana regime by the 1990s indicates. Rwandans are also capable of judging their acts and possess moral systems; they are not devoid of moral values.

The main problem with all the psychological explanations pre-sented—the banality of evil thesis, or its opposite, the irrationality, pathological one—is that they are overly general and undetermined, with little explanatory power. For these reasons, most social scientists have concluded that psychological factors play no role in the explanation of large-scale phenomena such as genocides (Jonassohn 1992)—a tradition dating back at least to Emile Durkheim's injunction a century ago that social facts must be explained by other social facts, not psychological ones (Ross 1993, 52, 180). Moreover, in the specific context of discussions on the genocide in Rwanda, many of these explanations have the side effect of removing all blame from the organizers and the perpetrators, for either uncontrollable, irrational forces overtook Rwanda like a dark storm, sweeping away all resistance, or all people in general are capable of engaging in genocide if told to do so, especially if they have an obedient traditional culture (which could be said of many of the world's peoples).

Yet, while asserting that explanations that rely solely on general statements about people's psychological attributes are reductionist and simplistic, it seems wrong to exclude psychological factors entirely from the analysis. The motivations and emotions of people engaged in genocides must be of a particular nature. In other words, there is a social-psychological component in answering the question why ordinary people—individuals with families, religious beliefs, values, and ideals—are willing to set aside the norms against cruelty and murder and to slaughter innocent, unarmed children, women, and men. I believe that these factors need to be sought in the level of frustration and alienation in a society in which structural violence is widespread and in the sociopsychological racist imagery already discussed in Chapter 2.

We saw how, in Rwanda, basic psychocultural images of the Tutsi and the Hutu have been a prime element of society for decades. These profound images treat Hutu and Tutsi as radically and unchangeably different, in their history as well as in their character and their moral, intellectual, and social attributes and roles. Even those who deliberately seek to avoid racism, those who advocate power sharing, those who are opposed to violence, have to position themselves in relation to these basic images, deal with them, and refer to them.

This racism lay dormant for more than a decade, meaning that it was less visible, less of a priority to people, less needed by both those in power and the masses—but not that it was abandoned. Prejudice toward a group can exist without showing itself in day-to-day behavior toward all members of that group; it can even exist while allowing exceptions for specific people (Duckitt 1992–93; Gamson 1995, 11; this is also Goldhagen's controversial 1996 argument). It was reactivated in the 1990s through hate speech and sporadic violence against Tutsi, rendering the Tutsi "socially dead." Its rapid reactivation is testimony to its widespread and profoundly ingrained nature, even during the first fifteen years of the Habyarimana regime.

In the 1990s, this ideology radicalized, leading to the genocide that began on April 7, 1994. This process of radicalization fed on two basic forces: one emanating from government and the elites, and one from the needs of ordinary people. Both these processes were necessary to create genocide. For decades, anti-Tutsi racism had served as a deliberately maintained strategy of legitimization of the powers that be and was kept alive through a systematic public structure of discrimination and education, in which the different and problematic identity of all Tutsi was constantly being referred to. Under threat by political and economic processes, parts of the elite increased their use of the old strategy and effectively spread it throughout society. This had been done before (in 1959 and 1973), and it still worked because so little had changed in Rwanda.

At the same time, racist prejudice was a means for ordinary people, subject to structural violence and humiliation, to make sense of their predicament, to explain their ever-growing misery through projection and scapegoating. The state-supplied racism provided poor Hutu with a sense of value, as well as an "explanation" for the maldevelopment they faced daily. As Simpson and Yinger (1953, 83) stated in their seminal work on prejudice: "the designation of inferior groups comes from those on top—an expression of their right to rule—as well as from frustrated persons often near the bottom, as an expression of their need for security."

Psychologists have documented how the designation of inferior groups, and their more or less active exclusion, serves important functions of projection and scapegoating. Marc Ross (1993, 178), who was quoted at length in Chapter 2, adds:

> These shared images of the world and plans for action are predicated on a common perception of the differences between one's own group and outsiders. The interpretative processes involved in intense conflict situations emphasizes the homogeneity of each party, often using minor objective differences to mark major social distinctions. Outsiders then can serve as objects for externalization, displacement, and projection of intense negative feelings, which are also present but denied within the group.

Ervin Staub, one the foremost psychologists to have studied "the roots of evil," similarly describes in detail how devaluation of others and scapegoating are strategies for coping with the stress of persistent life problems, frustration, and lack of self-esteem (Staub 1989, chap. 3; Staub 1990).

Sociologists use different terms to describe similar processes. At the end of the nineteenth century, Durkheim, studying suicide, coined the term *anomie*, or normlessness, referring to a condition of instability resulting from a breakdown of standards and values or from a lack of purpose or ideals. The concept has remained important in sociology, both at the level of societies and at the level of individuals, referring in the latter case to a personal sense of rootlessness or the breakdown of an individual's sense of attachment to society (Srole 1956). Robert Merton (1968) found that anomie is greatest in the United States in persons who do not have acceptable means of achieving their cultural goals, leading to crime, delinquency, and suicide. Elwin Powell (1970) describes how anomie leads to war and violence against outsiders as a means of reducing anxiety and promoting social cohesion. Among the components of anomie (defined as a breakdown of an individual's sense of attachment to society), sociologist Leo Srole distinguished political powerlessness, social powerlessness, the experience of socioeconomic regression, loss of a sense of life's meaningfulness, and social isolation (Srole 1956; see also Merton 1968, 218). These are precisely the processes discussed earlier.

Additional Factors of Importance

There is a set of other factors that contributed to the genocide in Rwanda. These factors are complementary; that is, they did not by themselves supply sufficient dynamics to cause the genocide, but they added to the previously described processes. I discuss four such factors here: opportunism, the effects of past occurrences of violence, the absence of external constraints, and the colonial legacy.

The first one, quite often discussed in the literature, is opportunism, or the search for personal gain. Whenever violence seems to be a socially acceptable option, some people will join in to appropriate someone else's money, possessions, or land. This argument has often been invoked for the case of Rwanda. In Kigali, during the height of the genocide, massive looting of government offices, international aid agencies, and businesses took place. André and Platteau (1995, 34–35), in their excellent study of a commune in northern Rwanda, demonstrate how all the Hutu who were killed there during the genocide (only one

Tutsi woman lived in the village, and she was murdered too) tended to be either the wealthier ones or social outcasts, suggesting that "the 1994 events provided a unique opportunity to settle scores or to reshuffle land properties." More generally, quite a few people have mentioned land grabbing as one reason for participation in the genocide, and even as a cause of it, although none supplied any proof of this statement (Kabirigi 1994, 4; Reyntjens 1994, 192). And Claudine Vidal (1985, 168), discussing the 1972–73 violence in Rwanda, mentions "suivisme et opportunisme" and racism as major factors.

The personal gain motive was apparent for militia members, who, in both Burundi and Rwanda, were at the forefront of the radicalization and the killing. The main militia operating in Burundi in 1995, for example, emanated from a number of urban gangs that used to be biethnic but became monoethnic and better equipped after the 1993 unrest (Cros 1995; Dans un maquis hutu 1995). In Rwanda too, it seems that many of the youth gangs that worked with or for the militias, and eventually became one with them, were originally no more than gangs of small-time criminals, young thugs who worked for the highest bidder (Nayigizente 1995, 46). For them, little changed, apart from marching behind a different banner. They were still out to loot and steal and did so with great regularity and impunity.

However, the importance of opportunism and the desire for enrichment should not be overestimated. For opportunism to exist, there must be a process of violence into which opportunists can insert themselves and do their dirty work; opportunism, by definition, cannot be the primary explanation for the process (Goldhagen 1996, 382). As Du Preez (1994, 35) rightly says, "one should not imagine that genocide is purely practical. It requires a great vision to justify a great wrong." Moreover, it is an explanation that is situated at the level of people's motives and, as such, is hard to verify or falsify. In the case of Rwanda, with the exception of the studies by André and Platteau (1995) and Longman (1995b), we do not possess the microdata necessary to test it. Thus we run the risk of adopting this explanation simply because it seems plausible and convenient. Indeed, Feagin and Hahn (1973, 127 ff.) point out that urban violence in the 1960s and 1970s in the United States has often been explained by similar factors—they mention the so-called riffraff theory and the wild youngsters theory—without any proof apart from its political convenience. Hence, we can conclude that opportunism played a role but is not the crucial dynamic in the genocide.

Another factor that seems relevant to explaining mass participation in genocide in Rwanda is the dynamics set in motion by past occurrences of violence. As the saying goes, violence begets violence. Once a serious episode of violent conflict occurs, it leaves a persistent residue in people's memories and attitudes. For a long time afterward, it can be invoked by leaders to justify political action (Gurr 1993, 126–27). This works through four mechanisms, involving both the victims and the executors of violence.

Acts of violence have psychological consequences for the people and groups that commit them as well as for those at whom they are directed. The more violent a group has been against another group, the more it needs to justify that violence to itself, seeking to balance those acts with its self-perception of being moral and right.[1] Moroever, on a practical level, perpetrators of violence come to fear revenge and may have to engage in all kinds of behaviors, including so-called preventive attack, to defend themselves.[2] This explanation is more important if the society is characterized by widespread impunity, as both Burundi and Rwanda are.

Moving to the victims' side, psychologists have observed a strong relation between victimization and the commission of violence. In other words, people who have been victims of violence or close witnesses of it, especially during childhood, tend to repeat the same behavioral patterns throughout their lives (McKendrick and Hoffmann 1990, 471). For adults, victimhood—especially if the perpetrator goes unpunished—weakens the institutions and norms that counter violence. It is easier to justify violence against a person or group who has used violence against oneself—or, taking the October 1990 invasion as the starting point of our story, who has instigated violence. Without the FPR invasion, the Habyarimana regime would in all likelihood have fallen slowly, under a combination of internal and external pressure, and the genocide would not have taken place—which is not to say that Rwanda would have been a democratic, peaceful place. The October 1990 invasion by the FPR was the ideal occasion for the government to recreate its legitimacy, to unite part of the population around itself, and to increase the level of violence, fear, and control in society.

In the case of Rwanda, there is an important twist to the "violence begets violence" argument: namely, the dynamics between Rwanda and Burundi. Indeed, the destructive, mirrorlike situation of these two countries is unique and has dramatic effects. Both countries represent each other's worst fears, and events in one country are interpreted and used by its (radical) neighbors to confirm their worst suspicions and fears. The rulers in Rwanda have been able to reinforce the "truth" of their racist ideology by pointing to the massacres of Hutu (by the Tutsi-dominated army) in Burundi in 1965, 1972, 1988, 1989, and 1993, "proving" that all Tutsi seek the ruthless oppression of the Hutu. Vice versa, Tutsi rulers in Burundi have pointed since 1960 to Rwanda's example to demonstrate that, if given the chance, all Hutu are out to kill them. Although these occurrences of violence along ethnic lines may have been no more than part of a strategy of aspiring elites to conquer or maintain power, they became a traumatic part of the culture of prejudice in both countries. In the words of Volkan (1994, xxv; see also Bar-Tal 1990), "the group draws the mental representation of a traumatic event *into its very identity*. It passes the mental representation of the event—along with associated shared feelings of hurt and shame, and defenses against the perceived shared conflicts they initiate—from generation to generation." Moreover, the most radical elements of both sides tended to seek refuge in the neighboring country (as well as Zaire, Tanzania, Kenya, and Uganda), where they sought to destabilize the neighbor's government. Hence, more than any other place in the world, these two countries are caught in a mutually reinforcing mirror of violence and prejudice.

A third element that contributed to the genocide is the absence of external constraints. One of the three factors that promote genocide, according to Harff (1987, 43), is the "lack of external constraints on murderous regimes."[3] Helen Fein (1993, 86, 99) has shown that most governments committing mass violence are repeat offenders, partly because they saw that their previous uses of violence were condoned by the international community. Along the same lines, Physicians for Human Rights (1994) argues that "the massacres were used by government officials to settle political scores for which no one has ever been punished: the international community viewed them as an internal affair and the government was never likely to punish that which it had ordered." What we are talking about, then, is an internationalized form of impunity.

In the case of the Rwandan genocide, this factor was very important. The carnage in Burundi in 1993 had shown the Rwandan leadership that the international community, lip service to democracy and human rights notwithstanding, would not intervene if massive violence were used to reverse democratic change. The recent case of Somalia also demonstrated that the international community would quit any country immediately if only a few of its peacekeepers were hurt; for that reason, the killing of ten Belgian peacekeepers was one of the first actions on April 7, 1994. And the total absence of any condemnation during the first few days and even weeks of the genocide—including the infamous Clinton administration memo forbidding officials to use the term *genocide*—gave the interim government the clearest possible signal that it could continue the genocide without being bothered.

There is one more factor that needs to be taken into consideration. Although it cannot be said to have caused the genocide or even contributed to it in any direct manner, it is crucial to understanding Rwanda and the dynamics that eventually led to genocide. That factor is the colonial legacy, and it affects our subject matter in many ways. We cannot understand the nature of ethnicity in Rwanda without understanding the practice of indirect rule. The differences between Hutu and Tutsi in all likelihood were not created ex nihilo by the colonizer, but indirect rule and the associated ideology of racial superiority have had lasting consequences on the nature of social relations in the postcolonial state.

The nature of Rwanda's political system is also largely a continuation of colonial practice. The centralizing, omnipresent state—with its administrative complexity, its top-down functioning, and its control over the bulk of distributional benefits in the country—as well as the restrictions on the expression of political demands and the lack of democracy, are continuations of colonial practice. In Rwanda, as in so many other colonies, the colonial state served the interests of one ethnic group, the Bazungu, and ethnic division was used by the Bazungu to strengthen their rule (Nevitte and Kennedy 1986).

The colonial legacy also shows up in the economic policies followed by independent Rwanda and the way the interaction between the state and its citizens was structured. In Rwanda's dependence on coffee and tea exports; its top-down, constraining, and condescending extension system; its *umuganda* system; and the specific techniques proposed to fight erosion, contemporary Rwanda bears a close resemblance to colonial Rwanda (World Bank 1987, 4; Willame, 1995a, 113). To a certain extent, this can be explained by arguing that it makes sense, given Rwanda's constraints (that is, one could argue for example that the system of living hedges introduced by the colonizer is the best thing to do and thus needs to be continued). To a larger extent, however, this is the result of the constraints imposed by colonial legacy, which limited the margin for maneuver of the new power holders—all the more so in countries that were desperately poor, with almost no educated leadership. Like anywhere, the combination of inertia, habit, and the vested interest that some have in the status quo is hard to overcome. It is symptomatic, for that matter, that, over the years, the foreign aid system has not proposed anything radically different from a continuation of colonial policy either. The top-down extension system, the dependence on a few cash crops, did not seem to bother it unduly.

To understand the genocide, then, three elements are necessary: the anomie and frustration caused by the long-standing condition of structural violence; the strategies of manipulation by elites under threat from economic and political processes; and the existence of a sociopsychological, widespread attachment to racist values in society. It is the specific interaction of these three processes that allowed the genocide to occur in Rwanda.

Four other factors are of secondary importance; they contributed to the genocide but did not cause it directly. Foremost among them is the occurrence of past violence, both in Rwanda and in Burundi. The others are opportunism, the absence of external constraints, and the colonial legacy. Virtually all these factors far predate the 1990s. Many of them involve the international community. This is what I turn to in the final chapter.

Notes

1. See Bar-Tal 1990 and Warren 1993, 9, writing about people's "struggles to make sense of their own violence." See also Lauer 1989; Striker 1992, chap. 5 for the case of South Africa.
2. This explanation is very important for understanding the dynamics of current violence in Burundi. (See Uvin forthcoming; Archer n.d.); for the case of the Armenian genocide, Libaridian (1987, 210–11) describes how "previous occurrences of victimization make the Armenians more dangerous in the eyes of the powerholders." In general, see Fein 1993, 99.
3. The other two factors are structural change (a necessary but not sufficient condition) and sharp internal cleavages combined with a history of struggle between groups.

11

DEVELOPMENT AID:
CONCLUSIONS AND PATHS
FOR REFLECTION

In this chapter, I begin by recapitulating the answers to the basic question of this book: what was the role of development aid in the processes that led to genocide in Rwanda (processes analyzed in the previous chapter)? Two very different answers to this question coexist, and I discuss the implications of this ambiguous situation. In the rest of this chapter, I deal with a few broad themes that have emerged from the analysis, centering around the political nature of development; human rights, democracy, and civil society; and political conditionality. Occasionally, I outline some suggestions for change. This chapter does not, however, contain a consultant list of recommendations; the kind of changes required are, in my mind, too fundamental to be described in a short list of doable recommendations. Moreover, any such changes should emerge from discussions among the people concerned, including both development practitioners and the poor themselves.

The Dual Role of Aid

Parts II and III of this book dealt with different time periods and different types of violence, yet both were intimately connected to the 1994 genocide. Part II explained the recent political and economic processes that precipitated the genocide. It discussed the many faces of acute violence: civil war, arbitrary imprisonment, mob violence, pogroms against the Bagogwe and Tutsi, hate speech, and the militarization of society. Through this crescendo of acute violence, the Tutsi as a category were dehumanized, and violence against them was routinized, culminating in the genocide in which hundreds of thousands of innocent people were killed in a few months, merely for being of the wrong ethnic group. Part III documented the existence of structural violence, a much more long-standing and often invisible situation of inequality, exclusion, and humiliation, in which millions of people were deprived of their dreams, opportunities, and self-respect. I argued that the concept of structural violence provided one part of the puzzle necessary for understanding the 1994 genocide. In both these parts, I analyzed the role of foreign aid. From this analysis, two quite different images, or realities, of development aid emerged.

THE USUAL IMAGE OF FOREIGN AID

The first image is the most common and most easily understandable; it is associated with Part II of this book. In this image, development aid is external, whereas the political processes that caused the genocide—civil war, competition for power, racism, ideological radicalization, militarization, human rights violations—are internal. Starting from this image, the debate usually becomes about the capacity and desirability of *foreign* aid to *intervene* in what are considered *domestic* political issues.

Typically, the discussion then turns to the issue of political conditionality. Can foreign aid influence domestic political processes in recipient countries? Should it try to do so? If so, what tools are available to do that? When should aid be cut? These questions have recently been asked not only about Rwanda but also about many developing countries in Africa and Asia. The answers tend to be careful and rather minimalistic. Aid has little leverage or capacity to steer domestic political processes in different directions, and if it does attempt to do so, this often produces distorted, partial results (Uvin 1993; Uvin and Biagiotti 1996).

These answers seem relevant for the case for Rwanda too. It has been said that cutting development aid in the early 1990s could have been counterproductive, for it could have decreased foreign agencies' leverage with the government or hurt the chances for democratization to take place. Yet Chapter 5 documented that on the two occasions when the international community did put pressure on the Rwandan government to end human rights violations, the government *did* change its behavior, at least temporarily. Others have suggested, however, that this international pressure together with the forced negotiations in Arusha, may have radicalized certain factions within Rwanda even further, pushing them to increasingly radical actions to preserve their power and privileges. Clearly, there is no easy answer to this issue; I will come back to it later.

AID AND THE STATE: TWO
SIDES OF THE SAME COIN

The second image of development aid emerges out of Part III of this book. From this perspective, development aid interacts in manifold and important ways with profound social processes of inequality, exclusion, humiliation, impunity, and despair, on which the genocidal edifice was built. What emerges is a picture of Rwanda as a country where foreign aid is so important that it is nearly impossible, or meaningless, to separate it from the socioeconomic and political processes that take place domestically. For decades, foreign aid contributed to structural violence both directly and indirectly, through action and inaction, through its mode of functioning and its ideology. The reach of the state, the survival and reproduction of the elite, the unfolding of the processes of exclusion, inequality, and humiliation are all so intertwined with the presence of foreign aid—and in some cases, impossible to envision without foreign aid—that any separation between them is artificial if not meaningless. This point merits further explanation.

The case of Rwanda shows how difficult it is to grasp with any degree of exactness the relative importance of the foreign aid system and the state system in the construction of the processes of exclusion, inequality, and structural violence. On the one hand, the foreign aid system has a discourse that privileges the laudable (albeit often conflicting) objectives of poverty reduction, popular participation, capacity building, and non-intervention. Projects are justified on the grounds that they implement the government's overall development policies and strengthen its capacities to promote sustainable development; great care is taken to avoid any impression of lack of respect for the government's sovereignty.

On the other hand, the donor community is clearly not a passive reflection or a powerless appendix of the government. Being responsible for as much as 80 percent of the total investment budget of the government, as well as a significant fraction of its current (operating) budget, the donor community's influence is large. There is no way that the government could implement any policy, coherent or not, without the assistance of the foreign aid community; as a matter of fact, there is no way that significant parts of the government bureaucracy could even exist without international aid. In countries such as Rwanda and many other African countries, development aid is the fuel that allows the government machinery to exist, to expand, to control, to implement.

Donor governments often use the resulting influence for a variety of purposes: to modify specific project objectives, to acquire personnel changes, to support the adoption of structural adjustment, or, more recently, to push through changes in the mode of governance in recipient countries. The fact that donor governments choose not to use this influence for certain purposes does not mean that it does not exist. This influence is even stronger at the level of the state class, the group that largely sets, executes, and benefits from public policy. As most aid ends up with the upper crust in the cities—in the form of training, salaries, per diems, transportation, and entrepreneurial income—the elite could not live its lifestyle, make its money, buy its consumption products, and so forth without the support of the aid system.

Moreover, it can easily be said that the government's policies in fields such as agricultural development, environmental protection, health, or urban development amounted to little more than the sum total of the projects implemented in that sector. And in this case, unlike in the gestalt theory, the total is definitely *not* more than the sum of the parts. There are literally hundreds of projects in Rwanda, and by and large, they make their own interpretations of the government's policies and how to implement them.[1] They hire their own people, pay salaries that differ from the government's salary caps, privilege their own specific approaches and goals, and so forth. Often, key people in the government have only the vaguest idea of the precise goals, budgets, or outcomes of projects under their responsibility. Similarly, the sectors that foreign aid neglects—in Rwanda, for example, the strengthening of justice systems, the reintegration of refugees, or the promotion of civil society through education for peace and human rights (Cart 1995, 482)—look very different from those that it concentrates on.

At the end of the day, the outcomes described earlier are the result of neither foreign aid being forced to accept such modalities by powerful and untouchable governments nor innocent governments being unwillingly dragged into this by the financial powerhouse of the aid agencies. They are truly the outcome of the interactions between both—one integrated system in which external and internal forces intermesh profoundly, where it makes little sense to seek to discover the original sin. Peasants know this: they make no distinction between the aid system and the state system—in Burundi, farmers lump them both together under the name *Leta*, "the state" in Kirundi. As Ngwabije (1995, 39) observed, for the farmers, both the state and the aid system seem identical and equally remote from their concerns and lives. This was directly experienced by the many technical assistants who were ill received by farmers in places where the latter considered themselves hurt by the state.

In the image just described, aid is deeply and inherently political—not only when it seeks to influence political matters (as in the first image), but by definition, for it profoundly influences and is influenced by the distribution of scarce resources in society. From this perspective, also, the distinctions between internal and external factors that were so evident in the first image become problematic. The policies and institutions that led to structural violence cannot be separated from international aid, and vice versa. Domestic politics are inseparable from external aid; foreign aid is constitutive of domestic processes.

COULD AND SHOULD AID
HAVE ACTED DIFFERENTLY?

Both these divergent images are correct at the same time. In other words, *aid is at the same time external to the political processes that caused the genocide and constituent of them.* This conclusion has some fascinating implications for the concept of sovereignty, the cornerstone of the contemporary international political system; however, developing these is not my aim here. Rather, I wish to analyze in more detail what this means for development aid and for the international community's capacities and obligations to influence domestic political processes in developing contries.

In the case of the genocide, one can ask two sets of questions, related to the two images or realities. One set deals with the way development aid influenced the processes of preparation for a genocide in the 1990s. The second set relates to foreign aid's participation in the processes of structural violence that provided an important part of the social basis on which genocide rested. Typically, for both these issues, one can ask four related questions: Did aid seek to impact these processes, presumably to halt them? Did aid have an impact on these processes without intending to do so? Should aid have gone about this matter differently? And could aid have done so?

The answers to the first set of questions, dealing with the preparation for acute violence in the 1990s, must start from the observation that it is difficult and quite artificial to separate the aid enterprise from the broader foreign relations between Rwanda and the Western countries; the behavior of France is especially important—and reprehensible—here. As to the first question—did aid seek to stop the genocidal processes in the 1990s?—it is clear that the development aid milieu did not react much at all to the human rights abuses, racism, and militarization of society that were constitutive elements of the drive to genocide, and neither did the international diplomatic community. The latter did, however, put significant effort into promoting democratization and peace in Rwanda, although it was unwilling to commit itself to much, as the UNAMIR history shows. As to the second question—did aid impact the processes in the 1990s without seeking to do so?—the military and diplomatic support to the regime by some countries, as well as the general passivity toward the rights abuses, racism, and militarization inside the country by the entire international community, undoubtedly facilitated if not encouraged the forces of genocide to reach their final conclusion. The fact that the development business continued as usual while government-sponsored human rights violations were on the rise sent a clear signal that the international community did not care too much about the racially motivated and publicly organized slaughter of citizens. Note that the cases of Burundi, where such slaughter had taken place a few months before, and Serbia, where the international community substituted relief for political action, only added fuel to this belief. But aid did not create these forces, nor, it must be admitted, were they easily controllable.

This brings us to the third question: should aid have acted differently when faced with the preparation for the genocide in the 1990s? Most Western aid agencies are legally obliged to act when faced with grave and systematic human rights violations, and their discourse at the time—after the end of the cold war—suggested that human rights matters had moved to the top of the agenda.[2] Clearly, this was not the case in Rwanda, and this is one more instance in which rhetoric and practice differ markedly. However, the international community may have considered that its support for democratization and peace was sufficient to end the human rights violations and the racism. This may have seemed a reasonable assumption to most of the people involved, especially before 1994, when the possibility of genocide was truly unthinkable.

The fourth question—could aid have positively influenced the processes that led to genocide had it sought to do so?—immediately brings us to the issue of political conditionality. On the one hand, on the few occasions that the international community used its leverage to force change from the Rwandan government, it was quite successful. In 1991, most arbitrarily arrested Tutsi were released, and in 1993, human rights violations subsided for some months. Seemingly, the Rwandan government felt vulnerable because of its tarnished image and was capable of being influenced by international threats. On the other hand, even highly aid-dependent Third World governments have relative political, economic, and ideological autonomy from the external actors on which they depend for financial survival. If the international community had used aid conditionality to wrestle more than small concessions from the Rwandan government, it is by no means sure that it would have been successful. In all likelihood, the president would have made promises that he was unwilling to honor. Another possibility, to be seriously considered in the case of Rwanda, is that even if the president or the prime minister had truly wished to act in accordance with international desires to stop racism, militarization, or human rights abuses, it is not sure that he or she would have been successful; the clique of people behind the scenes who masterminded the genocide were probably uncontrollable by any one person, including the president. Knowing all that, one could concur that there were good arguments for employing political conditionality only sparingly in Rwanda. Political conditionality is a two-edged sword, difficult to handle and with uncertain results.

However, besides the use of negative conditionality, the international community can employ other instruments to influence social processes in recipient countries. The development aid agencies could have continued to assist the Rwandan population toward development but adapted their goals, strategies, and allocations to the new realities and challenges the country faced. In the 1990s, it seems, these challenges were rapidly becoming those of violence, hatred, manipulation, conflict, human rights abuses, and militarization. New projects could have been started to intervene in these factors, or existing projects could have been reoriented to take more account of them. This is not necessarily easy to do— indeed, there are no clear-cut, pre-packaged solutions to these challenges —but it was imperative to try. Faced with the disintegration of Rwandese society, the development community should have tried to rethink its mission and reorient its actions. It did not do so.

The second set of questions deals with development aid's role in structural violence. The answer to the first question—did aid seek to stop the processes of structural violence that existed long before the 1990s?—is negative. As I documented in detail, most development aid shared these biases, was blind to them, or did not consider them serious enough to warrant profound changes in the way the development game was played. The second question—did aid impact structural violence without intending to do so?—must be answered strongly affirmatively. In a nutshell, my analysis has shown that aid financed much of the machinery of exclusion, inequality, and humiliation; provided it with legitimacy and support; and sometimes directly contributed to it. To their credit, some aid agencies—some nongovernmental organizations (NGOs) foremost among them—may have had different impacts; they may have softened some parts of the crises faced by ordinary Rwandans. Yet, by and large, aid was an active and willing partner in the construction of structural violence in Rwanda, as it is elsewhere in Africa.

The third question asks whether aid should have acted differently. I personally believe so, and others, such as Robert Chambers (1995) have made strong arguments in favor of change. The notion of "development" defined as economic growth, mainly at the macro level, is meaningless if it can coincide with increases in inequality, disempowerment, alienation, violence, and frustration. It seems to me that the study of Rwanda makes one more strong case for a broadening of the concept of development, one that includes eradication of the features of structural violence discussed in Part III. Intellectually, this is not a new project (see Nussbaum and Sen 1993), and to a certain extent, aid agencies pay lip service to it, but its practical, operational implications have still not been well understood. Here lies an important area for further reflection by development practitioners.

The fourth question—could aid have acted differently regarding the processes of structural violence in Rwanda?—is harder to answer, for the problem is not one of development aid to Rwanda solely but of the whole development enterprise. Indeed, the mechanisms through which aid interacted with structural violence, and the blindness to its consequences, are profoundly ingrained in the institutional, ideological, and political fundaments of the development enterprise. Aid behaves in much the same way throughout Africa (and in other poor and weak countries), with largely the same effects. Any change is thus bound to be a fundamental matter, with major implications for all players concerned, going beyond the specific case of Rwanda. Change has to be about a different vision of what development is, how it is achieved, and the place of the poor in it. Such a vision can be constructed, and a number of people have made major contributions to it, but its widespread adoption in practice is still a major challenge. In the next pages, I make a few points that emerged from the analysis I made in this book and that may constitute parts of such a new vision for development practice.

The Politics of Development Interventions

One of the foremost conclusions of this book is that all development aid constitutes a form of political intervention. This holds as much for bilateral and multilateral aid as for nongovernmental development aid. It is also the case at all levels, from the central government to the local community. Ethnic and political amnesia does not make development aid and the processes it sets in motion apolitical; it just renders these processes invisible.

This has manifold effects, which go far beyond those expected. It leads to project or program failure, that is, to projects or programs not achieving their stated objectives, or doing so only in a limited and unsustainable fashion. But it does more: it creates other outcomes that are often unrecognized. In other words, its effects are not only the failure to achieve progress but also the creation of new dynamics that may act as brakes on future progress, if not actually promote regression. They do so by providing opportunities for arbitrariness and illegality; by strengthening ethnic, regional, or social inequality; or by reinforcing the humiliation and dehumanization brought about by authoritarian, top-down, controlling development agencies. Apolitical development is not only ineffective but also oppressive and often regressive. This is becoming increasingly recognized in the development community, and the case of Rwanda has contributed to that (it did exactly the same to the relief community in 1994–97, but that is another matter). Many people involved in Rwanda, both foreigners and locals, told me that this is one of the prime lessons they learned from the Rwandan catastrophe.

While many may share this diagnostic, things become more difficult when we seek to draw operational lessons. If all aid is political, how should the aid enterprise be managed so as to take account of this and to promote optimal outcomes? Should development agencies become players in the political arena of recipient countries? Should aid agencies support candidates for political office? This seems far-fetched and undesirable. What concrete consequences follow, then, from the notion that all aid, all development, is political?

I can see three levels of consequences. The lowest level is that we must analyze, and be aware of, the political nature of any development intervention and seek to design interventions in such a way as to maximize the chances of political processes being beneficial to the poor and the excluded. Blindness to politics often achieves the inverse result and hurts those we seek to help. The philosophical basis of such a change could be the rediscovery of solidarity, rather than technocracy, as the foundation for action by aid agencies and the people working for them. This is probably easiest to accomplish for NGOs and least likely for international organizations, with bilateral agencies falling in between, but *all* have room for improvement.

At the intermediate level, the consequence is an increase in the allocation of development resources to what used to be called "political development," involving widespread and appropriate information about democracy and human rights; strengthening of the free press; the initiation of conflict-resolution as well as compromise and peace-building initiatives; support to civil society organizations beyond their service-delivery functions; work with the judicial system, bar associations, police forces, and legal defense organizations; and the application of consistent human rights standards to all development projects and programs. Democracy building and human rights improvements are by no means easy areas, but neither is promoting economic growth; I return to this later.

At the highest level, the consequence is the integration of foreign policy into the development toolbox, together with financial support and technical advice. It means putting foreign policy at the service of development considerations, "moralizing foreign policy." There are two major difficulties with this. First, it seems fraught with ethical dangers: who are we to define political or social morality for other countries? I disagree with that position of cultural relativity, no matter how sympathetic I am to its overall undercurrent of respect for social differences. The act of providing aid—in the case of Rwanda, in such amounts that we could call it the act of helping regimes and public institutions to survive—is, by definition, a political one. Blindness means acquiescence to values and behaviors that are often inimical to our goals and unacceptable to our values, as well as not conducive to development. Development is not a neutral, apolitical, technical matter. We make political choices, in our own societies and elsewhere, and the development enterprise is no exception to that rule. In the field of development cooperation, these choices may be difficult to define or implement, but we cannot be absolved from making them by pretending that they do not exist.

The second problem is that many people within the development community fear the imposition of foreign policy objectives on development programs by people with limited knowledge of conditions on the ground and with a vested interest in defending Western powers' economic and strategic interests. It is for this reason that the separation of the development cooperation agencies from the departments of foreign affairs in many countries has been hailed as a victory for development. If one needed any proof of the dangers inherent in linking foreign policy and development establishments, the behavior of France in Rwanda or of the United States during the cold war in Central America should act as a powerful reminder.

Both these objections are valid, but do not fundamentally undermine the argument: if the foreign policies of donor countries are often inimical to development goals, then people committed to development should attempt to modify these policies. This will not happen soon or definitively, but it ought to be a constant goal.

Democratization and Civil Society

The dangers in intervening from the outside in support of political goals such as democracy are perfectly illustrated by the case of Rwanda. The international community's heavy pressure for a rapid peace-plus-democracy settlement in Arusha is considered by many to have been crucial in pushing part of the elite toward extremist solutions. As the negotiation process was the result of external pressure rather than internal realignments of power and interest, significant and powerful groups that would have lost from the negotiations set out to undermine the outcome. Those groups in favor of change were not sufficiently powerful to challenge the former and neutralize them. That, then, is a profound problem with external interference in democratization: it sets in motion processes that go beyond the domestic alignments of power and preference (this is more or less always the case, for if the domestic alignments of power and preference had already changed in favor of democracy, external pressure would not be required). The result may be that powerful groups end up with their backs against the wall, forced to deploy strategies of increasing terror and violence, human rights violations, or manipulation of social divisions. Especially in those cases in which the international community is unwilling to address the latter processes— and doing so is difficult as well as costly, in money and possibly in lives—the end result could be an increase in violence and instability. The case of Rwanda illustrates this problem, but there is more.

We saw that most opposition parties in Rwanda rapidly split into so-called Hutu power wings and moderate wings; all political parties also created militias, and used violence both within the party (between leaders of the two wings, for example) and against outsiders. We also saw how large segments of civil society at large—NGOs, the church, and so forth—adhered to the genocidal values. In other words, adherence to an undemocratic and genocidal ideology and willingness to use violence and human rights abuses in the quest for power were not confined to those who controlled the state. They were widespread among opposition parties as well as civil society organizations. There are two main reasons for this. First, most people within the opposition parties and in civil society at large shared the racist ideology that had been dominant in Rwanda for so long. It was thus easy and logical for them to follow the trend toward radicalization. Second, many of the leaders of these opposition parties or NGOs were more committed to themselves than to any social cause: if racism and genocidal talk were what paid off, they were willing to embrace it. External pressure for democracy and negotiations abroad cannot change these factors; hence, the risk of derailment. In other words, if there is no genuine, popularly-based, clear alternative to the status quo, external pressure for political change may only yield more of the same, or even exacerbate the situation.

Finally, it has been widely observed that the democratization process was of little interest or relevance to the rural masses—the large majority of the population. It was an urban game, with foreign rules and referees (Reyntjens 1994, 221; 1995c). Rural people were badly informed about democratization and cared little about it. More generally, there was little if anything about civil society that represented the interest of the vast majority of the population: the poor, farmers, women, minorities (including the Twa), for example. As we saw, the many NGOs that did exist largely limited their mandate to participating in the development business. The political parties were urban and were mainly vehicles for the power dreams of big men, almost all of them formerly high dignitaries in the Habyarimana regime. Few of the conditions necessary for democracy to take hold in society were united. It is little wonder, then, that the process of democratization degenerated into racial hatred and political manipulation.

External pressure for democratization is thus a risky matter, fraught with difficulties and risks of derailment. This is all the more so when the international community typically displays incoherent, contradictory, partial, and ambiguous behavior and refuses to intervene when it is most needed. In the case of Rwanda, that was very clear. Notwithstanding the well-documented rise in government-sponsored racism and human rights violations, development aid from almost all countries increased, and military support from most countries continued and from at least one increased significantly. When foreign commitments were required to monitor the peace process and protect civilians, UNAMIR failed miserably, never receiving the mandate and the resources required and promised in Arusha. When the democratization process in Burundi was violently halted in September 1993 the international community stood by and did nothing, thus setting a major example for radical elements in Rwanda. Finally, when the genocide began in earnest, the international community evacuated its nationals and looked the other way. It seems reasonable to conclude that the international community's inconsistency and passivity at the very least facilitated the execution of the genocide.

Hence, outside pressure for democracy is a tricky business. It tends to take more time, consistency, knowledge, finesse, and commitment than the international community typically has. It risks setting in motion political and social processes one does not expect or cannot master. If nothing is done about these processes—in other words, if the international community is unwilling to defend the democratic changes it set in motion when they are threatened—the end result may be a much worse situation, as the case of Rwanda shows.

Aid and Political Conditionality

We need to return one more time to the issue of political conditionality, for the picture that has emerged seems inconclusive and unclear. Strong arguments have been advanced on either side of the divide—should and could development aid be used to push for changes in governments' human rights and democracy records, or not?—and no side has emerged victorious. This seems to reflect the state of the debate in the foreign policy and development communities also. However, three important observations have emerged from this case study; they may allow us to better understand the margin for action in conditions like Rwanda's and militate in favor of a redefinition of the development mandate in general.

First, it is important to remember that negative political conditionality was never really implemented in Rwanda; there were few credible threats and even less action to diminish Rwanda's financial lifeline. After all, we should not forget that aid to Rwanda greatly increased during the period under consideration—admittedly for other, unrelated reasons, most notably, structural adjustment. In so doing, the aid system sent a message, however, and it essentially said that, on the level of practice and not discourse, the aid system did not care unduly about political and social trends in the country, not even if they involved government-sponsored racist attacks against Tutsi, many of whom were aid employees or partners. The problem is that we tend to conceptualize our choices as between negative conditionality and the continuation of business as usual. The former is clearly an action fraught with risks and uncertainties, while the latter is perceived to be neutral—amounting to no action at all. That is wrong: the continuation of business as usual *is* a form of action, it *does* send signals, and it *has* an impact on local political and social processes.

In heavily aid-dependent countries like Rwanda, where the lifestyle, income, travel, education, and networks of clientelism of the elite exist by and large with aid's blessings, people look carefully at the actions and inactions, the trends and discourses of the aid system. All of them, including inaction, send messages and constitute political acts. This is not to say that these messages or these acts are all-powerful and or that they directly determine outcomes. Yet they are part of the constraints and opportunities faced by local elites. This argument, then, strongly pleads in favor of political conditionality: although it may not be directly effective in producing the political outcomes desired, it does send signals of disapproval and avoids international complicity.

A second important observation that emerged from this case study relates to the existence of an entirely different set of actions that the international aid community could have undertaken but largely failed to. Faced with the disintegration of Rwandese society and systems of governance, existing projects could have been modified, or new ones created, to attempt to intervene in favor of forces of moderation and compromise, peaceful conflict resolution, human rights education, democracy awareness, political scaling up of NGOs, and so forth. A bit of this did happen, to be sure: some European NGOs financed a few activities in these fields; the U.S. Agency for International Development (USAID) prepared, but did not execute, a project to do so; and the Swiss Development Cooperation agency increased its funding to human rights NGOs.

Yet, all in all, this amounted to no more than 1 percent of all aid, if that. At no point did the aid community sit down and try to fundamentally redefine its mission, goals, and functioning. This, then, is a strong plea in favor of so-called positive conditionality, whereby aid resources are used to strengthen the social and political conditions for improved policies rather than to force governments to adopt such policies. Note that such policies should not be adopted only when society is about to disintegrate in violence but should be an integral part of *all* development aid at all times.

A third observation adds nuance to this. As we saw, there were few strong and well-organized forces of moderation, pluralism, and tolerance in Rwanda. The broad concept of civil society, to which we tend to ascribe many positive functions in promoting these outcomes, did not live up to its expectations (expectations that, as I argued in Chapter 8, were exaggerated) Foreign aid cannot substitute for the presence of internal forces in favor of pluralism, moderation, and tolerance. Worse, under such circumstances, negative conditionality risks producing only Pyrrhic victories and may set in motion unexpected counterprocesses. Yet we know that in Rwanda there were many people, at all levels of society, who would have preferred harmony over hatred, increased popular participation over authoritarian government, peace over war. It is only when their voices are strengthened and organized, when their weight is felt in the political process, that sustainable changes will take place. This, again, pleads in favor of defining all development, and all development aid, in more holistic and political terms, at both the intellectual and the operational level.

Notes

1. Voyame and others 1996, 163, observe that "the content of the projects was largely determined by the technical assistants themselves"—and this in an agency that was more advanced than most in seeking to strengthen local capacity. See also Godding 1983.
2. Since 1974, the U.S. Foreign Assistance Act, for example, specifies that "no assistance may be provided . . . to the government of any country which engages in a consistent pattern of gross violation of internationally recognized human rights." Most European countries added similar clauses to their development aid policies, albeit later. See Uvin and Biagiotti 1996.

BIBLIOGRAPHY

ACORD. 1995. *Politique Stratégique Regionale d'ACORD (Pays des Grands Lacs). Phase II.* N.p.: ACORD.

Adelman, Howard, and Astrid Suhrke. 1996. *Early Warning and Conflict Management.* Vol. 2 of *The International Response to Conflict and Genocide: Lessons from the Rwanda Experience.* Copenhagen: DANIDA.

African Rights. 1994. *Rwanda. Death, Despair and Defiance.* London: African Rights.

Africa Watch, International Federation of Human Rights, InterAfrican Union of Human Rights, and International Center of Rights of the Person and of Democratic Development. 1993. *Report of the International Commission of Investigation of Human Rights Violations in Rwanda since October 1, 1990.* N.p.

Allport, Gordon W. 1954. *The Nature of Prejudice.* New York: Anchor Books.

Amselle, Jean-Loup. 1988. Le Développement Vu du Village. *Sociologia Ruralis* 28, no. 2/3: 176–81.

Anderson, Benedict. 1991. *Imagined Communities.* New York: Verso.

André, Catherine, and Jean-Philippe Platteau. 1995. *Land Tenure under Unendurable Stress: Rwanda Caught in the Malthusian Trap.* Namur, Belgium: University of Namur, Centre de Recherche en Economie du Développement, Faculty of Economics.

Archer, Robert. N.d. *Burundi. Vivre dans la peur.* N.p.: Christian Aid/Church World Action.

Arendt, Hannah. 1963. *Eichmann in Jerusalem: A Report on the Banality of Evil.* New York: Viking Press.

Article 19. 1996. *Broadcasting Genocide. Censorship, Propaganda and State-Sponsored Violence in Rwanda 1990–1994.* London: Article 19, the International Centre against Censorship.

Bagiramenshi, J., and C. Bazihizina. 1985. *Le cas Gitarama.* N.p.: Groupe de Labeaume.

Banton, M. 1983. *Racial and Ethnic Competition.* Cambridge: Cambridge University Press.

239

Barrère, Bernard, Juan Schoemaker, and others. 1992. *Enquête Démographique et de Santé, Rwanda 1992*. Kigali, Rwanda: Office National de la Population and Demographic and Health Surveys Macro International Inc.

Bart, François. 1993. *Montagnes d'Afrique, terres paysannes. Le cas du Rwanda*. Bordeaux, France: Presses Universitaires de Bordeaux.

Bar-Tal, Daniel. 1990. Causes and Consequences of Delegitimization: Models of Conflict and Ethnocentrism. *Journal of Social Issues* 46, no. 1: 65–81.

Barth, Fredrik. 1969. *Ethnic Groups and Boundaries: The Social Organization of Cultural Differences*. Boston: Little, Brown.

Bayart, Jean-François. 1986. Civil Society in Africa. In *Political Domination in Africa: Reflections on the Limits of State Power*, edited by P. Chabal. Cambridge: Cambridge University Press.

Bayart, Jean-François. 1991. La problématique de la démocratie en Afrique noire. "La Baule, et puis après?" *Politique Africaine* 43 (October): 5–20.

Bernstein, Jerome. 1995. The Psychology of Genocide. In *Workshop on Rwanda. Final Report*. Leuven, Belgium: CIDSE/CARITAS.

Bienen, Henry. 1993. Leaders, Violence and Absence of Change in Africa. *Political Science Quarterly* 108, no. 2 (summer): 271–82.

Bizimungu, Télésphore, Octavien Bisa-Samali, Emmanuel Bugingo, and Charles Ntampaka. 1991. *Politique et priorités de la coopération technique au Rwanda*. Kigali, Rwanda: PNUD.

Bonneux, Luc. 1994. Rwanda: A Case of Demographic Entrapment. *Lancet* 344, no. 17 (December 17): 1689–90.

Boutros-Ghali, Boutros. 1996. Introduction. In *The United Nations and Rwanda 1993–1996*. New York: United Nations Department of Public Information.

Braeckman, Colette. 1994. *Génocide au Rwanda*. Paris: Fayart.

Braeckman, Colette. 1995. Autopsie d'un génocide planifié au Rwanda. *Le Monde Diplomatique* (March): 8–9.

Braeckman, Colette. 1997. Le retrait qui tue. Commission Rwanda: C'est le sprint final. *Le Soir* (December 6).

Braun, E. 1990. Une bonne association pour une autopromotion efficace. *Dialogue* 142 (September–October): 37–39.

Brown, L. David, and Darcy Ashman. 1996. *Intersectoral Problem-Solving and Social Capital Formation: A Comparative Analysis of African and Asian Cases*. Boston: Institute of Development Research.

Brusten, Robert, and Nelson Bindariye. 1997. *Les Politiques des ONG Belges au Rwanda de 1969 à 1994*. Brussels: ATOL/South Research, étude commanditée par le NCOS.

Bugingo, Emmanuel, and Charles Ntampaka. 1991. *Document-Synthèse des études préparatoires au séminaire sur la coopération technique au Rwanda*. Kigali, Rwanda: United Nations Development Programme.

Bugingo, Emmanuel, Emmanuel Gahungi, and others. 1992. *Etude sur la commune du Rwanda*. Kigali.

Cambrézy, L. 1984. *Le surpeuplement en question: Organisation spatiale et écologie des migrations au Rwanda*. Paris: ORSTOM Coll. Travaux et Documents Vol. 182.

Campbell, David J. 1994. *Environmental Stress in Rwanda*. Preliminary

Analysis No. 1, Rwanda Society–Environment Project Working Paper 4. East Lansing: Michigan State University, Department of Geography and the Center for Advanced Study of International Development.

Cart, Henri-Phillipe. 1995. La coopération suisse au Rwanda ou les limites de l'aide extérieure. In *Les crises politiques au Burundi et au Rwanda (1993–1994)*, edited by A. Guichaoua. Lille, France: Karthala and Université des Sciences et Technologies de Lille.

Caviezel, Lothard, and Pascal Fouga. 1989. *L'ajustement structurel, l'emploi et la pauvreté au Burundi*. Bujumbura, Burundi: Bureau International du Travail.

Centre Nord-Sud. 1994. *Le Rwanda dans son Contexte Regional: Droits de la personne, réconciliation et rehabilitation. Document de synthèse préparé pour la conférence de La Haye, 16–17 Sept. 1994.* The Hague: Centre Nord-Sud, Centre Europeen pour l'Interdependence et la Solidarite Mondiales, Conseil de l'Europe, NCOS.

CePeD. 1994. *La démographie de 30 Etats de l'Afrique et de l'Ocean Indien*. Paris: Centre Français sur la Population et le Développement.

Cernea, Michael. 1993. Culture and Organization: Social Sustainability of Induced Development. *Sustainable Development* 1, no. 2: 18–29.

Chambers, Robert. 1983. *Rural Development: Putting the Last First*. Essex: Longman.

Chambers, Robert. 1995. *Poverty and Livelihoods: Whose Reality Counts?* Discussion Paper vol. 347. Sussex: Institute of Development Studies.

Chatterjee, Partha. 1993. *The Nation and Its Fragments. Colonial and Post-colonial Histories*. Princeton, N.J.: Princeton University Press.

Chossudovsky, Michel. 1994. Les fruits empoisonnés de l'ajustement structurel. *Le Monde Diplomatique* (November): 21.

Chrétien, Jean-Pierre. 1985. Hutu et Tutsi au Rwanda et au Burundi. In *Au coeur de l'ethnie. Ethnies, tribalisme et Etat en Afrique*, edited by Jean-Loup Amselle and E. M'Bokolo. Paris: La Découverte.

Chrétien, Jean-Pierre. 1991. Presse Libre et propagande raciste au Rwanda. *Politique Africaine* 42 (June): 109–20.

Chrétien, Jean-Pierre. 1993a. Le Rwanda et la France: La democratie ou les ethnies? *Journal* (March–April): 190–95.

Chrétien, Jean-Pierre. 1993b. Tournant historique au Burundi et au Rwanda. *Marchés Tropicaux* 20–24.

Chrétien, Jean-Pierre, and others. 1995. *Rwanda. Les médias du génocide*. Paris: Karthala.

CIDSE and CARITAS Internationalis. 1995. *Workshop on Rwanda. Final Report*. Leuven, Belgium: CARITAS Internationalis.

CIM (Comité des Institutions Missionaires). 1994. Wie sprak er over vrede en rechtvaardigheid? *Informissi* 144 (October): 2–6.

Clay, Daniel C., and Jim McAllister. 1991. Family Development Cycle, Social Class, and Inequality in Rwanda. *Rural Sociology* 56, no. 1: 22–40.

Clay, Daniel, Thomas Reardon, and Jaakko Kangasniemi. 1995. *Sustainable Intensification in the Highland Tropics: Rwandan Farmers' Investments in Soil Conservation and Fertility*. Staff Paper vol. 95-21. East Lansing: Michigan State University, Department of Agricultural Economics.

Clay, Daniel C., François Byiringiro, Jaakko Kangasniemi, and others. 1995. *Promoting Food Security in Rwanda through Sustainable Agricultural Productivity: Meeting the Challenges of Population Pressure, Land Degradation, and Poverty*. Staff Paper vol. 95-08, East Lansing: Michigan State University, Department of Agricultural Economics.

CNDC. 1995. *Rwanda Memorial Day 7 Avril 1995. Le génocide*. Brussels: EUROSTEP.

Cobb, Clifford, Ted Halstead, and Jonathan Rowe. 1995. *The Genuine Progress Indicator. Summary of Data and Methodology*. San Fransisco: Redefining Progress.

Cochet, Hubert. 1996. *Burundi: La paysannerie dans la tourmente*. Paris: Fondation Progrès de l'Homme.

COOPIBO. 1980. *Rapport de la session d'études de COOPIBO 2 nov.–12 nov. 1980. Les programmes économiques dans les projets de développement*. Heverlee, Belgium: COOPIBO.

Corrèze, Annette, Dominique Gentil, and Michel Barnaud. 1982a. *Rapport d'évaluation Projet Agricole Kibuye. Tome I. Synthèse*. Montpellier, France: Institut de Recherches et d'applications de méthodes de développement (IRAM), pour la DDA et le MINAGRI-Rwanda.

Corrèze, Annette, Dominique Gentil, and Michel Barnaud. 1982b. *Rapport d'évaluation Projet Agricole Kibuye. Tome II. Eléments d'analyse et résultats de l'enquête en milieu rural*. Montpellier, France: Institut de Recherches et d'applications de méthodes de développement (IRAM), pour la DDA et le MINAGRI-Rwanda.

Corrèze, Annette, and Jean-Pierre Lemelle. 1985. *Le développement communal: Exigences et perspectives*. Montpellier, France: IRAM.

Coser, Lewis A. 1956. *The Functions of Social Conflict*. Glencoe, Ill.: Free Press.

Cros, Marie-France. 1995. Burundi: Le règne des milices. *La Libre Belgique* (March 21).

Dahrendorf, Ralph. 1995. *Economic Opportunity, Civil Society and Political Liberty*. Discussion Paper vol. 58. Geneva: UNRISD.

Dans un maquis hutu. 1995. *Libération*. (January 19).

de Heusch, Luc. 1994. Anthropologie d'un génocide: le Rwanda. *Les Temps Modernes* 49, no. 579 (December): 1–19.

de la Masselière, Charley Bernard. 1992. Le resserrement de l'espace agraire au Rwanda, les paysans dans la crise. *Etudes Rurales* 125–126: 99–115.

de la Masselière, Charley Bernard. 1993. Du versant terroir aux territoires fragmentés. Organisation, dynamique et crise de l'espace agraire au Rwanda. *Cahiers Sciences Humaines* 29: 661–94.

Delor-Vandueren, Annick, and Jose Degand. 1991. *Burundi: Demographie, agriculture et environment*. Louvain-la-Neuve, Belgium: Universite Catholique de Louvain, Unité d'économie et de sociologie rurales, Cahiers du CIDEP 14.

de Ravignan, François. 1980. L'Afrique des paysans. *Dialogue* 82 (September–October): 3–22.

Derenne, Benoît. 1989. De la chicotte aux billons. Aperçu des méthodes de lutte contre l'érosion au Rwanda et au Burundi du XIXe siècle à nos jours. *Genève-Afrique* 27, no. 1: 45–72.

Derrier, Jean-François. 1985. Public works programmes in Rwanda: Conditions for popular participation. *International Labour Review* 124, no. 5: 611–21.

des Forges, Alison. 1994. *Human Rights in Burundi and Rwanda and U.S. Policy*. Washington, D.C.: Senate Foreign Relations Committee, Crisis in Africa Session, July 26.

des Forges, Alison. 1995. Face au genocide, une réponse désastreuse des Etats-Unis et des Nations Unies. In *Les crises politiques au Burundi et au Rwanda (1993–1994)*, edited by André Guichaoua. Paris and Lille: Karthala and Université des Sciences et Technologies de Lille.

des Forges, Alison L. 1996. Making Noise Effectively: Lessons from the Rwanda Catastrophe. In *Vigilance and Vengeance. NGOs Preventing Ethnic Conflict in Divided Societies*, edited by Robert I. Rotberg. Washington, D.C., and Cambridge: Brookings Institution Press and World Peace Foundation.

Destexhe, Alain. 1994. *Rwanda. Essai sur le génocide*. Bruxelles: Editions Complexe.

d'Hertefelt, M. 1971. *Les clans du Ruanda ancien. Eléments d'ethnosociologie et d'ethnohistoire*. Tervuren, Belgium: Musée Royal de l'Afrique Centrale.

Downs, R. E., and Stephen P. Reyna. 1988. Introduction. In *Land and Society in Contemporary Africa*, edited by S. P. Reyna and R. E. Downs. Hanover: University Press of New England.

Duckitt, John. 1992–93. Prejudice and Behavior: A Review. *Current Psychology* 11, no. 4 (winter): 291–307.

Dupaquier, Jean-François. 1996. Droit de réponse. *Dialogue* 190 (April–May): 150.

Du Preez, Wilhelmus Petrus. 1994. *Genocide. The Psychology of Mass Murder*. London: Boyars/Bowerdean.

Ehrlich, Paul R., and Anne H. Ehrlich. 1990. *The Population Explosion*. New York: Simon and Schuster.

Elias, M., and D. Helbig. 1991. Deux mille collines pour les petits et les grands. Radioscopie des stéréotypes hutu et tutsi au Rwanda et au Burundi. *Politique Africaine* 42: 65–73.

Engelman, R., and P. LeRoy. 1995. *Conserving Land: Population and Sustainable Food Production*. Washington, D.C.: Population Action International.

Ennals, M. 1988. Ethnic Conflict Resolution and the Protection of Minorities. The Quest for NGO Competence Building. In *Ethnic Conflict and Human Rights*, edited by K. Rupesinghe. Tokyo: United Nations University and Norwegian University Press.

Eriksson, Johnand, and others. 1996. *Synthesis Report*. Vol. 5 of *The International Response to Conflict and Genocide: Lessons from the Rwanda Experience*. Copenhagen: DANIDA.

Erny, Pierre. 1994. *Rwanda 1994*. Paris: L'Harmattan.

Erny, Pierre. 1995. Catégories spatiales et structures mentales au Rwanda. *Cahiers de Sociologie Economique et Culturelle* 24 (December): 87–94.

Erpicum, R. 1986. Le paysan et l'agronome. *Dialogue* 117 (July–August): 21–23.

Escobar, Arturo. 1995. *Encountering Development: The Making and Unmaking of the Third World*. Princeton, N.J.: Princeton University Press.

Eyoh, Dickson. 1996. From Economic Crisis to Political Liberalization: Pitfalls of the New Political Sociology for Africa. *African Studies Review* 39, no. 3 (December): 43–80.

FAO. 1982. *Report of the Rwanda Mission de reconnaissance. Programme de coopération FAO/FIDA Investment Support Programme.* Rome: FAO.

FAO. 1983. *Report of the Rwanda Mission d'identification FAO/FIDA. Programme national d'amélioration de la culture du mais, et projet d'appui à l'initiative communautaire dans les communes de Kinigi, Mukingo et Mkuli.* Rome: FAO.

FAO. 1990. *Aperçu Nutritionnel: Rwanda.* Rome: FAO.

FAO. 1994. *The State of Food and Agriculture, 1994.* Rome: FAO.

FAO-GIEWS. 1995. *Food Supply Situation and Crop Prospects in Sub-Saharan Africa.* Rome: FAO Global Information and Emergency Warning System.

Feagin, Joe R., and Harlan Hahn. 1973. *Ghetto Revolts: The Politics of Violence in American Cities.* New York: Macmillan.

Fein, Helen. 1993. Accounting for Genocide after 1945: Theories and Some Findings. *International Journal on Group Rights* 1: 79–106.

Fein, Helen. 1995. More Murder in the Middle: Life-Integrity Violations and Democracy in the World, 1987. *Human Rights Quarterly* 17: 170–91.

Feltz, Gaetan. 1995. Ethnicité, Etat-nation et Démocratisation au Rwanda et au Burundi. In *Démocratie et développement. Mirrage ou espoir raisonnable?* edited by M. Esoavelomandroso and Gaetan Feltz. Paris: Karthala.

Ferguson, Jonathan. 1990. *The Anti-Politics Machine. "Development," Depoliticization, and Bureaucratic Power in Lesotho.* Cambridge: Cambridge University Press.

FIAU. 1996. *Colloque International. Les principales crises de gouvernance au Rwanda et leurs déboires ethniques: fondements, pratiques et perspectives.* N.p.: Fondation Internationale Agathe Uwilingiyimana.

Fisher, R. J. 1990. Needs Theory, Social Identity and an Ecclectic Model of Conflict. In *Conflict: Human Needs Theory*, edited by John Burton. New York: St. Martin's Press.

Foote, K. A., K. H. Hill, and L. G. Martin, eds. 1993. *Demographic Change in Sub-Saharan Africa.* Washington, D.C.: National Academy Press, National Research Council Panel on the Population Dynamics of Sub-Saharan Africa.

Ford, Robert E. 1993. Marginal Coping in Extreme Land Pressures: Ruhengeri, Rwanda. In *Population Growth and Agricultural Change in Africa*, edited by B. L. Turner, G. Hyden, and R. W. Kates. Gainesville: University of Florida Press.

Ford, Robert E. 1995. The Population-Environment Nexus and Vulnerability Assessment in Africa. *Geo-Journal* 35, no. 2: 207–16.

Ford, Robert E. 1996. The Rwanda Tragedy: A Personal Reflection. *Hunger Notes* 21, no. 4 (fall): 12–14.

Foreign Broadcast Information Service Reports. 1990–96. *Africa (Sub-Sahara) and Western Europe.* Washington, D.C.: Global Newsbank.

Fox, Jonathan. 1996. How Does Civil Society Thicken? The Political Construction of Social Capital in Rural Mexico. *World Development* 24, no. 6: 1089–1103.

Franche, Dominique. 1995. Généalogie du génocide rwandais. Hutu et Tutsi: Gaulois et Francs? *Les Temps Modernes* 582: 169–226.

Franke, Richard W., and Barbara H. Chasin. 1980. *Seeds of Famine. Ecological Destruction and the Development Dilemma in the West African Sahel.* Totowa, N.J.: Rowman and Allanheld.

Fukuyama, Francis. 1996. *Trust. The Social Virtues and the Creation of Prosperity.* New York: Free Press.

Funga, François. 1991. Pouvoir, ethnies et régions. *Dialogue* 149 (November–December): 21–35.

Galtung, Johan. 1969. Violence, Peace, and Peace Research. *Journal of Peace Research* 6, no. 1: 167–91.

Galtung, Johan. 1990. Cultural Violence. *Journal of Peace Research* 27, no. 3: 291–305.

Galtung, Johan, and others. n.d. *Measuring World Development.* Vol. 2. Oslo: Chair in Conflict and Peace Research, World Indicators Program.

Gamson, William A. 1995. Hiroshima, the Holocaust, and the Politics of Exclusion. *American Sociological Review* 60: 1–20.

Gatwa, Tharcisse. 1996. Eglises au Rwanda: Des contributions de valeur? *Dialogue* 189: 29–41.

Gaud, Michel. 1995. La tragédie du Rwanda. *Problèmes Politiques et Sociaux* 752 (July 28): 1–5.

Geen voedselhulp meer voor Rwanda. 1993. *De Standaard,* (August 16).

Gil, D. G. 1970. *Violence against Children.* Cambridge: Harvard University Press.

Gizewski, Peter, and Thomas Homer-Dixon. 1995. *Urban Growth and Violence: Will the Future Resemble the Past?* Toronto: University of Toronto, Environment, Population and Security Project.

Godding, Jean-Pierre. 1983. Quand l'aide extérieure bloque le développement. *Dialogue* 99 (June): 65–87.

Godding, Jean-Pierre. 1985. Grains de levure dans la pate, ou la deuxième table ronde des ONG. *Dialogue* 113 (November–December): 13–20.

Goldhagen, David J. 1996. *Hitler's Willing Executioners. Ordinary Germans and the Holocaust.* New York: Alfred A. Knopf.

Gordon, Nick. 1992. *Murder in the Mist.* Boulder, Colo.: Westview Press.

Gourevitch, Philip. 1995. After the Genocide. *New Yorker* (December 18): 79–94.

Gourevitch, Philip. 1997. After Genocide. A Conversation with Paul Kagame. *Transition* 72: 162–94.

Green, Donald P., Jack Glaser, and Andrew Rich. 1996. *From Lynching to Gay-Bashing: The Elusive Connection between Economic Conditions and Hate Crime.* Working Paper vol. 96-05.1. New Haven, Conn.: Yale University, Institution for Social and Policy Studies.

Green, Donald P., Janelle Wong, and Dara Strolovitch. 1996. *The Effects of Demographic Change on Hate Crime.* Working Paper vol. 96-06.1. New Haven, Conn.: Yale University, Institution for Social and Policy Studies.

Grosse, Scott. 1994a. *More People, More Trouble: Population Growth and Agricultural Change in Africa* (draft). Ann Arbor: University of Michigan, Department of Population and International Health.

Grosse, Scott. 1994b. *The Roots of Conflict and State Failure in Rwanda: The Political Exacerbation of Social Cleavages in a Context of Growing Resource*

Scarcity. Ann Arbor: University of Michigan, Department of Population Planning and International Health, School of Public Health.

Grosse, Scott, Katharine Krasovec, and others. 1995. *Evaluating Trends in Children's Nutritional Status in Rwanda*. East Lansing: Department of Agricultural Economics, Michigan State University.

Groupe de Labeaume. 1985. *Approche du point de vue des paysans à propos du cas Gitarama*. N.p.: Groupe de Labeaume.

Groupe d'Ecoute et Réconciliation dans l'Afrique des Grands Lacs. 1995. *Pour en terminer avec la "culture de l'impunité" au Rwanda et Burundi*. Geneva: Institut Universitaire d'Etudes du Développement.

Guichaoua, André. 1987. *Les paysans et l'investissement-travail au Burundi et au Rwanda*. Geneva: International Labour Office.

Guichaoua, André. 1989. *Destins Paysans et Politiques Agraires en Afrique Centrale, L'Ordre paysan des hautes terres centrales du Burundi et du Rwanda*. Paris: Editions l'Harmattan.

Guichaoua, André. 1991. Les "travaux comunautaires" en Afrique Centrale. *Revue Tiers-Monde* 32, no. 127 (July–September): 551–75.

Guichaoua, André. 1995a. "Un lourd passé, un présent dramatique, un avenir des plus sombres." In *Les crises politiques au Burundi et au Rwanda (1993–1994)*, edited by A. Guichaoua. Paris and Lille: Karthala and Université des Sciences et Technologies de Lille.

Guichaoua, André. 1995b. Rwanda: de l'omniprésence des aides au désengagement international. *L'Afrique Politique* (1995): 13–27.

Gurr, Ted R. 1970. *Why Men Rebel*. Princeton, N.J.: Princeton University Press.

Gurr, Ted R. 1993. *Minorities at Risk. A Global View of Ethnopolitical Conflicts*. Washington, D.C.: U.S. Institute of Peace Press.

Hancock, Graham. 1989. *Lords of Poverty: The Power, Prestige, and Corruption of the International Aid Business*. New York: Atlantic Monthly Press.

Hanssen, Alain. 1989. *Le désenchantement de la coopération. Enquête au pays des milles coopérants*. Paris: L'Harmattan.

Hardin, Garrett. 1993. *Living within Limits: Ecology, Economics, and Population Taboos*. New York: Oxford University Press.

Harff, Barbara. 1987. The Etiology of Genocides. In *Genocide and the Modern Age. Etiology and Case Studies of Mass Death*. edited by I. Wallimann and M. N. Dobkowski. New York: Greenwood Press.

Hayter, Theresa, and C. Watson. 1985. *Aid Rhetoric and Reality*. London: Pluto Press.

Heilbrunn, J. R. 1993. Social Origins of National Conferences in Benin and Togo. *Journal of Modern African Studies* 31, no. 2: 277–99.

Heimo, M-C. 1994. La tragedie Rwandaise est-elle explicable? *CIVITAS* 49: 193–99.

Hétier, Antoine. 1985. *Les journées de créativité*. N.p.: Groupe de Labeaume.

Hiebert, Paul G., and B. Hiebert-Crape. 1995. The Role of Religion in International Development. *The Conrad Grebel Review. A Journal of Christian Inquiry* 13, no. 3 (fall): 281–98.

Hirschman, Albert O. 1967. *Development Projects Observed*. Washington, D.C.: Brookings Institution.

Hobart, Mark. 1993. Introduction: The Growth of Ignorance? In *An Anthropological Critique of Development. The Growth of Ignorance,* edited by Mark Hobart. London: Routledge.

Hoben, Susan J. 1989. *School, Work and Equity. Educational Reform in Rwanda.* African Research Studies vol. 16. Boston: Boston University, African Studies Center.

Hoffmann, Wilma, and Brian McKendrick. 1990. The Nature of Violence. In *People and Violence in South Africa,* edited by Brian McKendrick and Wilma Hoffmann. Cape Town: Oxford University Press.

Horowitz, Donald L. 1985. *Ethnic Groups in Conflict.* Berkeley: University of California Press.

Human Rights Watch. 1994a. Arming Rwanda: Arms Trade and Human Rights Abuses in the Rwandan War. *Human Rights Watch Africa* 6, no. 1 (January).

Human Rights Watch. 1994b. Genocide in Rwanda, April–May 1994. *Human Rights Watch Africa* 6, no. 4 (May).

Human Rights Watch. 1995. *Slaughter among Neighbors. The Political Origins of Communal Violence.* New Haven, Conn.: Yale University Press.

Humana, Charles. 1984. *World Human Rights Guide.* New York: Pica Press.

Humana, Charles. 1992. *World Human Rights Guide,* 3d ed. New York: Oxford University Press.

Huntington, Samuel P. 1968. *Political Order in Changing Societies.* New Haven, Conn.: Yale University Press.

ICHRDD. 1995. *Pour un système de justice au Rwanda.* Montreal: International Centre for Human Rights and Democratic Development and Centre International des Droits de la Personne et du Développement Démocratique.

IFAD. 1988. *Report and Recommendations to the Executive Board on a Proposed Loan to the Rwandese Republic for the Gikongoro Agricultural Development Project.* Rome: International Fund for Agricultural Development.

IFAD. 1990. *Report and Recommendations to the Executive Board on a Proposed Loan to the Rwandese Republic for the Byumba Agricultural Development Project—Phase II.* Rome: International Fund for Agricultural Development.

IFAD. 1991. *Soil and Water Conservation since Independence: Selected Country Summaries.* Rome: International Fund for Agricultural Development.

IFAD. 1992. *Report and Recommendations to the Executive Board on a Proposed Loan to the Rwandese Republic for the Intensified Land Use Management Project in the Buberuka Highlands.* Rome: International Fund for Agricultural Development.

IFRCRCS. 1994. Under the Volcanoes: Special Focus on the Rwandan Refugee Crisis. In *World Disasters Report.* Amsterdam: Martinus Nijhoff for the International Federation of Red Cross and Red Crescent Societies.

INADES. 1987. *Les ONG au Rwanda.* Kigali, Rwanda: INADES/Banque Mondiale.

Inter-Ministerial Committee of MINISANTE, MINAGRI, MINIPLAN, MININTER, MINICOM and MINIMART. 1991. *Analyse de la situation nutritionnelle au Rwanda.* Kigali.

International Institute for Labour Studies and United Nations Development

Programme. 1994. *Overcoming Social Exclusion. A Contribution to the World Summit for Social Development.* Geneva.

IRAM. 1985. *Réflexion sur les limites et possibilités d'intégration d'appuis extérieurs dans les responsabilités et compétences de la commune.* Paris: IRAM.

IWACU. 1991. Bilan de la pauvreté au Rwanda. In *Rapport du séminaire des agences du système des Nations Unies sur la lutte contre la pauvreté.* Kigali, Rwanda: United Nations.

Jackson, Robert H. 1990. *Quasi-States: Sovereignty, International Relations and the Third World.* Cambridge Studies in International Relations. Cambridge: Cambridge University Press.

Jonassohn, Kurt. 1992. What Is Genocide? In *Genocide Watch,* edited by Helen Fein. New Haven, Conn.: Yale University Press.

Kabirigi, Lindiro. 1994. *Génocide au Rwanda: Honte pour l'humanité. Réflexions d'un responsable d'une ONG sous-régionale.* Kigali, Rwanda: Programme Régional de Formation et d'Echanges pour le Développement (PREFED).

Kagabo, Jean, and Claudine Vidal. 1994. L'extermination des Rwandais Tutsi. *Cahiers d'Etudes Africaines* 34, no. 4: 537–47.

Kaljee, Linda M., Bonita Stanton, and others. 1995. Urban African American Adolescents and Their Parents: Perceptions of Violence within and against Their Communities. *Human Organization* 54, no. 4: 373–82.

Kaplan, Robert. 1994. The Coming Anarchy. *Atlantic Monthly* 273, no. 2 (February): 44–76.

Karemera, Emmanuel. 1988. *Une année du projet agricole de Gitarama.* Gitarama, Rwanda: Ministère de l'Agriculture, de l'élévage et des forêts, Projet Agricole de Gitarama.

Karemera, Gaspard. 1995. ONG rwandaises: rectifier le jugement. *Traits d'Union Rwanda* (March 1): 23–24.

Kayitesi, Christine. 1993. *Du project a l'appui institutionnel. Difficult és et objectifs. Le cas du PAK au Rwanda: 1980–1990.* Travail de recherche no. 82. Geneva: Institut Universitaire d'Etudes du Développement.

Kelman, Herbert C., and V. Lee Hamilton. 1993. Sanctioned Massacres. In *Political Psychology. Classic and Contemporary Readings,* edited by Neil J. Kressel. New York: Paragon House.

Khan, Rasheeduddin. 1978. Violence and Socio-economic Development. *International Social Science Journal* 30, no. 4: 834–57.

King, Maurice. 1994. Rwanda, Malthus and Medicus Mundi. *Medicus Mundi Bulletin* 54 (August): 11–19.

Kressel, Neil J., ed. 1993. *Political Psychology. Classic and Contemporary Readings.* New York: Paragon House.

Krishna, Kumar (team leader). 1996. *Rebuilding Post-War Rwanda.* Vol. 4 of *The International Response to Conflict and Genocide: Lessons from the Rwanda Experience.* Copenhagen: DANIDA.

Kuper, Leo. 1977. *The Pity of It All.* Minneapolis: University of Minnesota Press.

Lauer, Robert H. 1989. *Social Problems and the Quality of Life,* 4th ed. Dubuque, Iowa: Brown Publishers.

Lemarchand, René. 1966. Power and Stratification in Rwanda: A Reconsideration. *Cahiers d'Etudes Africaines* 24, no. 6: 592–610.

Lemarchand, René. 1970. *Burundi and Rwanda*. New York: Praeger.

Lemarchand, René. 1982. *The World Bank in Rwanda. The Case of the Office de Valorisation Agricole et Pastorale de Mutara (OVAPAM)*. Bloomington: University of Indiana, African Studies Program.

Lemarchand, René. 1992. Uncivil State and Civil Societies: How Illusion Became Reality. *Journal of Modern African Studies* 30, no. 2: 177–91.

Levinson, Jerome. 1992. Multilateral Financial Institutions: What Form of Accountability? *American University Journal of International Law and Policy* 891: 39–64.

Lewis, Lawrence A. 1994. *Environmental Data Needs for Assessing Agricultural Land Degradation in the Rwandan Context*. Rwanda Society–Environmental Project Working Paper 10. East Lansing: Michigan State University, Department of Geography and the Center for Advanced Study of International Development.

Lewis, Lawrence A., Daniel C. Clay, and Y. M. J. Dejaegher. 1988. Soil Loss, Agriculture and Conservation in Rwanda: Toward Sound Strategies for Soil Management. *Journal of Soil and Water Conservation* 43: 418–21.

Lewis, Lawrence A., and V. Nyamulinda. 1989. Les relations entre les cultures et les unites topographiques dans les régions agricoles de la bordure du Lac Kivu et de l'Impara au Rwanda: Quelques stratégies pour une agriculture soutenue. *Bulletin Agricole du Rwanda* 22, no. 3: 143–49.

Lewis, Lawrence A., and V. Nyamulinda. 1996. The Critical Role of Human Activities in Land Degradation in Rwanda. *Land Degradation and Development* 7: 47–55.

Libaridian, Gerard J. 1987. The Ultimate Repression: The Genocide of the Armenians, 1915–1917. In *Genocide and the Modern Age. Etiology and Case Studies of Mass Death*, edited by I. Wallimann and M. N. Dobkowski. New York: Greenwood Press.

Linguyeneza, Vénuste. 1996. Les divisions dans l'Eglise du Rwanda. *Dialogue* 189: 3–14.

Lipton, Michael. 1988. *The Poor and the Poorest*. Staff Working Paper. Washington, D.C.: World Bank.

Little, Peter, and Michael Horowitz. 1987. Subsistence Crops Are Cash Crops: Some Comments with Reference to East Africa. *Human Organization* 46, no. 3: 254–57.

Long, Norman, and Magdalena Villarreal. 1993. Exploring Development Interfaces: From the Transfer of Knowledge to the Transformation of Meaning. In *Beyond the Impasse. New Directions in Development Theory*, edited by Frans J. Schuurman. London: Zed Books.

Longman, Timothy P. 1995a. *Christianity and Crisis in Rwanda: Religion, Civil Society, Democratization and Decline*. Madison: University of Wisconsin Press.

Longman, Timothy P. 1995b. Genocide and Socio-political Change: Massacres in Two Rwandan Villages. *Issues* 23, no. 2: 18–21.

Louvel, Roland. 1994. *Quelle Afrique pour quelle coopération? Mythologie de l'aide française*. Paris: L'Harmattan.

Machipisa, Lewis. 1997. *Development: Knowledge, a Weapon against Poverty*. N.p.: Inter Press Service Press Report.

Malkki, Liisa H. 1995. *Purity and Exile: Violence, Memory, and National Cosmology among Hutu Refugees in Tanzania.* Chicago: University of Chicago Press.

Mamdani, Mahmood. 1996. *Citizen and Subject. Contemporary Africa and the Legacy of Late Colonialism.* Princeton, N.J.: Princeton University Press.

Maquet, Jaques. 1961. *The Premise of Inequality in Ruanda: A Study of Political Relations in Central African Kingdom.* London: Oxford University Press.

Maquet, Jaques. 1969. Institutionalisation feodale des relations de dependance dans quatre cultures interlacustres. *Cahiers d'Etudes Africaines* 35, no. 3: 403–14.

Margalit, Avishai. 1996. *The Decent Society.* Cambridge: Harvard University Press.

Marmor, Judd. 1992. Cultural Factors in the Darker Passions. *Journal of the American Academy of Psychoanalysis* 20, no. 3: 325–34.

Marysse, Stefaan. 1982. *Basic Needs, Income Distribution, and the Political Economy of Rwanda.* Antwerp: University of Antwerp, Centre for Development Studies.

Marysse, Stefaan, T. De Herdt, and E. Ndayambaje. 1993. *Appauvrissement de la population rurale et ajustement structurel: causalité ou coincidence? Le cas de Kirarambogo (Rwanda).* Antwerp: University of Antwerp, Centre for Development Studies.

Marysse, Stefaan, T. De Herdt, and E. Ndayambaje. 1995. *Rwanda: Appauvrissement et ajustement structurel.* Brussels and Paris: Institut Africain-CEDAF, L'Harmattan.

Marysse, Stefaan, E. Ndayambaje, and E. Waterloos. 1992. *Revenus ruraux au Rwanda avant l'ajustement structurel. Cas de Kirarambogo.* Louvain-la-Neuve, Belgium: CIDEP, Cahiers du CIDEP.

Mason, John, Urban Jonsson, and Jo-Anne Csete. 1996. Is Childhood Malnutrition Being Overcome? In *The Hunger Report 1995,* edited by Ellen Messer and Peter Uvin. New York: Gordon and Breach.

Maton, Jef. 1994. *Développement economique et social au Rwanda entre 1980 et 1993. Le dixième décile en face de l'Apocalypse.* Ghent: State University of Ghent, Faculty of Economics, Unit for Development Research and Teaching.

Mattheiem, Nathalie. 1991. Le ministre belge de la coopération est à Washington. *Le Soir* (May 17).

May, John. 1995. Policies on Population, Land Use, and Environment in Rwanda. *Population and Environment* 16, no. 4: 321–34.

Mbonimpa, Melchior. 1994. *Ethnicité et démocratie en Afrique. L'homme tribal contre l'homme citoyen?* Paris: L'Harmattan.

McCullen, H. 1995. *The Angels Have Left Us. The Rwandan Tragedy and the Churches.* Risk Book Series no. 66. Ferney, Switzerland: World Council of Churches Publishers.

McHugh, Heather S. 1995. USAID and Ethnic Conflict: An Epiphany? Paper presented at a Cornell University conference on development assistance and ethnic conflict, Washington, D.C.

McKendrick, Brian, and Wilma Hoffmann. 1990. Towards the Reduction of Violence. In *People and Violence in South Africa,* edited by Brian McKendrick and Wilma Hoffman. Cape Town: Oxford University Press.

Médard, Jean-François. 1991. Autoritarismes et démocraties en Afrique Noire. *Politique Africaine* 43 (October): 92–104.

Merton, Robert King. 1968. *Social Theory and Social Structure*, enlarged ed. New York: Free Press.

Michel, Roger. 1984. *Bilan de deux années à la coopération technique suisse au Rwanda au projet agricole de Kibuye.* Geneva: Institut Universitaire d'Etudes du Développement, Mémoire presentée pour le diplôme de recherche en études du développement vol. 20.

Milgram, Stanley. 1974. *Obedience to Authority: An Experimental View.* New York: Harper and Row.

Miller, Arthur G. 1986. *The Obedience Experiments. A Case Study of Controversy in Social Science.* New York: Praeger.

Minear, Larry, and Philippe Guillot. 1996. *Soldiers to the Rescue: Humanitarian Lessons from Rwanda.* Paris: Organization for Economic Cooperation and Development.

Ministère des Affaires Étrangères et de la Coopération Internationale. 1990. *Rapport Annuel 1990. Tome III. Coopération Internationale.* Kigali: République Rwandaise.

Ministère de l'Agriculture, de l'Elévage et des Forêts. 1985. *Résultats de L'enquête nationale agricole 1984.* Kigali: République Rwandaise.

Ministère de l'Agriculture, de l'Elévage et des Forêts. 1992. *Enquête nationale agricole 1990: Production, superficie, rendements, élevage et leur évolution.* Kigali: République Rwandaise.

Ministère de l'Interieur et du Developpement Communal. N.d. *Rapport d'une étude de milieu réalisée par 11 formateurs CCDFP de la préfecture Gisenyi sur quelques problèmes rélatifs au foncier.* Gisenyi: République Rwandaise.

Ministère du Plan. 1988. *La situation économique du Rwanda en 1987.* Kigali: Ministère du Plan.

Ministère du Plan. 1989. *La situation économique du Rwanda en 1988.* Kigali: Ministère du Plan.

Ministère du Plan. 1993. *Evolution de la situation économique du Rwanda 1988–91 et tendances 92.* Kigali: République Rwandaise, Direction de la Politique Economique.

Minot, N. 1991. *La consommation et les sources de revenu des menages en milieu rural.* Presented to the Seminaire sur les resultats de l'Enquete Nationale sur le Budget et de la Consommation des Menages, Kigali, October 14–16.

Misser, Francois. 1993. Will the Ceasefire Hold? *New African* 308 (May 1): 32–36.

Mitchell, B. R. 1995. *International Historical Statistics, 1750–1988: Africa, Asia, Oceania.* New York: Stockton Press.

Mitchell, Christopher. 1990. Necessitous Man and Conflict Resolution: More Basic Questions about Basic Human Needs Theory. In *Conflict: Human Needs Theory*, edited by John Burton. New York: St. Martin's Press.

Mkundabigenzi, F. 1961. *Le Rwanda politique (1958–1960).* Brussels: CRISP.

Moore, Robert I. 1987. *The Formation of a Persecuting Society.* Cambridge: Blackwell.

Moore-Lappé, Frances, Joseph Collins, and D. Kinley. 1980. *Aid as an Obstacle.* San Francisco: Institute for Food and Development Policy.

Mugesera, Antoine. 1983. Pourquoi le sous-développement? A qui la faute? *Dialogue* 99 (June): 13–16.

Mugesera, Antoine. 1987. Le mouvement coopératif au Rwanda. *Dialogue* 123 (July–August): 62–78.

Mugwaneza, Callixte. 1994. Nos critiques et nos attentes. Ecrit d'un paysan rwandais. *Traits d'Union Rwanda* (December 27): 26–27.

Mukene, P. 1993. Une semaine de la non-violence à la paroisse St. André de Gitarama. *Dialogue* 170 (September–October).

Mummendeny, Amelie, and Sabine Otten. 1993. Aggression: Interaction between Individuals and Groups. In *Aggression and Violence: Social Interactionist Perspectives*, edited by James Tedeschi and Richard Felson. Washington D.C.: American Psychological Association.

Munyakazi, L. 1993. La question ethnique: un problème mal-posé. *Dialogue* 170 (September–October): 9–11.

Munyantwari, F. 1992. Structuration du mouvement coopératif rwandais. *Dialogue* 132 (January–February): 58–63.

Nayigizente, Ildefonso. 1995. *Rwanda: une jeunesse sacrifiée pour des fantasmes*. N.p.: Parti Democrate.

Ndegwa, Stephen N. 1996. *The Two Faces of Civil Society. NGOs and Politics in Africa*. West Hartford, Conn.: Kumarian Press.

Nelson, Paul J. 1995. *The World Bank and Non-Governmental Organizations. The Limits of Apolitical Development*. New York: St. Martin's Press.

Netherlands Development Cooperation. 1992. *Sector Programme for Rural Development. Summary Evaluation Report*. The Hague: Ministry of Foreign Affairs, Directorate General International Cooperation, Operations Review Unit.

Nevitte, Neil, and Charles Kennedy. 1986. Introduction. In *Ethnic Preference and Public Policy in Developing Societies*, edited by Neil Nevitte and Charles Kennedy. Boulder, Colo.: Lynne Rienner.

Newbury, Catharine. 1988. *The Cohesion of Oppression. Clientship and Ethnicity in Rwanda 1860–1960*. New York: Columbia University Press.

Newbury, Catharine. 1992. Rwanda: Recent Debates over Governance and Rural Development. In *Governance and Politics in Africa*, edited by Michael Bratton and Goran Hyden. Boulder, Colo.: Lynne Rienner.

Ngwabije, R. 1995. Le paysan rwandais et la problématique du developpement agricole et rural: hiérarchisation des contraintes et esquisse des voies de solution. *Bulletin des Séances de l'Academie Royale des Sciences de l'Outre-Mer* 40, suppl. 1: 35–65.

Niyibizi, T. 1986. Sensibilisation et participation communautaire dans les actions de développement. In *Consultation sectorielle des bailleurs de fonds dans le domaine de l'approvisionnement en eau potable et de l'assainissement. Rapport de synthèse*. Kigali: Republique Rwandaise, Ministère des Travaux Publics et de l'Energie.

Nkeshimana, A. 1987. Vulgarisation agricole: deficience d'un système. *Dialogue* 123 (July–August): 83–86.

Nkubito, Alphonse-Marie. 1992. Rwanda: Violations des droits de l'homme. *Dialogue* 152 (March): 20–23.

Nkubito, Alphonse-Marie. 1995. Le rôle de la justice dans la crise rwandaise. In *Les crises politiques au Burundi et au Rwanda (1993–1994)*, edited by André Guichaoua. Lille and Paris: Karthala and Université des Sciences et Technologies de Lille.

Nkunzumwami, Emmanuel. 1996. *La tragédie Rwandaise. Historique et Perspectives.* Paris: L'Harmattan.

Nshimiyunurenyi, Benoît. 1993. *Le développement rural au Rwanda: bilan de l'intégration et perspectives pour l'auto-promotion régionale.* Geneva: Institut Universitaire d'Etudes du Developpement.

Ntagungiro, Carpophore. 1991. Les paysans, le crédit et la coopération internationale au Rwanda. Ph.D. diss., Graduate School of International Studies, Geneva.

Ntamahungiro, J. 1988. Eloge du paysan rwandais. *Dialogue* 130 (September–October): 7–12.

Ntavyohanyuma, P. 1987. *Inventaire des coopératives et groupements a vocation coopérative, 1985.* Kigali, Rwanda: IWACU.

Ntezilyayo, Anastase. 1995. L'agriculture: une priorité dans la reconstruction nationale. In *Les crises politiques au Burundi et au Rwanda (1993–1994)*, edited by André Guichaoua. Paris: Karthala and Université des Sciences et Technologies de Lille.

Nussbaum, Martha C., and Amartya K. Sen. 1993. *The Quality of Life.* Oxford: Clarendon Press.

Nzisabira, Jean. 1992. *Participation populaire au processus de développement du Rwanda. Les idées et les faits.* Louvain-la-Neuve, Belgium: Cahiers du CIDEP vol. 13.

OECD. *Creditor Reporting System of the Development Assistance Committee.* On-line: www.oecd.org/dac/.

Olivier de Sardan, Jean-Pierre. 1995. *Anthropologie et développement. Essai en socio-anthropologie du changement social.* Paris: Karthala.

Olson, Jennifer M. 1994a. *Demographic Responses to Resource Constraints in Rwanda.* Rwanda Society–Environment Project Working Paper vol. 7. East Lansing: Michigan State University, Department of Geography and the Center for Advanced Study of International Development.

Olson, Jennifer M. 1994b. *Land Degradation in Gikongoro, Rwanda: Problems and Possibilities in the Integration of Household Survey Data and Environmental Data.* Rwanda Society–Environmental Project Working Paper vol. 5. East Lansing: Michigan State University, Department of Geography and the Center for Advanced Study of International Development.

Olson, Jennifer M. 1995. Behind the Recent Tragedy in Rwanda. *Geo-Journal* 35, no. 2: 217–22.

Opotow, Susan. 1995. Drawing the Line. Social Categorization, Moral Exclusion, and the Scope of Justice. In *Conflict, Cooperation and Justice: Essays Inspired by the Work of Morton Deutsch*, edited by Barbara Benedict Bunker and Jeffrey Rubin. San Francisco: Jossey-Bass.

Organization for Economic Cooperation and Development (OECD). 1991. *Development Assistance 1991. Efforts and Policies of the DAC Member States.* Paris: OECD.

Oxfam. 1996. *Rwanda Never Again—The Search for Durable Solutions in the African Great Lakes Region*. London: Oxfam International Position Paper.

Pabanel, J-P. 1995. Bilan de la deuxième République rwandaise: du modèle de développement à la violence générale. *Politique Africaine* 57 (March): 112–23.

Pace, Sonja, and Barbara Schoetzau. 1995. Africa's Hutu vs. Tutsi Struggle. Voice of America radio broadcast, 12:44 UTC, April 28.

PAK. 1980. *Concours agricoles, Jan. 1980*. Kibuye, Rwanda: Projet Agricole Kibuye.

Patterson, J. 1995. Rwandan Refugees. *Nature* 373: 185.

Percival, Valerie, and Thomas Homer-Dixon. 1995. *Environmental Scarcity and Violent Conflict: The Case of Rwanda*. Toronto: University of Toronto, Environment, Population and Security Project.

Physicians for Human Rights. 1994. *Rwanda 1994. A Report of the Genocide*. London: Physicians for Human Rights.

Powell, Elwin H. 1970. *The Design of Discord. Studies of Anomie*. New York: Oxford University Press.

Prunier, Gerard. 1995. *The Rwanda Crisis: History of a Genocide*. New York: Columbia University Press.

Putnam, Robert D. 1993. *Making Democracy Work*. Princeton, N.J.: Princeton University Press.

Quarles von Ufford, Philip. 1993. Knowledge and Ignorance in the Practices of Development Policy. In *An Anthropological Critique of Development. The Growth of Ignorance*, edited by Mark Hobart. London: Routledge.

Rader, Victoria. 1990. Human Needs and the Modernization of Poverty. In *Conflict: Human Needs Theory*, edited by John Burton. New York: St. Martin's Press.

Ranger, Terence. 1993. The Invention of Tradition in Colonial Africa. In *The Invention of Tradition*, edited by Eric Hobshawn and Terence Ranger. Cambridge: Cambridge University Press.

Rawls, John. 1971. *A Theory of Justice*. Cambridge: Harvard University Press.

Reardon, Thomas, Valerie Kelly, and Eric Crawford. 1995. *Promoting Investment in Sustainable Intensification of African Agriculture*. MSU Staff Paper vol. 95-18. East Lansing: Michigan State University.

Reyntjens, Filip. 1994. *L'Afrique des Grands Lacs en crise. Rwanda, Burundi: 1988–1994*. Paris: Karthala.

Reyntjens, Filip. 1995a. Akazy, "escadrons de la mort," et autres "Réseau Zéro": un historique des résistances au changement politique depuis 1990. In *Les crises politiques au Burundi et au Rwanda (1993–1994)*, edited by André Guichaoua. Paris and Lille: Karthala and Université des Sciences et Technologies de Lille.

Reyntjens, Filip. 1995b. Rwanda. In *Trois jours qui ont fait basculer l'histoire*. Paris and Brussels: Karthala and CEDAF Cahiers Africains vol. 16.

Reyntjens, Filip. 1995c. Rwanda. Background to a Genocide. *Bulletin des Séances de l'Académie Royale des Sciences d'Outre-Mer* 41, no. 3: 281–92.

Renard, Robrecht, and Filip Reyntjens. 1993. Aid and Conditionality: The Case of Belgium, with Particular Reference to Policy vis-a-vis Burundi, Rwanda, and Zaire. Paper presented at the EADI Workshop, Berlin.

Robins, Edward. 1990. The Lesson of Rwanda's Agricultural Crisis: Increase Productivity, Not Food Aid. In *African Food Systems in Crisis. Part Two: Contending with Change*, edited by Rebecca Huss-Ashmore and Solomon H. Katz. New York: Gordon and Breach Science Publishers.

Ross, Marc H. 1993. *The Culture of Conflict. Interpretations and Interests in Comparative Perspective*. New Haven, Conn., and London: Yale University Press.

Rossel, Hubert. 1992. Le Rwanda et le Burundi à la vieille de leur 30e année d'Indépendance. *Genève-Afrique* 30, no. 2: 11–74.

Rueschemeyer, Dietrich. Forthcoming. The Self-Organization of Society and Democratic Rule: Specifying the Relationship. In *Participation and Democracy East and West: Comparisons and Interpretations*, edited by Dietrich Rueschemeyer, Marilyn Rueschemeyer, and B. Wittrock. Armonk, N.Y: M. E. Sharpe.

Rupesinghe, Kumar. 1988. Theories of Conflict Resolution and Their Applicability to Protracted Ethnic Conflicts. In *Ethnic Conflict and Human Rights*, edited by Kumar Rupesinghe. Tokyo: United Nations University and Norwegian University Press.

Rwanda: French Agenda. 1992. *Africa Confidential* 33, no. 5 (March 6).

Rwanda: La machète et le goupillon. 1995. *Golias* 43 (July–August): 22–58.

Rwanda: Third Degree. 1991. *Africa Confidential* 32, no. 21 (October 25).

Rwanda: Wrapping Democracy in Violence. 1992. *Africa Confidential* 33, no. 20 (October 9).

Rwandan Churches Culpable, Says WCC. 1994. *Christian Century* (August 24): 778–80.

Sabini, John P., and Maury Silver. 1993. Destroying the Innocent with a Clear Conscience: A Sociopsychology of the Holocaust. In *Political Psychology. Classic and Contemporary Readings*, edited by Neil J. Kressel. New York: Paragon House.

Sangpam, S. N. 1993. Neither Soft nor Dead: The African State Is Alive and Well. *African Studies Review* 36, no. 2 (September): 73–94.

Sauer, Christian. 1996. Hilflos oder Blind? Ruandas deutsche Partner. *Der Uberblick* 32, no. 1 (March): 27–30.

Scheper-Hughes, Nancy. 1992. *Death without Weeping: The Violence of Everyday Life in Brazil*. Berkeley: University of California Press.

Scheper-Hughes, Nancy. 1996. Small Wars and Invisible Genocides. *Social Science and Medicine* 43, no. 5 (September): 889–900.

Scherr, Sara J., and Peter B. R. Hazell. 1994. *Sustainable Agricultural Development Strategies in Fragile Lands*. Discussion Paper no. 1. Washington, D.C.: International Food Policy Research Institute, Environment and Production Technology Division.

Schilder, Kees. 1994. *Quest for Self-Esteem: State, Islam, and Mundang Ethnicity in Northern Cameroon*. Aldershot, England: Avebury.

Schoepf, Brooke G. 1995. Genocide and Gendered Violence in Rwanda, 1994. Paper read at the annual meeting of the American Anthropological Association, Washington, D.C.

Schürings, Hildegard. 1995. La coopération de la République fédérale d'Allemagne avec le Burundi et le Rwanda. In *Les crises politiques au Burundi et au Rwanda (1993-1994)*, edited by A. Guichaoua. Paris and Lille: Karthala and Université des Sciences et Technologies de Lille.

SDC. Various years. *Annual Report*. Berne: Swiss Development Cooperation, Federal Department of Foreign Affairs.

Seruvumba, Anastase. 1992. *Les ONG et les initiatives locales: quel appui? Cas du Rwanda*. Genève: Institut Universitaire d'Etudes du Développement.

Seruvumba, Anastase. 1992-93. *L'Ambiguité des ONG d'appui du sud, entre l'autonomie et les objectifs sociaux de promotion*. Genève: Institut Universitaire d'Etudes du Développement.

Shorris, Earl. 1997. *New American Blues. A Journey through Poverty to Democracy*. New York: W. W. Norton.

Simon, Julian L. 1981. *The Ultimate Resource*. Princeton, N.J.: Princeton University Press.

Simons, Anna. 1995. *Networks of Dissolution: Somalia Undone*. Boulder, Colo.: Westview Press.

Simpson, George Eaton, and J. Milton Yinger. 1953. *Racial and Cultural Minorities: an Analysis of Prejudice and Discrimination*, 3d ed. New York: Harper and Row.

SIPRI (Stockholm International Peace Research Institute). Various years. *SIPRI Yearbook: World Armaments and Disarmament*. Stockholm and New York: Almquist and Wiksell and Humanities Press.

Sollors, Werner. 1996. Foreword: Theories of American Ethnicity. In *Theories of Ethnicity. A Classical Reader*, edited by Werner Sollors. New York: New York University Press.

Sommers, Marc. 1996. *The Mending of Hearts: Conflict Resolution and Reconciliation Activities among Rwandan Refugee Religious Groups in Ngara District, Tanzania (a Preliminary Field Report)*. Working Paper no. 207. Boston: Boston University African Studies Center.

Sorg, Jean-Pierre. n.d. Problèmes forestiers au Rwanda. *Bulletin Agricole du Rwanda*, 4-9.

Spitz, Pierre. 1978. Silent Violence: Famine and Inequality. *International Social Science Journal* 30, no. 4: 867-92.

Srole, Leo. 1956. Social Integration and Certain Corollaries: An Exploratory Study. *American Sociological Review* 21: 709-16.

Staub, Ervin. 1989. *The Roots of Evil: The Origins of Genocide and Other Group Violence*. Cambridge: Cambridge University Press.

Staub, Ervin. 1990. Moral Exclusion, Personal Goal Theory and Extreme Destructiveness. *Journal of Social Issues* 46, no. 1: 47-64.

Stavenhagen, Rodolfo. 1988. Ethnic Conflict and Human Rights. Their Interrelationship. In *Ethnic Conflict and Human Rights*, edited by Kumar Rupesinghe. Tokyo: United Nations University and Norwegian University Press.

Stavenhagen, Rodolfo. 1990. *The Ethnic Question. Conflicts, Development, and Human Rights*. Tokyo: United Nations University Press.

Striker, Gill. 1992. *Faces in the Revolution. The Psychological Effects of Violence on Township Youth in South Africa*. Cape Town and Athens, Ohio: David Philip and Ohio University Press.

Tedeschi, James, and Mitchell Nesler. 1993. Grievances: Development and Reactions. In *Aggression and Violence: Social Interactionist Perspectives*, edited by James Tedeschi and Richard Felson. Washington, D.C.: American Psychological Association.

Tetzlaff, Rainer. 1991. Politisierte Ethnizität—eine unterschätzte Realität in nachkolonialen Afrika. *Afrika Spectrum* 26, no. 1: 5–28.

Theunis, Guy. 1993. Rwanda: Eglise du silence? *Dialogue* 171 (November–December): 17–31.

Theunis, Guy. 1995. Le rôle de l'Eglise catholique dans les événements récents. In *Les crises politiques au Burundi et au Rwanda (1993–1994)*, edited by André Guichaoua. Paris and Lille: Karthala and Université des Sciences et Technologies de Lille.

Tiffen, Mary, Michael Mortimore, and Francis Gichuki. 1994. *More People, Less Erosion: Environmental Recovery in Kenya*. Chichester, England: Wiley.

Tomasevski, Katarina. 1989. *Development Aid and Human Rights, A Study for the Danish Center of Human Rights*. New York: St. Martin's Press.

Ugirashebuya, Octave. 1996. Causes et facteurs du déchainement génocidaire au Rwanda. *Dialogue* 190 (April–May): 33–38.

UNDP. 1987. *Republique du Rwanda: Renforcement Institutionnel du Ministère de L'Agriculture, de L'Elevage et des Forêts*. Kigali, Rwanda: UNDP.

UNDP. 1995. *Human Development Report 1995*. Oxford: Oxford University Press.

UNDP. 1996. *Human Development Report 1996*. Oxford: Oxford University Press.

UNDP. Various years. *Compendium of Ongoing Projects*. New York: UNDP Bureau for Programme Policy and Evaluation.

UNDP Resident-Representative. Various years. *Rapport Annuel sur l'assistance au développement. Rwanda 1992*. Kigali, Rwanda: United Nations Development Programme.

UNICEF. 1995. *State of the World's Children 1995*. Oxford: Oxford University Press.

United Nations. 1991. *Rapport du séminaire des agences du système des Nations Unies sur la lutte contre la pauvreté*. Kigali, Rwanda: Nations Unies.

United Nations. 1993. *Report by the Special Rapporteur on Extrajudicial, Summary or Arbitrary Executions on His Mission to Rwanda, 8–17 April 1993*. New York: United Nations.

United Nations. 1996. *The United Nations and Rwanda 1993–1996*. New York: Department of Public Information.

United Nations. Various years. *African Statistical Yearbook, Part 4*. New York: United Nations.

United Nations, Department of International Economic and Social Affairs. 1991. *The Sex and Age Distributions of Population. The 1990 Revision of the UN Global Population Estimates and Projections*. Population Studies vol. 122. New York: United Nations.

United Nations Resident Coordinator of the UN System Operational Activities in Rwanda. Various years. *Annual Report of the Resident Coordinator of the UN System Operational Activities in Rwanda*. Kigali, Rwanda: United Nations.

University of Rwanda. 1983. *Rapport général et actes du 1er séminaire sur les apports des énergies renouvelables à la gestion de l'énergie et de l'environnement au Rwanda tenu à Kigali du 10 au 15 janvier 1983*. Butare: Université Nationale du Rwanda.

U.S. Department of State. 1993. *Country Reports on Human Rights Practices for 1993*. Report Submitted to the Committee on Foreign Affairs U.S. House of Representatives and the Committee on Foreign Relations U.S. Senate. Washington, D.C.: Government Printing Office.

USAID. 1981. *Draft Environmental Profile on Rwanda*. Washington, D.C.: USAID, Office of Forestry, Environment, and Natural Resources.

USAID. 1991. *Natural Resource Management: Issues and Lessons from Rwanda*. Evaluation PN-ABC-904. Washington, D.C.: USAID.

USAID. 1992. *Democratic Initiatives and Governance Project*. Washington, D.C.: USAID.

USAID. 1994. *U.S. Overseas Loans and Grants and Assistance from International Organizations/Obligations and Loan Authorizations July 1, 1945–Sept. 30, 1993*. CONG-R-0105. Washington, D.C.: Office of Budget, Bureau for Management, USAID.

USAID. Various years. *Annual Report*. Washington, D.C.: USAID.

Uvin, Peter. 1993. Do as I Do, not as I Say: The Limits of Political Conditionality. *European Journal of Development Research* 5, no. 1 (June): 63–84.

Uvin, Peter. 1994a. *The International Organization of Hunger*. London: Kegan Paul.

Uvin, Peter. 1994b. Violence and UN Population Data. *Nature* 372 (December 8): 495–96.

Uvin, Peter. 1996a. Tragedy in Rwanda: The Political Ecology of Conflict. *Environment* 38, no. 3 (April): 6–15, 29.

Uvin, Peter. 1996b. *Violence, Aid, and Conflict. Reflections from the Case of Rwanda*. Helsinki: United Nations University and World Institute of Development Economics Research.

Uvin, Peter. Forthcoming. Ethnicity and Power in Burundi and Rwanda: Different Paths to Mass Violence. *Comparative Politics*.

Uvin, Peter, and Isabelle Biagiotti. 1996. Global Governance and the "New" Political Conditionality. *Global Governance* 2, no. 3 (fall): 377–400.

Uwizeyimana, Laurent. 1991. Démocratie et développement: deux concepts indissociables. *Dialogue* 144 (January–February): 19–24.

Uwizeyimana, Laurent. 1996. *Crise du café, faillite de l'Etat et explosion sociale au Rwanda*. GEODOC no. 42. Toulouse, France: Université de Toulouse-Le Miral, documents de recherche de l'UFR Géographie et Aménagement.

van den Berghe, Pierre L. 1967. *Race and Racism: A Comparative Perspective*. New York: Wiley.

Van der Merwe, Hendrik. 1989. *Pursuing Justice and Peace in South Africa*. London: Routledge and Kegan Paul.

van Hoof, Frans. 1994. Rwanda: vers l'auto-détermination. *Défis-Sud* (December): 35–36.

Verschave, Francois-Xavier. 1995. Connivences françaises au Rwanda. *Le Monde Diplomatique* (March 10): 10.

Vidal, Claudine. 1974. Economie de la société féodale rwandaise. *Cahiers d'Etudes Africaines* 14, no. 1.

Vidal, Claudine. 1985. Situations ethniques au Rwanda. In *Au coeur de l'ethnie. Ethnies, tribalisme et Etat en Afrique*, edited by Jean-Loup Amselle and E. M'Bokolo. Paris: La Découverte.

Vidal, Claudine. 1991. *Sociologie des passions. (Côte d'Ivoire, Rwanda)*. Paris: Karthala.

Vis, Henri L., Ph. Goyens, and D. Brasseur. 1994. Rwanda: The Case for Research in Developing Countries. *Lancet* 345: 957.

Vis, Henri L., Ph. Goyens, and D. Brasseur. 1995. Ter gelegenheid van een brief aan de Lancet: "Rwanda: The Case for Research in Developing Countries." *Bulletin des Séances de l'Académie royale des Sciences d'Outre-Mer* 41, no. 3: 367–87.

Volkan, Vamik D. 1994. *The Need to Have Enemies and Allies. From Clinical Practice to International Relationships*. Northvale, N.J.: Jason Aronson.

von Benda-Beckman, Franz. 1993. Scapegoat and Magic Charm: Law in Development Theory and Practice. In *An Anthropological Critique of Development. The Growth of Ignorance*, edited by Mark Hobart. London: Routledge.

Voyame, Joseph, Richard Friedli, Jean-Pierre Gern, and Anton Keller. 1996. *La coopération suisse au Rwanda*. Berne: Département Fédéral des Affaires Etrangères.

Wade, Robert. 1996. The World Bank and the Art of Paradigm Maintenance. *New Left Review* 217 (fall): 1–32.

Warren, Kay B. 1993. *The Violence Within: Cultural and Political Opposition in Divided Nations*. Boulder, Colo.: Westview Press.

Washington Office on Africa. 1994. *Conflict Resolution: A High Priority in Rwanda and the Region*. Washington, D.C.: Washington Notes on Africa Update.

Watson, Catherine. 1991. *Exile from Rwanda*. Washington, D.C.: U.S. Committee for Refugees.

Weinstein, Warren, and Robert Schrire. 1976. *Political Conflict and Ethnic Strategies: A Case of Burundi*. New York: Syracuse University, Maxwell School of Citizenship and Public Affairs.

Wetherell, Margaret, and Jonathan Potter. 1992. *Mapping the Language of Racism: Discourse and the Legitimation of Exploitation*. Chichester, England: Columbia University Press.

Willame, Jean-Claude. 1995a. *Aux sources de l'hécatombe rwandaise*. Cahiers Africains vol. 14. Paris and Brussels: Karthala and CEDAF.

Willame, Jean-Claude. 1995b. La Belgique et le "Muyaga" des Grands Lacs. In *Les crises politiques au Burundi et au Rwanda (1993–1994)*, edited by A. Guichaoua. Lille and Paris: Karthala and Université des Sciences et Technologies de Lille.

Woodward, David. 1996. *The IMF, the World Bank and Economic Policy in Rwanda: Economic, Social and Political Implications*. Oxford: Oxfam.

Working Group on Demographic Effects of Economic and Social Reversals. 1993. *Demographic Effects of Economic Reversals in Sub-Saharan Africa*.

Washington, D.C.: National Academy Press, National Research Council Panel on the Population Dynamics of Sub-Saharan Africa.

World Bank. 1976. *Memorandum on the Economy of Rwanda.* Washington, D.C.: Eastern Africa Country Programs II.

World Bank. 1979. *Mutara Agricultural and Livestock Development Project—Phase II. Staff Appraisal Report.* Washington, D.C.: Eastern Africa Region, Central Agricultural Division.

World Bank. 1981. *Mutara Agricultural Development Report (Credit 439-RW). Project Performance Audit Report.* Washington, D.C.: Operations Evaluation Department.

World Bank. 1983. *Rwanda Economic Memorandum. Recent Economic and Sectoral Developments and Current Policy Issues.* Washington, D.C.: Division C, Country Programs II, Eastern Africa Region.

World Bank. 1984. *Rwanda Population, Health and Nutrition Sector Review.* Washington, D.C.: Population, Health and Nutrition Department.

World Bank. 1986a. *Rwanda Economic Memorandum. Recent Economic Developments and Current Policy Issues.* Washington, D.C.: Country Programs II, Eastern and Southern Africa.

World Bank. 1986b. *Rwanda Family Health Project. Staff Appraisal Report.* Washington, D.C.: Population, Health and Nutrition Department.

World Bank. 1986c. *Rwandese Republic. A Third Education Project. Staff Appraisal Report.* Washington, D.C.: Education and Manpower Development Division, Eastern and Southern Africa Regional Office.

World Bank. 1987. *Rwanda. The Role of the Communes in Socio-Economic Development.* Washington, D.C.: South, Central and Indian Ocean Department.

World Bank. 1989a. *Rwanda Agricultural Services Project. Staff Appraisal Report.* Washington, D.C.: Agricultural Operations Division, South Central and Indian Ocean Department, Africa Region.

World Bank. 1989b. *Rwanda Public Expenditure Program. An Instrument of Economic Strategy. Volume I.* Washington, D.C.: South Central and Indian Ocean Department, Africa Region.

World Bank. 1989c. *Rwanda Public Expenditure Program. An Instrument of Economic Strategy. Volume II.* Washington, D.C.: South Central and Indian Ocean Department, Africa Region.

World Bank. 1991a. *Mutara Agricultural and Livestock Development Project—Phase II. (Credit 937-RWA). Project Completion Report.* Washington, D.C.: Agricultural Operations Division, South Central and Indian Ocean Department, Africa Regional Office.

World Bank. 1991b. *Republic of Rwanda. First Education Sector Project. Staff Appraisal Report.* Washington, D.C.: Population and Human Resources Division, South Central and Indian Ocean Department, Africa Region.

World Bank. 1991c. *Rwanda Agricultural Strategy Review.* Washington, D.C.: Agriculture Operations Division, South Central and Indian Ocean Department, Africa Region.

World Bank. 1991d. *Rwanda Financial Sector Review.* Washington, D.C.: Industry and Energy Operations Division, South Central and Indian Ocean Department, Africa Region.

World Bank. 1991e. *Rwanda First Population Project. Staff Appraisal Report.* Washington, D.C.: Africa Region, South, Central and Indian Ocean Department, Population and Human Resources Division.

World Bank. 1991f. *Trends in Developing Economies 1991.* Washington, D.C.: World Bank.

World Bank. 1993. *World Development Report 1993.* Oxford: Oxford University Press.

World Bank. 1994a. *Adjustment in Africa: Lessons from Country Case Studies.* Washington, D.C.: World Bank.

World Bank. 1994b. *Rwanda Poverty Reduction and Sustainable Growth.* Washington, D.C.: Population and Human Resources Division, South Central and Indian Ocean Department, Africa Region.

World Bank. 1995. *World Development Report 1995.* Oxford: Oxford University Press.

World Bank. 1996. *World Debt Tables 1995–96.* Oxford: Oxford University Press.

World Resources Institute. 1996. *World Environmental Tables.* Washington, D.C.: WRI, UDP, UNEP.

Wozniak Schimpp, Michele. 1992. *Aid and Democratic Development: A Synthesis of Experience and Literature.* Washington, D.C.: USAID.

INDEX

ABOUT THE AUTHOR

NANCY SOUKUP

Peter Uvin is associate professor (research) at the Watson Institute of International Studies at Brown University. He has worked in a number of African countries for a Swiss NGO. He has published extensively on issues related to development, aid, food, NGOs, capacity building, and Rwanda. His books include *The International Organization of Hunger* (1994) and *The Hunger Report 1995*. He holds a Ph.D. in international relations from the Graduate School of International Studies in Geneva, Switzerland.

Books of related interest
from Kumarian Press

Players and Issues in International Aid
Paula Hoy

This one-stop source of introductory information provides a basic overview of the issues surrounding development assistance with multiple perspectives on the complexities of international assistance and aid.

US $21.95 Paper 1-56549-073-8
US $45.00 Cloth 1-56549-072-X

Nongovernments: NGOs and the Political Development of the Third World
Julie Fisher

This definitive work on nongovernmental organizations provides a complete overview of the composition and the types of NGOs that have emerged in recent years. Julie Fisher describes in detail the influence these organizations have had on political systems throughout the world and the hope their existence holds for the realization of sustainable development.

US $24.95 Paper 1-56549-074-6
US $45.00 Cloth 1-56549-075-4

Achieving Broad-Based Sustainable Development Governance, Environment and Growth With Equity
James H. Weaver, Michael T. Rock, Kenneth Kusterer

This comprehensive and multidisciplinary work provides an excellent overview of economic development and the results of

growth. The authors provide a model which looks through economic as well as social, political and environmental lenses.

US $26.95 Paper 1-56549-058-4
US $38.00 Cloth 1-56549-059-2

Beyond the Magic Bullet: NGO Performance and Accountability in the Post-Cold War World
Michael Edwards, David Hulme

In the volume, experts review the issues of NGO performance and accountability in international development assistance and provide guidance with respect to the process of assessment. Case studies from Central America, Asia, South America, East Africa and North Africa.

US $18.95 Paper 1-56549-051-7
US $38.00 Cloth 1-56549-052-5

Governance, Administration and Development: Making the State Work
Mark Turner, David Hulme

Provides a comprehensive introduction to public policy and management in developing countries and transitional economies. The book assesses both traditional and new models of public administration with particular emphasis on the challenge to the centrality of the state in development and current debates about the conditions of effective governance.

US$24.95 Paper 1-56549-070-3
US$48.00 Cloth 1-56549-071-1

Management Dimensions of Development: Perspectives and Strategies

Milton J. Esman

The author critiques the thinking of the founding development administration practitioners and emerging generations and demonstrates how to go beyond early development approaches. Esman builds a case for multiorganizational strategies sensitive to all players within a society—government, private enterprise, and voluntary organizations.

US$16.95 Paper 0-931816-64-5
US$30.00 Cloth 0-931816-65-3

Promises Not Kept: The Betrayal of Social Change in the Third World
Fourth Edition

John Isbister

This book develops the argument that social change in the Third World has been blocked by a series of broken promises, made explicitly or implicitly by the industrialized countries and also by Third World leaders themselves.

This newly updated fourth edition reexamines the plight of Third World countries in light of recent events and trends of the post–cold war world—population growth, pollution, poverty, and the widening gap between rich and poor.

US$21.95 Paper 1-56549-078-9

Kumarian Press, Inc.
14 Oakwood Avenue
West Hartford, CT 06119-2127
USA

Inquiries: 860-233-5895
Fax: 860-233-6072
Order toll free: 800-289-2664

e-mail: kpbooks@aol.com
internet: www.kpbooks.com

Kumarian Press is dedicated to publishing and distributing books and other media that will have a positive social and economic impact on the lives of peoples living in "Third World" conditions no matter where they live.

As well as books on International Development, Kumarian Press publishes books on the Environment, Nongovernmental Organizations, Government, Gender, Peace, and Conflict Resolution.

To receive a complimentary catalog or to request writer's guidelines, call or write:

Kumarian Press, Inc.
14 Oakwood Avenue
West Hartford, CT 06119-2127 USA

Inquiries: 860-233-5895
Fax: 860-233-6072
Order toll free: 800-289-2664

e-mail: kpbooks@aol.com
internet: www.kpbooks.com